GIN & TONIC

THE COMPLETE GUIDE FOR THE PERFECT MIX

GIN & TONIC

FRÉDÉRIC DU BOIS & ISABEL BOONS

LANNOO

This symbol indicates that you can visit the distillery.

"The gin and tonic has saved more Englishmen's lives, and minds, than all the doctors in the Empire."

Winston Churchill

PREFACE

"I like
large parties.
They're so
intimate.
At small parties
there's never
any privacy."

Just like the character of Jordan Baker – played by Elizabeth Debicki in the 2013 film of *The Great Gatsby* – we know how to throw one hell of a party. Don't misunderstand us, there is nothing wrong with an intimate party with a few friends, but in this book we are pulling out all the stops and won't let anyone go thirsty. We don't care where and with whom you drink your gin & tonic; what does interest us is how you take your gin & tonic. What slides out of your glass should dance on the tongue and extend the boundaries to fill you with passion. So...let's get the party rolling!

Where others stop, we go further. Our book answers those questions that still burn on the lips of anyone who is passionate about gin & tonic: "Which gin do I combine with which tonic, and what garnish do I add?" Well, after reading this book you will be able to amaze your friends and foes with a heavenly gin & tonic: perfectly mixed with the right utensils and the best tasting garnish 'popped' on top!

Throughout the book you will discover more than fifty tonics and one hundred and ten gins and at the back you will find a comprehensive 'Gincyclopedia'.

This book pays homage to the immensely popular drink, and is your guide on the quest for the ultimate gin & tonic. First, we will catapult you back in time and get thoroughly 'gin soaked' before we resume our journey and take you to 'tonic land'. Read and learn. Then we will take you into the passionate relationship between gin & tonic. We will blow you away with a cornucopia of information, guidelines and sensations. We will show you how to find your ideal match, and top it off with the right garnish.

To make the party complete, we will combine various meals with gin & tonic. We will discover that our favourite drink is at home in any situation and can complement all kinds of dishes. We round it up with eighteen must-visit bars. After that, it is up to you: taste, discover and experience.

This book is for those who never leave a party early and like to slowly savour their drinks; for the free spirited and those who aspire to be so; for those in search of inspiration, information or who just want to use to book to get pleasantly light-headed; for those in search of a new love, or those who have already found their love.

But most of all, it's for those who prize passion and live life to the fullest.

Cheers to us all!

Note:
The author F. Scott Fitzgerald was a notorious gin lover...

GIN: SOME HISTORY

OR HOW THE JUNIPER BERRY CHANGED THE WORLD...

Before gin, there was genever or jenever. In Belgium it is called jenever with a 'j', while in the Netherlands it is often referred to as genever with a 'g'. The history of gin is not an entirely untroubled one: it is a story of courage, calamity and mishap, but also of new innovations, insights and trends, which continue to this day. While Whisky is associated with the Scottish Highlands, rum conjures up images of pirates and the shipping trade and vodka whispers of Siberian winters, the story of gin spreads from the Middle East to Europe and America, it's history completely changed the world.

BELGIUM OR THE NETHERLANDS

'der naturen bloeme'

Our favourite, gin is based on a famous drink which has its origins in the Low Countries (now Belgium and the Netherlands). The first mention of the juniper berry can be found in *Der Naturen Bloeme*, (The Flowers of Nature) written by Jacob van Maerlant in 1269. This encyclopaedia applauds the juniper berry for its many medicinal properties. Van Maerlant writes about juni-

per berries cooked in wine and how it is used as a medicine against cramps and stomach pains. A century later, jenever appear again in a booklet, this time as a medicine to cure the plague. The author, Jan van Aalter, was also the first to mention the euphoric effects of jenever. Both Jacob and Jan happened to be Flemish although jenever is well-known in both Great Britain and America, and to this day is called 'Dutch Courage' or 'Holland Gin', referring to its Low Countries heritage. During the siege of Antwerp in 1585, many fled to the Netherlands, taking their beloved jenever with them. The following century saw Belgium burdened by prohibition, while in the Netherlands the Golden Age was dawning, allowing the production methods of gin to develop.

YES WE CAN...

As people became more familiar with distillation methods and discovered that spirits could be made from anything that ferments, a world of possibilities unfolded. During the 14th and 15th centuries a lot of enthusiastic experimentation took place. In Poland and Russia they discovered the delights of a new use for the potato, and in Ireland and Scotland they were busy with barley. In the Low Countries brandy is a term used for a whole range of different spirits. Excise reports from 1492 show that significant amounts of grain-based spirits, particularly rye, were very commonly distilled. In 1582, the first technical description for how to distil spirits from grain appeared: *Guide to Distilling Korenbrandewijn* (corn brandy) by Casper Jansz.

THE MYTH OF DOCTOR SYLVIUS

The 17th century – the Golden Age in the Netherlands: the Dutch East India Company flourished to become the largest trading company in the world, Rembrandt painted his masterpieces, and medical science quickly evolved. It was at this time that Franciscus Sylvius (1614-1672), a professor at Leiden University, allegedly created 'Dutch Gin', however, this claim has been refuted. It is true that he used jenever as a medicine for kidney complaints and as a remedy for the plague, but it is highly unlikely that he was the inventor of gin. In his book *Een Constelijck Distileerboec* (1552), Philippus Hermanni refers to jenever or gin as 'Aqua Juniperi' and this was 98 years before Sylvius was born. There are also references to jenever/gin found in a medieval English cookery book, and also in the play *The Duke of Milan*, first published in 1632 when Doctor Sylvius was only nine years old.

DUTCH COURAGE

During the Thirty Years' War (1618-1648), a far reaching conflict in which most European powers were embroiled, English soldiers, stationed in the southern Netherlands to deal with the Spanish forces, were first introduced to jenever. These brave men certainly deserved a tipple before going into battle. However, the day after the battle, these heroes often found it hard to remember who they had fought. And so they christened this 'Dutch Courage', ginniver, an Anglicization of jenever which later became known simply as gin. They obviously took this habit back home with them. Yet jenever is not completely unknown in Great Britain, and is certainly familiar in London where, in 1571, six thousand Flemish Protestant refugees were provided a safe haven.

WILLIAM OF ORANGE AND THE MERRY BREWERS

England, 1688: William of Orange III ascended the throne, marking the beginning of a new era. English society underwent a major turnaround, not least in their drinking habits. The new king almost immediately encouraged the production of English spirits, and it became possible for anyone to brew gin without a licence. At the same time, import taxes on foreign drinks sky rocketed, resulting in an explosion of gin production as everyone takes up brewing.

GIN CRAZE

'Blue Ruin', 'Ladies' Delight', 'Cuckolds' Comfort' or 'Madam Geneva', the new drug of the 18th century had many nicknames, and England was in the grip of a drink craze like never before. London in particular will never be 'under the influence' like it was between 1720 and 1751, a period often compared to the crack epidemic of the 1980s in America. And indeed, Londoners were almost permanently high on gin. At that time, gin was cheap and readily available, but of poor quality. The malty complexity of the Dutch genever proved too much of a challenge for the local brewers, and often poor-quality grain was used to produce a neutral spirit, cut with oil of turpentine, oil of vitriol and alum. To mask the taste they used large amounts of sugar, limewater and rosewater. The consequences of this were devastating: gin was blamed for a number of woes, the rise in crime, prostitution and insanity, higher mortality rates and a

fall in the birth rate, as a huge proportion of the city's population drifted the streets from morning till night. The following facts shed light on the extent of the impact of this opium:

- *Between 1723 and 1733, the death rate in London far outweighed the birth rate.*
- *At one point, there were 7,044 recognized gin retailers and thousands of street sellers amongst a population of 600,000 Londoners.*
- *Between 1730 and 1749, 75% of children died before the age of five.*
- *Between 1740 and 1742, there were two funerals to every christening.*
- *As many as 9,000 children died from alcohol poisoning in 1751.*
- *In 1733, almost 47 million litres of legal gin were produced in London, an equivalent of 53 litres of gin per person per year.*
- *In 1740, no less than half of all the beverage establishments in London were so-called 'gin shops'.*

WILLIAM HOGARTH'S GIN LANE (1697-1764)

This historic engraving perfectly illustrates just how bad things had become, and there is no better depiction of the squalor and despair in London while in the grips of gin mania. It is easy to understand why reformers felt so desperate about the situation. *Gin Lane* depicts a busy street full of scenes of misery: a carpenter pawns his tools for money to buy gin; a little further on an undertaker is placing the body of an emaciated woman in a coffin; an addict has hung himself, while a mother feeds her child gin to lull it to sleep. And these depraved figures only form the back drop. In the foreground, amidst all the turmoil, a woman in a completely drunken stupor seems oblivious as her child slips out of her arms, about to fall over the balustrade.

GIN ACTS

Almost as tragic as the stories of the effects of gin in the 18th century, were the comical, frantic and unsuccessful attempts of the government to get a grip on gin consumption. In the period between 1729 and 1751, the British Parliament introduces no less than eight different Gin Acts, some more successful than others. The following is a summary of the most important ones.

In 1729, the first attempt was made to levy a tax on alcohol; however rich land owners appealed to their corruptible friends in high places, so that they were still able to sell their grain to the distilleries. Following a few further unsuccessful attempts, Parliament finally passed a new Gin Act in 1736. It was also around this time that the name 'Old Tom Gin' first appeared. The new Gin Act, which was motivated more by money than morals, placed such a hefty tax on the serving of gin, that in reality the law was more like prohibition, and those who broke the law faced heavy fines or even a prison sentence. The result of this was to drive the whole industry underground. Despite strong enforcement by the authorities, Londoners did not yield, and the Gin Act was often ignored. Finally, seven years later, the law was officially repealed. The Gin Act of 1751 was more successful since according to the law distillers could only sell their gin to bar owners with a licence. The licence fee was reasonable, and as a result of this action the quality of the gin improved, with only gradual price increases. The Gin Craze slowly ebbed away by the end of the 19th century, so it is not surprising that many of the great English distilleries date from this period.

GIN PALACES

While the British Empire reshaped the world, the Industrial Revolution completely restructured Great Britain itself. The emergence of factories brought many people to the towns and cities, and the rise of the working classes challenged the old way of thinking. This new technological age saw mass production of furniture for the first time, oil lamps were replaced by gas lighting and new ways of making glass were developed. All these new innovations led to the rise of the gin palaces: a new place where the working classes felt right at home, and probably nicer than their own homes at that. It was in 1829 that the first of these little gems appeared, such as Thompson and Fearon's. The glamour and atmosphere of the gin palaces gave gin's image a boost and drinking was considered more of a social occasion.

THE VERY FIRST GIN & TONIC

Meanwhile in India, events were taking place which couldn't be overlooked. Once again we had the soldiers to thank for a new evolution in drinking. At the beginning of the 19th century, the British of the East India Company took quinine to prevent malaria. Quinine is one of the main ingredients in tonic, but more about that later. To make the daily dose of quinine more palatable, they added water, sugar and lime, and it was soon followed by the addition of gin. So there we have it, the very first gin & tonic.

FROM OLD TOM TO LONDON DRY

Due to the rise in excise duty and quality controls, the government hoped that gin would never again be the 'killer' it once was. The premise was simple: since gin was more expensive to make, the quality of the gin had to be better so as to justify the higher price. 'Old Tom' was sold in large barrels to retailers, who then added sugar. During the Gin Craze, gin was sweetened to cover up the poor quality, but now it was sweetened purely to cater to people's taste. With the advent of new distillation equipment, such as the Coffey Still, also known as the Continuous or Patent Still, the distillates produced were of a higher quality, and so the dry, unsweetened style of gins that we now know as London Dry Gin, came into being. The upper classes preferred this gin to its sweet counterpart, and when people started to become aware of the concept of a healthy lifestyle during the Victorian era, the glory days of Old Tom were quickly over. The disappearance of Old Tom and the rise in popularity of dry gins was due to the fact that the dry varieties lent themselves better to mixing. In 1860, the cocktail trend blew across from America and it wasn't long before the fashion for mixing drinks spread throughout Europe. The English not only increased their exports of gin but also exported their drinking habits, such as in World War I, and in this way London

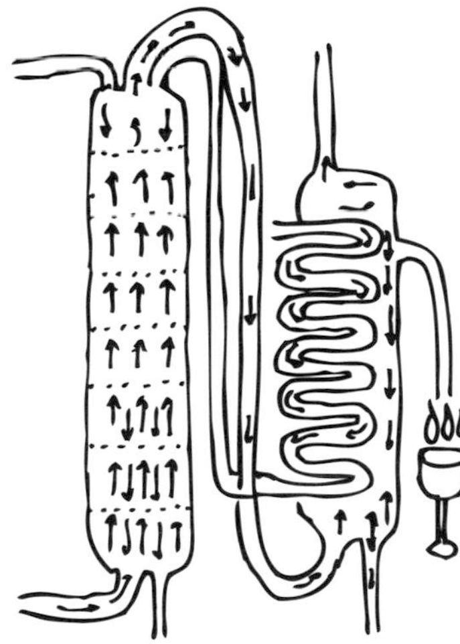

Dry gin became known worldwide. In the 1920s and 1930s, gin also becomes popular in America, where it was regularly used as a base in cocktails, perhaps the best known of all being the Dry Martini.

PROHIBITION AND 'BATHTUB GIN'

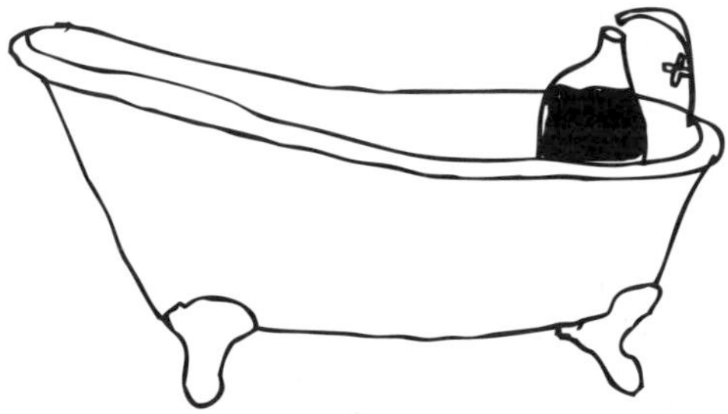

On 17th January 1920, American Congress passed the Volstead Act and prohibition comes into force. Yet what was forbidden became even more desirable and an entire generation of Americans plunged into criminality. Either they lived in the speakeasies where they could drink illegal alcohol, or they make their own at home, and 'Bathtub Gin' became very popular. This despicable combination of industrial alcohol, glycerine and juniper oil was prepared in large bottles, too large to be filled under the tap in the sink, and so were filled from the tap in the bath. Sometimes the gin was also fermented and distilled in the bath itself, hence the name 'Bathtub Gin'. As a result of prohibition, English distilleries feared they would lose this important export market. But in fact the opposite proved true as exorbitant prices were offered for the real stuff. Prohibition came to an end with President Franklin D. Roosevelt, and it is said that he even mixed the first legal martini in the White House himself.

THE ROARING 20S: THE GLORY DAYS

Think glitter, glamour, new movements in music, fast cars, fashion, art and cocktails ... a lot of cocktails. *The Great Gatsby* by F. Scott Fitzgerald paints a perfect picture of what it was like in this era. Incidentally, did you know that F. Scott Fitzgerald had a weakness for Gin Rickey? A gin cocktail, where half a lime is first squeezed and then dropped into the glass before topping up with soda water. It is rumoured that Fitzgerald was a gin lover because he believed that you couldn't detect gin on the breath. In the 20s, many bartenders left America – as they were no longer allowed to ply their trade – and ended up in London where they could share their skills. Cocktail parties in grand hotels were all the rage, replacing the more mundane afternoon tea. The driving force behind this party atmosphere: gin! The popularity of gin continued to grow and reached its peak in the 50s and 60s with Hollywood stars such as Errol Flynn and Humphrey Bogart seldom seen without a Gin Martini in their hand.

AND THEN CAME VODKA...

Gin continued to dominate the drinks world until after the 1960s, with probably half of all the existing cocktails using gin as their base at that time. And then vodka poked its head around the corner, and benefited from good marketing and a hip image. Gin began to be considered old-fashioned and stuffy. Luckily it is now back in fashion, and how!

TODAY'S GIN CRAZE

It wasn't until the end of the 20th century that gin distilleries were able to head off the vodka tsunami. What took them so long? Maybe it was a lack of imagination, or maybe the time simply wasn't right. Big brands such as Tanqueray Ten and Bombay Sapphire set the tone, and created spin-offs of their brands which were more suited to the tastes of vodka drinkers: softer and rounder. Bombay Sapphire breathed new life into the market, raising its profile with a square blue bottle, which was appreciated by the trendy crowd and bartenders alike. At the same time, other distilleries also began to stretch the boundaries by using new ingredients or by reinterpreting the classic gin recipes. Halfway through the noughties, Hendrick's developed a Super Premium Gin, and many followed this example. Today, it is impossible to keep up, as almost every week a new brand comes on the market. Too much? Perhaps. But we are certainly ecstatic about this revival.

BUT WHERE DOES THIS NEW GIN CRAZE COME FROM?

Since 2000, bartenders, chefs and enthusiasts in Spain have been inspired by gin, and in the last years we've also seen this trend make its way into Belgium and Germany. Nowadays, Holland, Italy and Portugal are experiencing the gin hype and in the UK gin is an historic product that has been loved for 400 years. Maybe it is due to their stoicism or pride that the British don't seem too bothered about this sudden surge in interest, although bartenders in the UK are cheering on this gin explosion as it offers them more room to experiment and show off their talents. Another explanation may be the new interest in food, with a preference for top quality products, new tastes and flavours – all unquestionably motivated by today's top chefs – which has led to greater awareness of what goes into our glasses as part of this gastronomic revolution. The mixing of all sorts of spirits, 'mixology', is currently reaching new heights and can certainly be referred to as gastronomy of the glass. Local bar culture is also playing

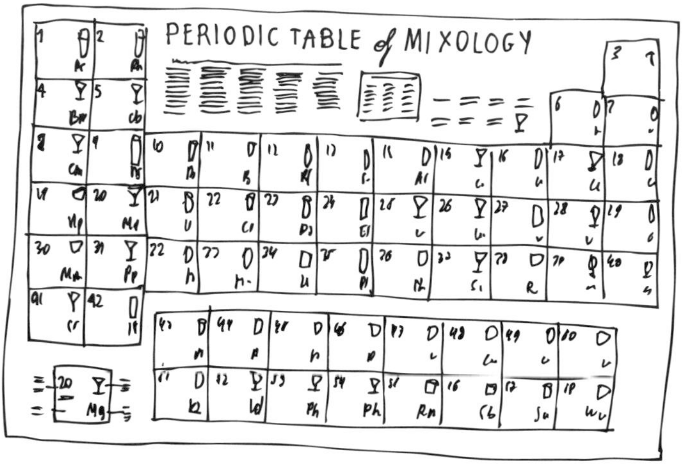

its role as the new generation of bartenders stimulate and motivate each other by 'sharing' their knowledge. In the age of social media, it is the most natural thing in the world for them to let everyone know about new discoveries, experiments and knowhow. New bar concepts, or old but revitalised bar concepts, are springing up everywhere. A good example which is growing daily in popularity is the speakeasy. During the years of prohibition, going to a speakeasy guaranteed a fun – if illegal – 'night out on the town'. Luckily nowadays, alcohol is no longer illegal and the term is used to describe a retro, 1920s ambiance bar, where mixed drinks of the highest quality are served. Speakeasies, like the originals, are shrouded in mystery: you may well have some difficulty finding the entrance, and even when you do, you may still not have actually reached the bar itself. Once inside however, you will be catapulted back in time: the décor, costumes and atmosphere will blow your mind. The drinks on offer are of the highest quality and tell the story of the classic recipes. It's worth a try in our opinion, as long as you can find the way in.

Hype? No, we believe that gin is here to stay, and this time for good. Sophisticated and well thought-out, with tonic as its ally, gin will undoubtedly, once again, conquer the world.

WHAT IS GIN?

THE LEGAL CONDITIONS FOR GIN

European legislation—just as for Amaretto or Champagne—has rules with which gin must comply to be allowed to call itself gin. In the EU, gin has to have a minimum alcohol percentage of 37.5%. In the United States, the legal minimum alcohol percentage is set at 40%. The second condition is that the juniper berry has to have a prominent presence, notably 51% per production unit.

THE DISTILLATION OF GIN: THE METHODS

POT STILLED GIN

Of all the methods used, the pot still, also known as batch distillation, is the most traditional distillation technique. The neutral grain alcohol, which has to be heated to at least 96 °C, is put in the pot still and 'thinned down' with water before the botanicals are added. Depending on the individual recipe the alcohol will be warmed and left to stand and steep for hours, sometimes even days. At the appropriate moment, the distillation process begins by applying heat—and in the case of gin—by a steam jacket underneath the pot still. Following this, the distiller adds steam to bring

the alcohol to the boil, which will then reach the top of the pot, and immediately reduce the pressure. The vapours then pass through a swan neck tube to a water-cooled condenser. This first part of the distillate, also known as the 'heads', often contains impurities and is therefore drained into another vessel. The pure gin follows at various concentrations until eventually a strength of 80% is achieved. When this level reduces to 60% again, the impurities reappear. This last part of the distillate known as the 'tails' is likewise drained into separate vats. The next stage is to increase the steam pressure again, resulting in only water and the residue of the botanicals being left behind in the pot still. The distillation process is then repeated with the heads and the tails in another still which has a long neck and plates to remove the impurities, and so this part can also be used to make gin. After this, the final distillate is mixed with water so that it can be brought back to the desired alcohol percentage.

COLUMN DISTILLED GIN

Column distilled gin is a term associated with the invention of the Coffey still, and is also known as continuous distillation. Neutral grain alcohol (mostly wheat-based) is distilled to 96%. This distillate is then diluted with water to make the ideal alcohol percen-tage of 60%, to which herbs and spices are then added. Following this, it goes though the distillation process again, whereby the essential oils of the botanicals are released.

Note:
In both pot stilled gin and column distilled gin the master distiller can apply two methods to combine the alcohol with the other ingredients or botanicals. 'Racking' means that the botanicals are placed in a copper rack—a so called 'gin basket'—positioned above the still, where the hot alcohol vapours can extract the aromatic components of the botanicals. In 'steeping', the botanicals are placed in the spirit in the bottom of the still and allowed to stand and infuse.

VACUUM DISTILLED GIN

Vacuum distilled gin is produced differently to the previous methods. Instead of using heat for the distillation of the botanicals, cold distillation is used. With this method the pressure above the distillation solution is cooled to about -5 °C. At this freezing temperature the spirit vaporises. Following this, at -100 °C a type of probe is inserted into the still and the vapours return to liquid form. The flavours of the botanicals are now perfectly embedded in the spirit. The whole process takes around five to six hours.

The great advantage to this method of cold distillation is that there are no 'heads' or 'tails', meaning virtually no wastage. But the real breakthrough is without a doubt in the taste of the gin. The theory is that in cold distillation the molecular structure of the botanicals is preserved and so too, the true original taste is guaranteed.

Examples of gins developed in this way are Sacred Gin and Oxley Gin.

Note:
Desmond Payne (master distiller at Beefeater) was the first to allow the botanicals to 'steep' in the alcohol for at least 24 hours prior to distillation, hence the name of their unconventional 'Beefeater24'. This technique has now been copied by countless gin makers. The time varies from distiller to distiller and can take anything from 6 to 24 hours.

GIN AND ITS BOTANICALS

The dominant juniper berry flavour is—as mentioned earlier—a legal requirement. As well as juniper berry, flavours such as orange or lemon peel, coriander seed, cardamom, caraway, cassia, cinnamon, angelica root and orris root, are commonly used botanicals in the new generation of gins. We have noticed that today, the average small batch (premium) gin uses some ten to twelve botanicals, almost becoming a standard, resulting in ever-increasing levels of quality.

Some of the most complex gins include Monkey 47 Gin with 47 botanicals, and Black Gin from the Gansloser Distillery with between 68 and 74 botanicals, depending on the source. These complex varieties are strongly reminiscent of herbal liqueurs such as Jägermeister. Both of these gins originate in the Black Forest region and will definitely appeal to a certain audience.

In what follows, we shortly describe the most used botanicals.

JUNIPER BERRY

The signature of every gin. The use of the juniper berry determines the character and taste of each individual gin. The bittersweet flavours of pine, lavender and camphor are all identifiable in the juniper berry. The tree or bush grows almost everywhere in the northern hemisphere, and is even found growing at heights of up to 3,500 metres. The juniper used to create gin is always carefully selected and processed by the manufacturers. Each having their own personal preference, from Italy to Macedonia, hand-picked and handled with care. Once in the distillery, the juniper berries are matured for up to two years until the oil reaches the maximum aromatic potential.

ANGELICA

Angelica is a biennial plant that, when growing in the wild, is most commonly found in moist, slightly acid, loamy soil. But it can also flourish just as well in the garden. According to legend, angelica can be used as a cure for the plague, or for protection against witchcraft. In gin, angelica root is used to make it 'dry'. The earthy notes help to support the botanic profile of a gin.

CITRUS FRUITS

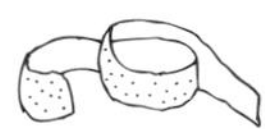

There is a definite trend to expand the citrus character of gin: bergamot orange, orange, lemon, lime, grapefruit, mandarin, etc. There is, however, a distinction made between the peel and the flesh or juice of the fruit.

CARDAMOM

Cardamom is a member of the ginger family, with a sweet, sharp fragrance and tastes of bergamot, lemon and camphor. It originates from the Far East and is, after saffron and vanilla, the most expensive spice in the world. Before distillation, the seeds are crushed in order to fully release their warm, spicy aromas which are then infused into the gin.

CARAWAY

Caraway is a biennial plant that is most commonly found in western Asia, Europe, and North Africa, where it grows in meadows, verges and dikes. Caraway seeds emit a spicy, sweet, aniseed flavour. Not to be confused with cumin, as the taste of caraway is much more pungent.

CINNAMON

The cinnamon tree grows predominantly in Sri Lanka, but can also be found on Java, in Brazil and Egypt. The cinnamon tree will only grow in a tropical climate, and preferably on the coast. Cinnamon has a warm and spicy taste and has many culinary uses.

CASSIA

Cassia is closely related to cinnamon and is similar in flavour and appearance. It is slightly hotter and sweeter than cinnamon and originates from Sri Lanka and China.

CORIANDER SEED

Coriander seed is a spice which is a favourite in many kitchens, originating from the Middle East and the Mediterranean region. Coriander has always played a leading role in several gin recipes. During distillation, coriander seeds release a herby, sage and lemon taste.

ORRIS ROOT

Orris root or iris root is used for many different purposes: in perfumes or potpourri, with the fragrance similar to violet. It is often included as one of the many ingredients in the Moroccan spice mix 'Ras el hanout'. In gin, orris root serves as a bonding agent for the other aromatics.

LIQUORICE

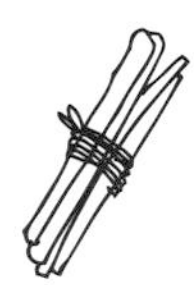

The root of the liquorice plant is used throughout the world as a treatment for bronchitis. Gin distillers mainly source their liquorice from the Middle East. Liquorice contains sugars, bitters and a substance that produces its distinctive woody taste. The use of liquorice in gin softens the mouth feel.

ALMONDS

The almond tree grows mostly in southern Europe. The bitter almond is used in gin, not the sweet variety. Almonds give gin a somewhat marzipan softness.

TONIC: SOME HISTORY

FROM MEDICINE TO PERFECT MIXER...

1638: THE MIRACULOUS CURE

Just like gin, tonic started life as a medicine. The legend takes us back to 17th century Peru. The countess Ana de Osorio del Chinchón was suffering from one of the most serious forms of the life-threatening disease, malaria. Her husband – whose name is unpronounceable – pleaded desperately with the local medicine man to find a cure for his wife's fever. Luckily, the medicine man was feeling generous and gave her a mysterious concoction made from the bark of the native 'Quinquina' tree. The Countess miraculously recovered. In honour of the Countess and in celebration of her recovery, the Spaniards re-christen the Peruvian tree, and it became known as the 'Cinchona' tree. They also eradicated the Incas, stole their gold and colonised their land!

EXPORT TRADE BOOMS

Meanwhile, the Countess Ana returned to her estate in Spain, taking a large quantity of the healing tree bark with her. The fame of this magical substance – which we now know as quinine – quickly spread throughout Europe, and this wonderful medicine also cured Charles II of England and the son of Louis XIV of France. The powder form of the tree bark became worth more than gold and demand quickly outweighed supply and the 'fever tree' was threatened with extinction.

1850:
SMUGGLING WAR

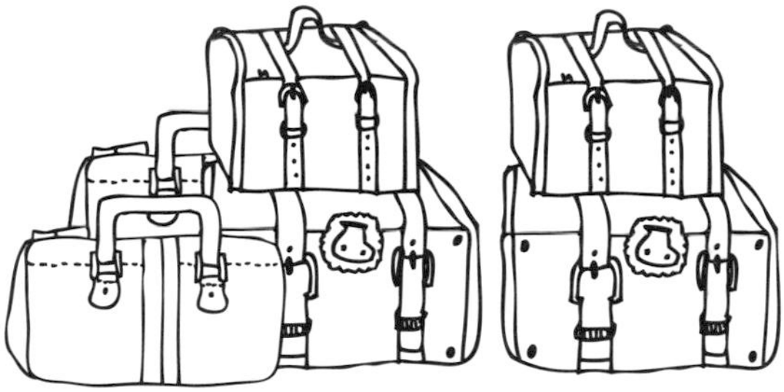

In the middle of the 19th century, the British and the Dutch come up with a splendid idea: to smuggle the seeds of the 'fever tree' out of Latin America. The British tried planting the trees in their own colonies in India and Ceylon, but were unsuccessful in producing quality quinine. The Dutch, however, fared better in colonial Java, where the trees grew and flourished to produce good quality quinine. By 1918, Java had become the biggest producer of quinine in the world.

SWEET MEDICINE

Meanwhile, quinine started to be used to also prevent, as well as cure, malaria. During this time of colonisation, malaria was widespread, and so quinine was popular stuff. The British occupiers in India masked the bitter taste of the quinine with sugar and diluted it with water. Soldiers and their commanders were given this medicine daily, and it wasn't long before some spirited soul was inspired to add gin to the mix. This rekindled the flame of enthusiasm, which has burned brightly ever since.

1858:
FIRST COMMERCIAL TONIC

The shrewd British businessman, Erasmus Bond was the first to see an opportunity in this trend among the British soldiers and officers, and in 1858 he produced the first commercial tonic: improved aerated tonic liquid. His invention was at first considered a health product, but it didn't take long before this first tonic moved from the medicine cabinet to the drinks cabinet.

1944:
SCIENCE KICKS IN

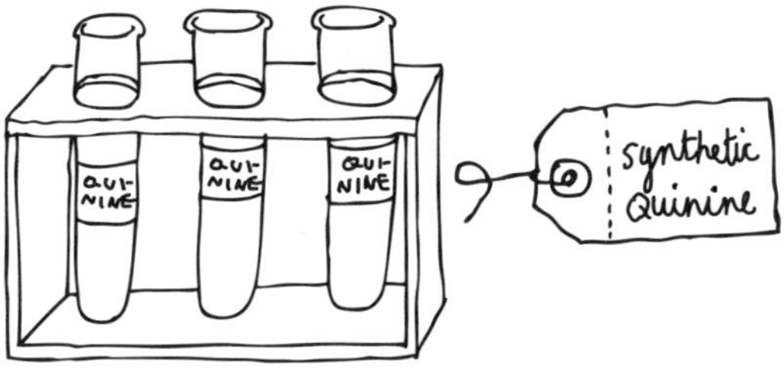

Until World War II, Indonesia produced more than 95% of the world's quinine. This however, came to an abrupt end when the Japanese occupied Java. This once again led to a shortage of quinine for medical use, so scientists were brought in to develop a synthetic alternative. By 1944, this synthetic variant had become a reality. Synthetic quinine is still used to this day to create certain types of tonic, but it goes without saying that the synthetic version tastes very different to the natural one.

TONIC TODAY

Gin is back; maybe bigger than ever. The evolution of more sophisticated and aromatic gin varieties logically demands that mixers are elevated to a new level. A new generation of tonics – undoubtedly with a view to forming the perfect partnership with gin – have been making their entrance over the last few years. And we can safely say they have been raising the bar even higher for the iconic long drink. Gin & tonic is the perfect example of a successful marriage that will last forever. Let's face it, separating this couple is simply unthinkable.

WHAT IS TONIC?

Tonic is a carbonated soft drink, whose bitter taste comes from the addition of our now well-known – if you have read the last few pages – quinine. In addition to quinine, tonic water is flavoured with sugar or sweeteners, and is often further enhanced by the addition of various fruit extracts. But let's get back to the quinine. Are you planning a trip to the tropics? Imagine some gin & tonic and you are protected against malaria. Well...you may need to consume two litres of tonic, containing natural quinine, a day, which is equal to ten gin & tonics. Is that a good idea? We'll leave that up to you.

GIN & TONIC THE IDEAL MATCH

Finding the ideal match rests on one basic principle, and that is the right combination of tastes. That is why we are categorizing the tonics as well as the gins according to their flavours. To create an explosive combination in your glass, we will blend the tastes by mixing the various types of gin with the most appropriate tonic.

And indeed, we are beginning with the tonic. Not that we want to be 'contrary' or attempt to paddle upstream, and we are certainly not suggesting a switch to 'tonic & gin'; not at all, the one and only reason is to make it easier for you. Consider it a warm up, or maybe a safeguard against too many premature hangovers, but above all, there can be no gin & tonic without the tonic. Although it is fair to say that tonic is, and will always be, the secondary ingredient in our favourite cocktail, but just as with gin, there are many differences in the quality and tastes. Failing to give some thought to the tonic is like not bothering about putting the right sort of fuel in the engine of your car.

With the re-birth, and explosion in the popularity of gin, tonic is similarly enjoying a serious resurgence. Tonic will always be a dominant flavour in our gin & tonic, and that is why we begin with this ode to tonic, for once bringing it out of gin's shadow. You will be introduced to an entire new generation of tonics, and believe us when we say, it will be both a fascinating and pleasurable experience, forming the basis of all your future creations. And maybe yes, we actually do enjoy paddling upstream, just a little...

TONIC:
CATEGORIZATION

For the perfect gin & tonic it is first important to know which flavours are in your tonic, and when armed with this knowledge you will be able to amaze your friends and foes alike. OK, gin is our protagonist, but a decent knowledge of tonic is also essential for creating your ultimate gin & tonic later. We categorize the new generation of tonics on the basis of their taste: **neutral**, **aromatic** and **fruity/floral**.

As we want to give you as detailed an overview as possible, we will not be concentrating too much on the big brands such as Kinley Tonic, Nordic Mist Tonic Water and Schweppes Indian Tonic. Instead we will focus in depth on the new generation of tonics, which mostly make use of natural ingredients and, as a consequence, really allow the gin to shine through.

So fasten your seatbelts and prepare for takeoff... Here we go!

NEUTRAL TONICS

UNITED KINGDOM

6 O'CLOCK INDIAN TONIC WATER

ORIGIN

The story of 6 O'Clock begins with gin, namely the recipe of Edward Kain, innovator, inventor and, above all, adventurer. Edward was a ship engineer in the 19th century, indeed the century in which malaria claimed many victims. Edward and his colleagues drank tonic water during their voyages to protect against malaria, and one fine day, Edward came up with the fantastic idea to add gin to the tonic. Hallelujah! Legend has it that from that day forward, every day at 6pm Edward would partake in a gin & tonic, thus the name 6 O'Clock. It was Edward's great grandson, Michael Kain, who years later brought 6 O'Clock gin and its partner tonic onto the market and developed the idea of creating the perfect match. 6 O'Clock is made in the Bramley and Cage distillery, a small producer in Great Britain. Their strategy is clear: You can't buy the gin without the tonic, or the other way around. Moreover, the gin and the tonic are only offered to bars and restaurants within Great Britain. Bramley and Cage are also developing a sloe gin.

INGREDIENTS

sparkling water
extract of lemon and lime
citric acid
sugar
natural quinine

6 O'Clock tonic contains no artificial sweeteners, or other flavourings.

TASTE AND AROMA

The pure taste is due to the use of natural quinine, with an exceptional twist of citrus. Beautifully balanced with a clear nose of lemon. A full-bodied tonic but surprisingly fresh.

ABBONDIO TONICA VINTAGE EDITION

ORIGIN

In business for over 120 years, Abbondio is one of the oldest drinks producers in Italy. Above all, this brand is seen as the most prestigious in the country. Angelo Abbondio set up his soft drinks factory in Tortona in 1889 and paid special attention to quality and traditional recipes. The pin-up pictures used on the bottles are quite striking. The Abbondio tonic was created at the beginning of the 20th century and was originally called 'bitter gazzosa'.

INGREDIENTS

carbonated water
cane sugar
quinine
natural flavourings

TASTE AND AROMA

The traditional formula seamlessly integrates the sour taste of the lemons with the cane sugar. Lightly carbonated and completely free of genetically modified products.

UNITED KINGDOM

BRITVIC INDIAN TONIC WATER

ORIGIN

In the middle of the 19th century, a British chemist began to experiment with the making of soft drinks at home. A little while later, James MacPherson & Co bought the recipes and introduced the drinks into the United Kingdom, under the name of British Vitamin Products. In 1971, the name changed from British Vitamin Products to Britvic and so the Britvic brand was born.

INGREDIENTS

carbonated water
sugar
citric acid
flavourings: including quinine
preservatives: potassium sorbate
saccharin

TASTE AND AROMA

On the nose, a real tonic: very lively citrus scent. In the mouth, sparkling with a dry and bitter finish. Big bubbles.

ITALY

CORTESE PURE TONIC

ORIGIN

Cortese Tonic is produced by Bevande Futuriste, a company inspired by the 18th century colonists in India and Africa who used to mix large quantities of water with quinine to obtain medicine against malaria. In addition to Pure Tonic, the company produces six other soft drinks and mixes.

INGREDIENTS

carbonated water ....
sugar ....
citric acid ....
quinine ....
natural flavourings ....

TASTE AND AROMA

A surprisingly fresh-sweet tonic, easy to drink and mix; a very smooth taste and nicely balanced.

FEVER-TREE INDIAN TONIC WATER

ORIGIN

The story begins with Charles Rolls, the man who brought Plymouth Gin back onto the market. After following a tonic-tasting course in 2000 with Tim Warrillow, they concluded that a lot of mixers used sodium benzoate or similar chemical substances as preservatives. Additionally, the use of cheap orange flavourings and artificial sweeteners jumped out at them, leading the men to exclaim "We can safely call this combination an attack on the taste buds". It was following this experience that the seeds of a simple yet brilliant idea began to grow: a gin & tonic is, after all, ¾'s tonic, why then is so little thought given to that tonic?! Fever-Tree Indian Tonic Water was launched in Great Britain in 2005 with the name deriving from the colloquial name for the Cinchona tree, the source of quinine. To do their tonic justice, Charles and Tim went in search of the best possible quality quinine, which they found in eastern Congo. Fever-Tree is therefore a tonic of premium quality, not only being served in seven out of the top ten restaurants in the world, but also in more than thirty countries worldwide. Sounds like a 'good' idea...

INGREDIENTS

spring water ....
cane sugar ....
citric acid ....
natural flavours ....
natural quinine ....

Fever-Tree Indian Tonic Water is made using a mix of eight botanical flavours, including rare ingredients such as extract of marigold and sour orange from Tanzania. Lemons from Sicily, thyme and rosemary from Provence in France, ginger from Nigeria and Ivory Coast... Need we say more?
Fever-Tree is made by 100% natural production methods and uses no artificial sweeteners or preservatives.

TASTE AND AROMA

The taste can be called, at the very least, soft. The authentic ingredients and production techniques from the world of perfumers provide a pure and subtle tonic with a sparkle similar to that in champagne. Refreshing, with a clear tint of citrus, perfectly supported by the natural bitterness of the quinine. The clean finish and the absence of a sticky mouth make this tonic a top notch mixer.

GERMANY

GOLDBERG TONIC WATER

ORIGIN

This German tonic was launched in 2013 and is made with natural quinine. In addition, MBG International Premium Brands puts additional Goldberg mixers on the market: Ginger Ale, Bitter Lemon, Intense Ginger and Soda Water. In 2013, Goldberg was awarded 'The Red Dot' award for the design of its bottle.

INGREDIENTS

carbonated water ....
citric acid ....
quinine ....
natural flavourings ....

TASTE AND AROMA

Goldberg is at the very least refreshing and that is also thanks to the use of bitter fruit. It has an aroma of mandarins and lime, with a citrus and bitter taste on the tongue. The aftertaste is dry, as befits tonic.

J.GASCO DRY BITTER TONIC

ORIGIN

J.Gasco Dry Bitter Tonic is an Italian tonic made from top-quality local ingredients. This tonic is just a touch drier and bitterer than its brother/sibling, the Indian Tonic version of J.Gasco. This Dry Bitter Tonic is perfect for lovers of a smoother, somewhat more floral and less sweet tonic. It consists of 100% natural ingredients without the addition of colouring and preservative agents. You can read the complete story behind these mixes under J.Gasco Premium Indian Tonic.

INGREDIENTS

carbonated water
citric acid
quinine
natural flavourings

TASTE AND AROMA

Neutral tonic, but somewhat bitterer, perfect for mixing; the bitterness adds finesse to the glass.

J.GASCO INDIAN TONIC

ORIGIN

This tonic has its origin in a bizarre dream J. Gasco had during his expedition to the forests of French Guiana, in search of the legendary green anaconda. The environmentalist from Piemonte in Italy was awoken one night by a dream, in which an obscure figure offered him a fantastically delicious drink. He couldn't get the dream out of his head and dedicated the rest of his life to recreating this magical drink. Today, J.Gasco's traditional recipes are still used as the basis for J.Gasco mixers.

INGREDIENTS

carbonated water ....
sugar ....
quinine ....
citrus essence ....

TASTE AND AROMA

A typically neutral tonic, perfect for use as a mixer

UNITED KINGDOM

LEDGER'S TONIC WATER

ORIGIN

In 1862 Charles Ledger went on a quest to Peru to find the mythical seeds of the cinchona tree. Two years later – when he explored Bolivia – he discovered a cinchona tree with a bark that has better and stronger quinine. This substance is classified under the name 'Cinchona Ledgeriana' in honour of the man who discovered it. Legend has it that Charles Ledger prevented the cinchona tree from becoming extinct. Together with his companion, Manuel, he collected the seeds of the cinchona tree and took them to London. He sold most of the seeds to the Dutch government, which planted them in Java, a Dutch colony. The rest of the seeds ultimately reached Australia and India. Ledger's Tonic is made with stevia instead of HFCS (high fructose corn syrup) or other artificial sweeteners, which means that a bottle of Ledger's Tonic contains only 23 calories, less than any other tonic in the market.

INGREDIENTS

carbonated water
stevia
citric acid
quinine from the Cinchona Ledgeriana
sodium citrate

TASTE AND AROMA

Ledger's tonic is subtly bubbled. The initial taste hints of orange. The quinine is not really noticeable and stevia gives it its sweet flavour. The aftertaste is citrus with subtle floral tones.

THE NETHERLANDS

LOOPUYT TONIC

ORIGIN

Loopuyt Tonic is obviously combined with the gin that bears the same name. The Loopuyt distillery began in 1772 and has recently been given a new life under the name P. Loopuyt & Co Distillers. During the summer of 2013, the company began developing a gin. This was followed by a matching tonic and eventually the market launch in December 2014. According to Jaco van de Leum, Master distiller at P. Loopuyt & Co, the combination of their gin with its tailor-made tonic produces a pleasant mix topped by refreshing tones of citrus and floral aromas.

INGREDIENTS

carbonated water ....
sugar ....
citric acid ....
quinine ....
natural flavourings ....

TASTE AND AROMA

Loopuyt Tonic water has a sparkling freshness to it, achieved by its high carbonated content and an obvious lemon aroma, giving a slightly sweet aftertaste.

ORIGINAL PREMIUM TONIC CLASSIC

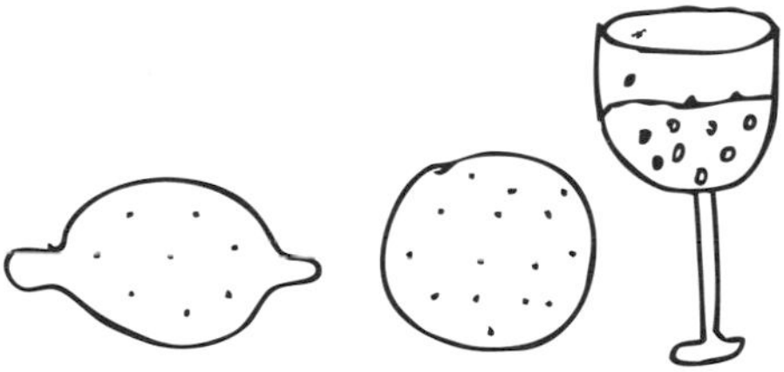

ORIGIN

Original Tonic Water Classic is produced by Magnifique Brands in Madrid.

INGREDIENTS

carbonated water
sugar
quinine
citrus
natural flavourings

TASTE AND AROMA

Crystal clear in appearance with a natural aroma and a big bubble. Lightly sweet in the beginning with hints of lemon and orange.

PETER SPANTON TONIC N°1

ORIGIN

After establishing the legendary bar, Vic Naylor's in 1986 in Clerkenwell, London, Peter Spanton was totally immersed in the world of alcoholic beverages, until 2005 when he experienced a revelation. Peter – who used to be an alcoholic – noticed that during the Christmas period, many businessmen consumed excessive amounts of alcohol. For the first time in his life, Peter despised the scene in which he lived. As an ex-alcoholic, he further noticed that the selection of sophisticated soft drinks was negligible. This led him to the conclusion that the 'hole in the market' was to be found in the non-alcoholic 'adults only' drinks, so he began experimenting in his own kitchen with various ingredients, including the Brazilian acai berry. This berry is considered a superfood, but it is difficult to process. After many failed attempts and just as many techniques, Peter threw all the ingredients into a muslin sack and two days later a certain liquid leaked out of the sack, which got him started. However, it took some time before Peter managed to create the right recipe. The acai berry is actually an acquired taste: chocolate with a metallic taste. Ultimately, he used Concord grapes to sweeten the drink and christened this potion Beverage N°7. This Acai Blend is the first creation of Peter Spanton Beverages. His London Tonic was designated Beverage N°1.

INGREDIENTS

- carbonated water
- lemon juice
- natural flavourings
- citric acid
- sucralose
- quinine

TASTE AND AROMA

The aroma of a real tonic, but the taste of quinine is compensated by Sicilian lemon oil and oil made from the peel of bitter orange.

SAN PELLEGRINO OLD TONIC

ORIGIN

San Pellegrino Old Tonic Water is the tonic made by the prestigious brand San Pellegrino. Its lasting success is deeply rooted in its exceptional heritage, symbolic value and legendary identity – each an expression of its unique Italian character. After all, since its creation in 1899, San Pellegrino has been a premium brand identified with style and refinement (cf. the annual publication of San Pellegrino's restaurant guide *The World's 50 Best Restaurants*). This effervesce water is praised worldwide for its exceptional quality. The water originates from a depth of 400 metres under the earth's surface where it is mineralized when it comes into contact with limestone and volcanic rock. It comes via the aquifer to the surface from three deep wells, with a temperature of 22-26°C. In addition the brand also markets a selection of lemonades: San Pellegrino Fruit Beverages. Their Tonic Water is made according to the 'Old Tonic' style and is characterised as somewhat bitter on the palate with a pleasant carbonation level.

INGREDIENTS

carbonated water ....
sugar ....
glucose syrup ....
quinine ....
citric acid ....
citrus aromas ....

TASTE AND AROMA

A mild bitter tonic with a crystal clear appearance; elegant with a fresh taste of citrus that leaves subtle, herbal hints in the background.

SCHWEPPES PREMIUM MIXER ORIGINAL

ORIGIN

In their premium range, Schweppes choose a formula based on natural sugars and ingredients from 100% natural sources. With this premium tonic, Schweppes tickles all the taste buds.

INGREDIENTS

carbonated water
sugar
citric acid
natural flavourings
quinine

TASTE AND AROMA

The formula guarantees the bubbles you would expect in Schweppes. This neutral tonic with a hint of lime gives a subtle and direct taste.

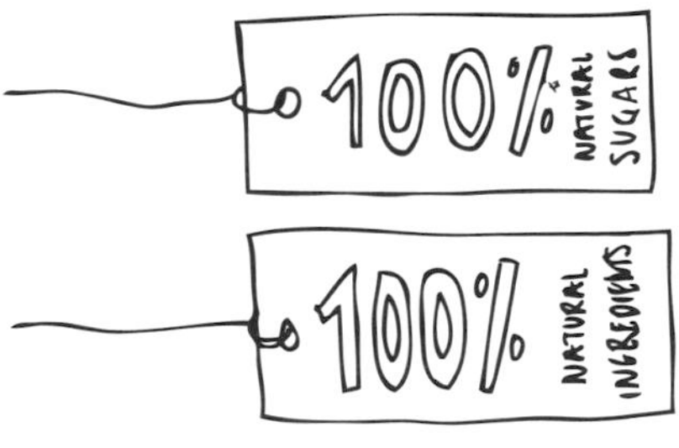

SEAGRAM'S PREMIUM TONIC

ORIGIN

The Seagram's brand came to life in the distillery of Joseph E. Seagram & Sons in Waterloo, Ontario, and takes its inspiration from the rugged Canadian wilderness. In 1928, Joseph E. Seagram & Sons was acquired by the Distillers Corporation Limited of Samuel Bronfman. After the death of Joseph Seagram, the distillery simply became known as Seagram Company Ltd., and so it is often wrongly claimed that Samuel Bronfman was the founder of Seagram. Over the years, Seagram Company Ltd. also acquired many shares in media companies such as Universal Studios, so it is somewhat surprising that Frankenstein wasn't saddled with alcohol problems... In 2000, the French concern Vivendi, gained a majority share in Seagram which heralded the end of the Canadian company. After the merger of Vivendi Universal, the various beverage divisions were sold in both public and closed auctions to PepsiCo, Diageo and Pernod Ricard. Acquired by Seagram in 1999, PolyGram merged with another Seagram music concern, MCA Music Entertainment to become Universal Music Group. Universal

Studios was then incorporated into Vivendi Universal Entertainment, later taken over by General Electric, and merged to become NBC Universal. Now enough of the film industry and back to the lesson. In 2002, the Coca-Cola Company acquired the mixer range, including Seagram's Premium Tonic Water, from Diageo and Pernod Ricard. And yet we are still not there... as far as gin is concerned. In 2006, Pernod Ricard announced plans to close Seagram's distillery in Lawrenceburg, Indiana. The distillery was temporarily taken over by CL Financial who, in turn, also went bankrupt, and from then on, the government took control of the company. Finally in 2011, MGP from Atchison, Kanas bought the distillery.

In an interview with *Globe and Mail*, Charles Bronfman, the son of Samuel Bronfman, declared: "The decisions that were made, led to Seagram becoming what it is now; they were a disaster, are a disaster, and will be a disaster..."

INGREDIENTS

sparkling water ....
fructose syrup..........................
citric acid.................................
quinine ....
potassium sorbate...................
sodium.......................................

TASTE AND AROMA

Complex and aromatic.
Spicy tints are clearly present.

THOMAS HENRY TONIC WATER

ORIGIN

In 1773, the name Thomas Henry, a well-known apothecary, could already be found on the label of a bottle in Manchester. And, like most apothecaries, he loved to experiment. Fortunately for us, as it was thanks to his experiments that the very first carbonated soft drink was born. Perhaps without Thomas Henry we would never have had our favourite, gin & tonic. Today, Thomas Henry is a German company, which makes many a Berlin bartender's heart beat faster. They really know how to throw a party in Berlin, and they are only too pleased to share it with the rest of the world. Sebastian Brack and Norman Stievert are now the inspiration behind Thomas Henry, after all these years. They may not be apothecaries, but they are soft drinks fanatics, and it has to be said, real marketing boys. They have managed to keep their recipe secret and launched their Tonic Water, amongst others, at the end of 2010.

INGREDIENTS

natural mineral water
sugar
carbonated water
citric acid
cinchona bark extract quinine

TASTE AND AROMA

It is safe to say that Thomas Henry Tonic Water is full of flavour. The unusually high quinine content gives an archetypal bitter taste. However the taste does not linger too long and it is refreshing, pure and surprisingly soft. A grown up tonic with extra freshness. The extract of cinchona bark quinine ensures the individual character of Thomas Henry Tonic Water.

AROMATIC TONICS

AQUA MONACO TONIC WATER

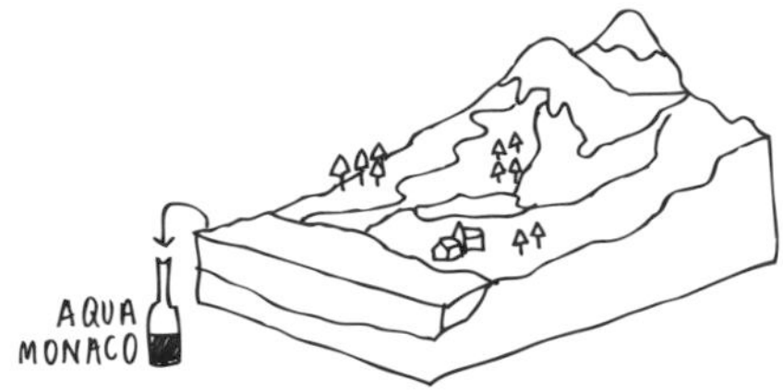

ORIGIN

The basis of this tonic is Aqua Monaco, a sodium-free water extracted from the 'Münchner Schotterebene'. The what? Well, the Münchner Schotterebene is a gravel bed that was formed millions of years ago, caused by the effects of glaciers in the Alps. The ice flowed off the glaciers, scraping over the ground and taking a mass of rock pieces and other debris along with it. When the glacier melted, the water was trapped in the rocky layers of the gravel bed. Today, the water used for Aqua Monaco Tonic Water is obtained from the 'Silenca Quelle' (a source formed by glacial water) of the privately owned brewery Schweiger who use it to brew their beer. The story behind the name Aqua Monaco is simple, but worth telling. The Italian for the capital of Bavaria is 'Monaco di Baviera' and the sound of the name suits the people particularly well. It is fresh and appealing, and reflects the spirit of the city perfectly: uncomplicated and brimming with confidence.

INGREDIENTS

natural spring water
a little sugar
quinine
citric acid
carbon dioxide
sage
Chinotto orange

TASTE AND AROMA

By using the purest of pure water, the best raw materials and a substantial reduction of the sugar content, the result is a particularly fine and delicious tonic. Very refreshing and brought to life by a slight acidity and a pleasant note of quinine. Extra carbon dioxide is added for that little extra sparkle.

FENTIMANS 19:05 HERBAL TONIC WATER

ORIGIN

Fentimans 19:05 Herbal Tonic Water is indisputably the tonic produced with the highest number of botanicals. The name refers to the year that Fentimans was founded, 1905. Fentimans Tonic Water is also a 100% botanical brew, which is brewed according to the traditional Fentimans method in the UK. The Fentimans family has been brewing for more than 100 years in the UK by using the best ingredients and natural aromas. You can read the complete story of Fentimans under Fentimans Tonic Water in neutral tonics.

INGREDIENTS

carbonated water
sugar
citric acid
natural flavourings
quinine
herbal infusions of lemon blossoms
myrtle
hyssop
fermented extracts of juniper extracts
orris root
lemon grass and kaffir lime leaves

TASTE AND AROMA

Fentimans 19:05 Herbal Tonic Water is a delicate herbal tonic with subtle sweetness of lime-tree blossoms that alternates with the bitterness of quinine. The juniper berries ensure that the tonic is not excessively herbal in taste.

Serve chilled
FENTIMANS
EST. 1905
BOTANICALLY
BREWED
TRADITIONAL
TONIC
WATER
Fermented Botanical
Tonic Water with Herbal
Extracts.
125ml℮
Best before: See neck

UNITED KINGDOM

FENTIMANS TONIC WATER

ORIGIN

In 1905, the Englishman Thomas Fentiman, using a traditional recipe which had been thrust under his nose as security on a loan, began brewing a botanical ginger beer. He started by grinding up ginger roots and boiled them in copper kettles to release the flavours. This syrup was then fermented in wooden barrels with brewer's yeast, sugar and botanicals such as ginger, juniper berry, veronica and yarrow extract. The loan was never repaid and so Thomas became the owner of this unique recipe and, with the aid of a horse and cart, he brought his ginger beer to the people. He bottled the beer in stone jars stamped with a picture of his dog 'Fearless'. Why his dog, I hear you ask? Well, Thomas was extremely proud of his dog, having twice won the prize for the most obedient dog at the famous dog show 'Crufts'. The depiction of Thomas' trusted four-footed friend is still used today in Fentimans logo. Now, more than 100 years later, the brewing process has of course been modernised. However, the recipe itself remains virtually unchanged, including fermenting the mixture for a week in a vat. Due to the addition of the natural flavourings and herbs, the alcohol percentage of Fentimans Tonic Water is reduced to less than 0.5% and therefore can be legally sold as a soft drink. So, never call Fentimans 'just a mixer'.

INGREDIENTS

soda water ....
sugar ....
citric acid ....
natural flavourings ....
quinine ....
spice infusions such as juniper berry, cinnamon and kaffir lime leaf

Fetimans Tonic Water is, without exception, manufactured using 100% natural ingredients such as Sicilian oranges

TASTE AND AROMA

The tonic has the spicy nose of lemon, lemongrass and ginger. As Fentimans Tonic Water is created with less quinine than some of its colleagues there is no 'metallic' aftertaste. The tonic clearly has many layers which are subtly released and brought to the forefront.

FEVER-TREE MEDITERRANEAN TONIC WATER

ORIGIN

Fever-Tree Mediterranean followed – along with seven other Fever-Tree mixers – a few years after the launch of the original version. For the complete Fever-Tree story, see the neutral tonics section.

INGREDIENTS

spring water
cane sugar
citric acid
natural flavourings
natural quinine
lemon oil from Sicily
geranium
rosemary
mandarin

TASTE AND AROMA

On the nose, clear aromas of thyme, with citrus and a hint of rosemary. The soft bitterness of the natural quinine and the elegant tastes of the herbs and citrus are accompanied by beautiful champagne-like bubbles.

UNITED KINGDOM

LEDGER'S TONIC WATER & CINNAMON

ORIGIN

Like Ledger's Tonic, Ledger's Tonic Water & Cinnamon is produced with stevia instead of HFCS (high fructose corn syrup) or other artificial sweeteners. The cinnamon in the tonic stimulates the gastric juices so you enjoy the gin that's mixed with it even better. You can read about the orgin of Ledger's Tonic under neutral tonics.

INGREDIENTS

carbonated water
sugar
citric acid
cinnamon aromas
potassium & sodium (salt)
quinine

TASTE AND AROMA

A very refined tonic with a subtle hint of cinnamon, but which you can nevertheless taste.

UNITED KINGDOM

LEDGER'S TONIC WATER & TANGERINE

ORIGIN

Like Ledger's Tonic, Ledger's Tonic Water & Tangerine is produced with stevia instead of HFCS (high fructose corn syrup) or other artificial sweeteners: A refreshing tonic that suggests warmer climates because it uses mandarins.

You can read the complete story behind Ledger's Tonic under neutral tonics.

INGREDIENTS

carbonated water ....
steviol ....
citric acid ....
quinine from Cinchona Ledgeriana ....
sodium ....
mandarin aromas ....

TASTE AND AROMA

A refreshing tonic, as tonic should be, with a distinct taste of mandarins and a touch of lemon in the background.

SPAIN

ME PREMIUM TONIC WATER

ORIGIN

The recipe for ME Tonic is based on the creativity of a number of professional cocktail specialists. The world of ME Tonic pays homage to contrasts by combining natural and exotic ingredients. ME Tonic is produced with natural quinine and Japanese yuzu, a citrus fruit that grows wild in Wakayama. Yuzu is handpicked – essential for improving the aromatic characteristics of ME Tonic.

INGREDIENTS

carbonated water ....
sugar ....
citric acid ....
aromas from citrus and black pepper ....
quinine ....
natural yuzu aromas ....

TASTE AND AROMA

ME Tonic has a refreshing and pure look. The bouquet is powerful and expressive with a powerful aroma. The mild aroma of citrus combined with a sweet nut aroma derives from the Japanese yuzu fruit. The taste is intensely refreshing and complex with a nice start of citrus and a fine, lasting, sparkling taste. The tonic is a perfect balance of sweet and sour with a dry aftertaste, thanks to the natural quinine.

ORIGINAL PREMIUM TONIC CITRUS

ORIGIN

Original Tonic Water Blue is produced by Magnifique Brands in Madrid.

INGREDIENTS

carbonated water
sugar
quinine
citrus
grapefruit

TASTE AND AROMA

Clear blue in appearance with a natural fragrance and a small bubble. Fresh tones of lime and sour lemon in the beginning, subsequently complemented by the bitter quinine taste, which is then followed by subtle hints of orange and grapefruit.

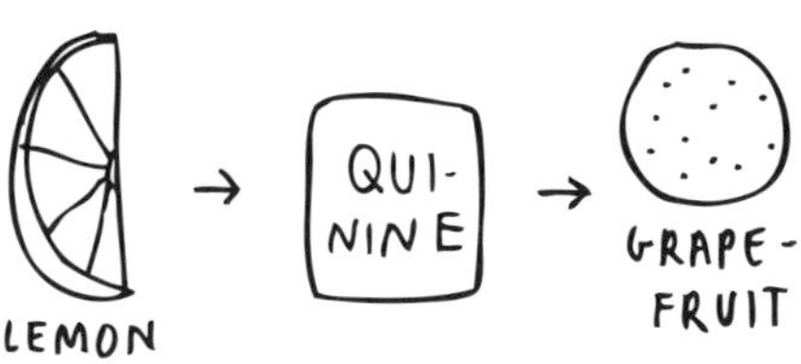

SPAIN

ORIGINAL PREMIUM TONIC MINT

ORIGIN

Original Mint Tonic Water is a premium tonic produced by Magnifique Brands in Madrid. Its green colour associates it immediately with mint, which gives it a subtle aroma.

INGREDIENTS

carbonated water
sugar
quinine
citric acid
mint aromas

TASTE AND AROMA

Like the other Original Tonics, Original Mint Tonic Water is lightly carbonated. With the first sip, you immediately taste the mint which gives the tonic exceptional freshness combined with a subtle citrus flavour. The mint is also noticeable in the aftertaste.

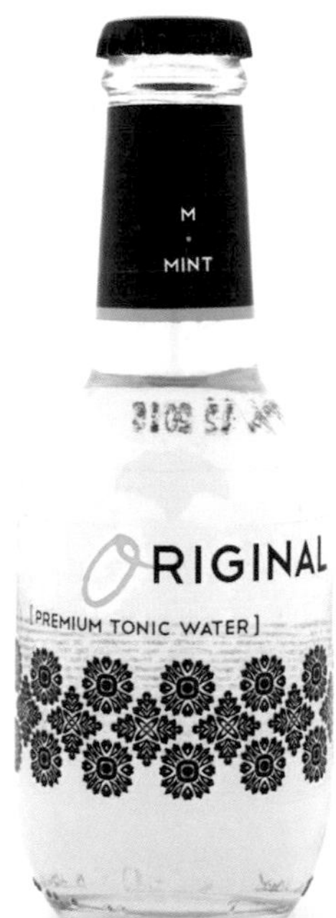

UNITED KINGDOM

PETER SPANTON TONIC N°4 CHOCOLATE

ORIGIN

Peter Spanton N°4 is a testimony of boldness: a blend of fresh mint and bitter chocolate. N°4 is astonishing and absolutely different from its predecessors – a unique combination of chocolate and mint. This tonic was developed mainly to enjoy in combination with darker spirits, such as rum, brandy and amaretto, but why not gin, too?

INGREDIENTS

carbonated water ....
sugar ....
citric acid ....
chocolate and mint aromas ....
quassia extract ....
potassium & sodium (salt) ....
quinine ....

TASTE AND AROMA

Your nose feels an aroma of fresh mint. Your lips and mouth feel a hint of bitter chocolate.

PETER SPANTON TONIC N°5 LEMONGRASS

ORIGIN

This tonic embraces the mild taste of lemon grass with a hint of warm ginger. N°5 is produced as a traditional tonic, yet slightly different, and mainly intended for combinations with vodka and vermouth. But it definitely also goes with a citrus gin.

The complete story behind Peter Spanton Tonic is under neutral tonics.

INGREDIENTS

carbonated water ....
sugar ....
citric acid ....
ginger and lemon grass aromas ....
potassium & sodium (salt) ....
quinine ....

TASTE AND AROMA

A true-blue tonic with a tinge of lemon in the mouth and a few remote tones of ginger.

UNITED KINGDOM

PETER SPANTON TONIC N°9 CARDAMOM

ORIGIN

Like all tonics in this range, Peter Spanton N°9 Cardamom is astonishing because of its subtle aromas. The use of cardamom gives the tonic a wonderful warm feeling; a superb tonic for mixing with herbal or complex gins or to counteract a soft gin. Find out for yourself.

You can read the complete story of Peter Spanton Tonic under neutral tonics.

INGREDIENTS

carbonated water ....
sugar ....
citric acid ....
cardamom aromas ....
potassium & sodium (salt) ....
quinine ....

TASTE AND AROMA

A tonic with the delicate taste of cardamom: both sweet and tangy. There is also a remote taste of cucumber.

SCHWEPPES PREMIUM MIXER GINGER & CARDAMOM

ORIGIN

In its premium range, Schweppes has opted for a formula based on 100% natural sugars and ingredients. In this aromatic tonic, it is the ginger and cardamom that produce its superior quality. The mix contains less sugar and more aromas.

INGREDIENTS

carbonated water ....
sugar ....
citric acid ....
natural aromas of quinine ....
ginger ....
cardamom ....

TASTE AND AROMA

Schweppes Premium Mixer Ginger & Cardamom is strongly carbonated, which enhances the aroma of gin. The 'nose' (or bouquet) is mainly cardamom, yet when drinking it, you mainly taste the ginger. This refreshing and exotic formula dazzles the taste of the flowery gin.

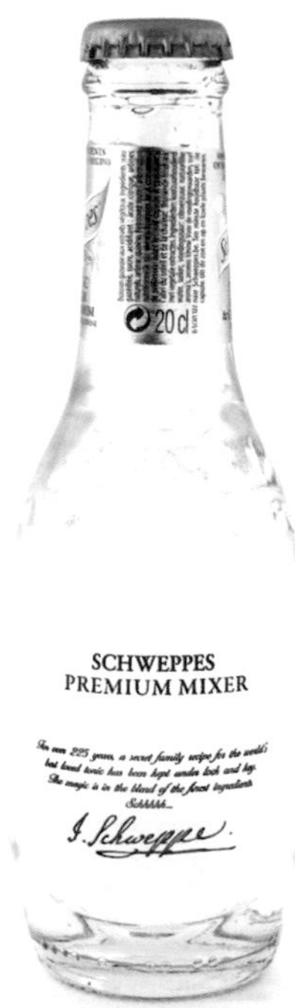

SYNDROME
Alpha Stimulus Euphoria

SYNDROME INDIAN TONIC VELVET

ORIGIN

The second tonic variant is the brainchild of the Antwerp catering entrepreneur, Serge Buss, better known for his bars Bounce and Tikibar in the South district of Antwerp and his BUSS N°509 gins (four by now). Syndrome is a true-blue Belgian tonic: all the ingredients are purchased in Belgium. It must be said that the clever addition of bitter oranges and thyme creates an innovative tonic.

INGREDIENTS

carbonated water ....
sugar ....
citric acid ....
quinine ....
natural aromas of orange and thyme ....

TASTE AND AROMA

With your first sip, you taste a tonic that strives towards delicate and somewhat dry, tingling tones. A strong and well-balanced injection of carbonate makes it a lasting and tingling experience. The long-lasting bitter taste is the result of adding raw quinine and orange, while the thyme gives it a very elegant, lightly herbal touch.

FRUITY/ FLORAL TONICS

CHILE

1724 TONIC WATER

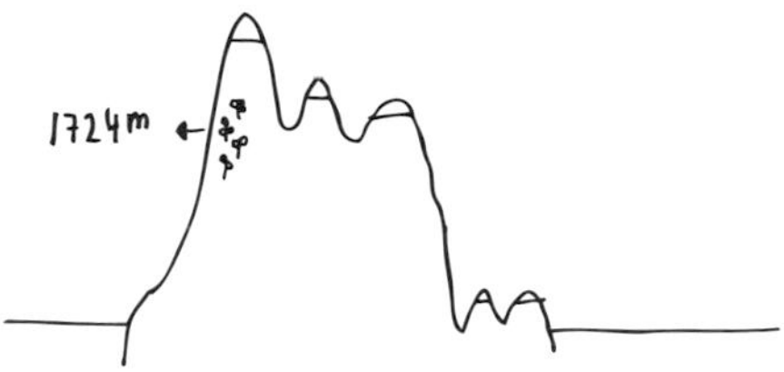

ORIGIN

In 2012, creators of Gin Mare brought the tonic 1724 to life. 1724 Tonic Water has been explicitly developed to partner the gin, and you can taste it! To find the essence of the quinine used for 1724 Tonic Water one has to climb high; 1724 metres above sea level to be precise... not a metre higher, not a metre lower! And you guessed it; this is how the name of the tonic came about. The quinine used is found in the Andes, on the so-called Inca trail, and is picked by hand... 1724 Tonic Water is produced in Chile.

INGREDIENTS

carbonated water
natural quinine
sugar
infusion of mandarin

TASTE AND AROMA

1724 Tonic Water takes you to completely new heights by finding the perfect balance between tradition and originality. The quinine is less bitter because of its Latin American origins. The balanced flavour is peppered with hints of rosemary and thyme. Lightly fruity with an elegant pearly bubble and a note of aniseed in the finish.

FEVER-TREE ELDERFLOWER TONIC WATER

ORIGIN

Fever-Tree Elderflower Tonic Water – along with other Fever-Tree mixers – was launched several years after the original version. The use of elderflower in this tonic gives it a very distinct floral touch. For this particular tonic, Fever-Tree uses elderflowers that are picked in the English countryside, more specifically in The Cotswolds, northwest of London. The subtle character of Fever-Tree Elderflower Tonic Water is perfectly balanced by the sweet taste of elderflower and the bitterness of quinine. You can read the complete story of Fever-Tree under neutral tonics.

INGREDIENTS

spring water ....
cane sugar ....
citric acid ....
natural quinine ....
elderflower extract ....

TASTE AND AROMA

This pure and crystal-clear tonic has a sweet and floral bouquet, which is combined with a light touch of citrus. The taste is perfectly balanced by the elderflower and quinine. The aftertaste is mild.

SWITZERLAND

GENTS SWISS ROOTS PREMIUM TONIC

ORIGIN

This tonic is produced by the start-up company Gents GmbH in Zurich. Its creator is journalist and communications expert Hans Georg Hildebrandt, alongside senior specialist Patrick Zbinden, the young chef Ralph Schelling and Markus Blattner, barman at the Widder Hotel, who lend their support to the basis of this tonic. The name 'Gents' was inspired by a local herb variety, the yellow gentian. This herb is widely used in a number of drinks from the Alpine region.

INGREDIENTS

carbonated water
sugar beet from Switzerland
lemon essence from Sicilian lemons
quinine from Peru
extract from the yellow gentian

TASTE AND AROMA

The harmonious mix of the ingredients ensures a good balance of flavours. Full and pleasantly sleek in the mouth, with a light floral hint.

INDI BOTANICAL TONIC

ORIGIN

Indi Tonic was launched in 2012 by Indi & Co and has its origins in Seville, Spain. In the quest for the perfect mixer, the Spanish developers have delved into their own culinary traditions, flavours and colours. In the Guadalquivir valley they have been drying aromatic herbs, oranges and lemons for hundreds of years, both for medicinal as well as culinary use. As it was not their intention to develop a medicine for headaches, the idea for Indi Tonic began to grow in the passionate minds of the Andalusians. By mixing age-old traditions with exotic ingredients like quinine and vanilla, the tonic is almost ready for the glass... almost...

The production in the Spanish village of El Puerto Santa Maria begins with a process of softening the botanical ingredients by macerating or soaking in cold water and alcohol. The resulting liquid is then distilled in a copper distillation kettle at a low temperature. This allows for a slower and finer distillate which ensures that the tastes and flavours are faithfully captured. Finally, purified water, white sugar and cane sugar are added.

INGREDIENTS

purified water

quinine

sugars

botanical spices: orange peel from Seville, kalonji (black cumin from India), kewra (Asian plant), cardamom from India

Indi Tonic is completely crafted by hand, and only contains 100% natural ingredients.

TASTE AND AROMA

Intense citrus with a hint of orange peel, setting the tone for perfect harmony with aromatic notes of cardamom and freshness from the kewra flower. Black cumin subtly prickles the tongue and perfectly combines with both the bitterness of the quinine and the sweetness of the sugars. Indi Tonic can certainly be consumed on its own, although we prefer the combination with gin.

LEDGER'S TONIC WATER & LICORICE

ORIGIN

Just like Ledger's Tonic, Ledger's Tonic Water & Licorice is produced with stevia instead of HFCS (high fructose corn syrup) or other artificial sweeteners. This tonic has great character and an even greater taste. The use of liquorice gives the mixer a subtle anise taste.

INGREDIENTS

carbonated water ....
sugar ....
citric acid ....
liquorice aromas ....
potassium & sodium (salt) ....
quinine ....

TASTE AND AROMA

The initial taste reminds you of oranges, after which there is a subtle hint of liquorice. Stevia provides the sweetness.

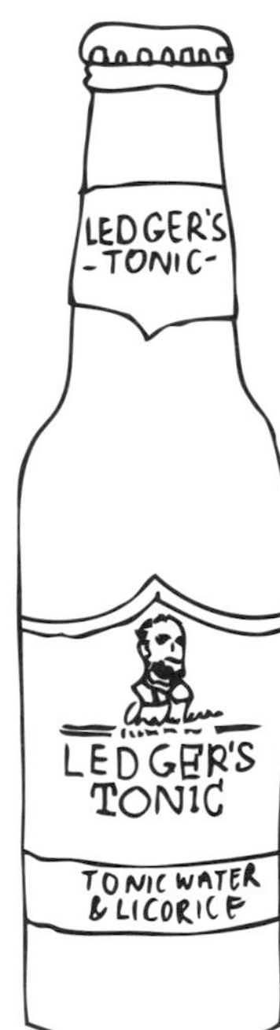

SPAIN

ORIGINAL PREMIUM TONIC BERRIES

ORIGIN

Original Tonic Water Pink is produced by Magnifique Brands in Madrid.

INGREDIENTS

carbonated water ....
sugar ....
quinine ....
citrus ....
red fruits ....

TASTE AND AROMA

This fruity tonic is soft pink in colour and naturally fragrant. A slightly larger bubble than the original version and with a perfect balance between bitter and sweet. The red fruits slowly emerge and then explode in the finish, with perfectly integrated citrus tones.

UNITED STATES

Q TONIC

ORIGIN

Q Tonic is the jewel in the crown of Q Drinks. The tonic was developed in Brooklyn, NY, by founder Jordan Silbert. The product is bottled in Worcester, Massachusetts. In 2002, Silbert began the process of developing, as it were, his tonic in his own garage, driven by his belief that too many soft drinks use synthetic quinine. He ordered the bark of the Cinchona tree online from Peru, for a mere ten dollars, which turned out to be a very good investment. In 2004, he asked for specialist help to further develop the recipe, leading to the addition of agave nectar to make the recipe sweeter. Q drinks finally opened for business in 2006.

INGREDIENTS

spring water with a high mineral content.........
citric acid..
Peruvian cinchona bark..
Mexican agave syrup..

TASTE AND AROMA

Q Tonic is soft yet pungent on the nose and is lightly salty in character. The tonic is certainly not sweet allowing the taste of the gin to remain unmasked. The earthy tone ensures that the quinine does not dominate the foreground.

UNITED KINGDOM

SCHWEPPES PREMIUM MIXER ORANGE BLOSSOM & LAVENDER

ORIGIN

For their premium range, Schweppes choose a formula based on 100% natural sugars and ingredients from 100% natural sources.

INGREDIENTS

lavender
orange blossom
carbonated water
sugar
citric acid
natural flavourings
quinine

TASTE AND AROMA

Make way for the flavours of the subtly processed lavender and orange blossom. The flowery notes completely unfold in the mouth and give a pleasant hint of the Mediterranean, coupled to his classic, bigger carbonate bubble.

UNITED KINGDOM

SCHWEPPES PREMIUM MIXER
PINK PEPPER

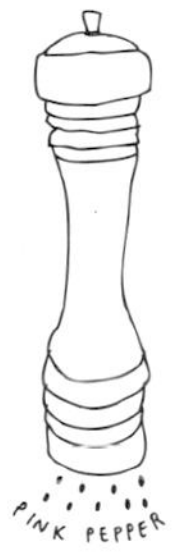

ORIGIN

For their premium range, Schweppes choose a formula based on 100% natural sugars and ingredients from 100% natural sources.

INGREDIENTS

carbonated water ....
sugar ....
citric acid ....
natural flavourings ....
quinine ....
pink pepper ....

TASTE AND AROMA

An adventurous taste, where the protagonist, the pink pepper, has been carefully studied, as it highlights the essence of an alcoholic drink and adds a fruity and rebellious touch.

BELGIUM

SYNDROME INDIAN TONIC RAW

ORIGIN

The catering entrepreneur from Antwerp, Serge Buss, better known for his bars Bounce and Tikibar in the South district of Antwerp and his BUSS N°509 gins (four by now), produced the very first Belgian premium tonic. Syndrome is a true-blue Belgian tonic: all the ingredients are purchased in Belgium. On the other hand, the crystal-clear water comes from Germany, where the tonic is also bottled. Syndrome Tonic favours the old school and is based on authentic chemist recipes from the 19th century. By adding the exotic fruit, Buddha's Hand – an unusual yellow citrus fruit segmented into finger-like sections from the Far East – Serge has succeeded in producing an astonishing tonic.

INGREDIENTS

carbonated water ....
sugar ....
natural quinine ....
Buddha's Hand ....

TASTE AND AROMA

With your first sip, you taste a tonic that strives towards mild and slightly fruity tones. A strong and well-balanced injection of carbonate makes it a lasting and tingling experience. The long-lasting bitter taste is the result of adding raw quinine.

THOMAS HENRY ELDERFLOWER TONIC

ORIGIN

Thomas Henry Elderflower Tonic is the most recent to be launched by the company. For more on the history of Thomas Henry, see the entry under 'Neutral Tonics'. The medicinal properties of elderflower have been known for centuries, but nowadays it is also used for many other purposes, including as an ingredient in liqueurs or cocktails and even in champagne. Thomas Henry Elderflower Tonic is also the ideal gin partner, as the floral touch wonderfully balances the juniper flavours.

INGREDIENTS

natural mineral water
sugar
carbonated water
citric acid
flavourings: quinine
elderflower

TASTE AND AROMA

Light and sweet floral

WORLDWIDE

KINLEY TONIC

ORIGIN

Kinley Tonic was first introduced into Germany in 1971 by the Coca-Cola Company and is now exported throughout Europe and Asia.

TASTE AND AROMA

Outspoken bitter tonic taste, with light sweet tones in the background

INGREDIENTS

- sparkling water
- sugar
- citric acid
- flavourings
- quinine
- preservative (kalium sorbate)
- antioxidant (ascorbic acid)

WESTERN EUROPE

NORDIC MIST TONIC WATER

ORIGIN

Nordic Mist Tonic Water was launched in 1992 by the Coca-Cola Company in New York, Boston, Pittsburgh and Philadelphia.

TASTE AND AROMA

Nordic Mist has a subdued nose with subtle notes of pine. The bitter taste of quinine is strongly present.

INGREDIENTS

sparkling water
sugar
citric acid
flavourings
quinine
sodium benzoate

WORLDWIDE

SCHWEPPES INDIAN TONIC

ORIGIN

Schweppes Indian Tonic is based on the drink the English colonists in India used, a mix of quinine, sugar and bitter orange peel, as a means of preventing malaria. This tonic was first produced by Cadbury Schweppes in London in 1870.

TASTE AND AROMA

Dry and an early bitter taste

INGREDIENTS

carbonated water
sugar
citric acid
natural flavouring
quinine flavouring

MAVERICKS

LIGHT TONIC: MAKES SENSE, OR IS IT NONSENSE?

Various brands market a light version of their tonic. Those which don't, will most likely follow suit. After all, is there any soft drink that's not available these days in a light or zero version? Sugars are replaced by synthetic sweeteners, fructose, agave syrup or stevia. This is not to say that synthetic sweeteners have not been under attack for a very long time. On the other hand, stevia claims to be healthy, or at least healthier. This herb is natural (it originates from a small South American evergreen shrub), 300 times sweeter than crystal sugar and absolutely free of calories. By now, there are several tonics on the market that use only this sweetener, for example Ledger's Tonic (see: neutral tonics). In terms of fructose and agave syrup, we will steer a middle course. But why would you ever want to make a gin & tonic with a light tonic? Not entirely because of the number of calories. Regular tonic contains an average of 35 kcal per 100 ml. Since a properly served gin & tonic contains around 150 ml tonic, which is roughly 53 kcal, the difference is negligible. So, why bother, unless you really like the taste of light tonic. A light tonic is just slightly 'lighter' (less sweet) than its classic sibling, which results in a greater emphasis on the taste of gin. This is why we have decided not to refrain from presenting a number of light tonics.

FENTIMANS LIGHT TONIC WATER

ORIGIN

The light version of Fentimans Tonic Water is brewed according to the traditional Fentimans method and uses only 100% natural ingredients. The taste is certainly not inferior to the classic version, but a bottle contains 33% fewer calories. You can read the full story of Fentimans under Fentimans Tonic Water.

INGREDIENTS

soda water
sugar
citric acid
natural flavourings
quinine
herbal infusions such as juniper berry
cinnamon
kaffir lime leaves

TASTE AND AROMA

This tonic has a herbal bouquet that smells of lemon, lemon grass and ginger. It has a typical Fentimans taste of citrus, yet somewhat less sweet.

FEVER-TREE NATURALLY LIGHT INDIAN TONIC WATER

ORIGIN

Fever-Tree Naturally Light Indian Tonic is 100% natural, light tonic water and is not inferior to the regular version. Fructose or fruit sugars rather than artificial sweeteners are used to manufacture this tonic, which contains only 41 kcal per 200 ml. bottle. You can read the full story of Fever-Tree under neutral tonics.

INGREDIENTS

spring water ....

pure fructose ....

citric acid ....

natural flavourings ....

natural quinine ....

TASTE AND AROMA

The taste is mild, to say the least, and has the same pure aftertaste as Fever-Tree, but with slightly more calories. The aroma has a scent of lime and a touch of citrus, which like its counterpart, is perfectly balanced by the natural bitterness of quinine. The pure aftertaste and the absence of a sticky mouthfeel, which is far more noticeable in this light version, make the Fever-Tree Naturally Light Indian Tonic Water an elegant topper.

NOT CONVINCED? MAKE YOUR OWN TONIC!

You can always make your own tonic. Surf the Internet and you will find various recipes that will get you a long way. And there is also an alternative: tonic syrups. Using tonic syrup can elevate your gin & tonic to a completely different level. The magic is in the taste; your personal taste. The syrup determines how your gin & tonic will taste. Tonic syrup can only be mixed with soda (carbonated) water; the quantity is entirely up to you. Too bitter? Add a bit more soda water. Too mild? Add more syrup. Can't be simpler than that. Furthermore, most tonic syrups are made with superior ingredients, which are 100% natural. Working with tonic syrup, gives your gin & tonic a completely different dimension. When we published the first edition of our book, there was only one tonic syrup available – John's Premium® Tonic Syrup. The biggest disadvantage was that this syrup was made in Phoenix, Arizona. The extra effort and the high import costs no doubt sent most of you to your local beverage retailer or gin specialist in order to obtain a premium tonic. We now have good news for you: You can now find dozens of non-alcoholic tonic syrups in the USA – be sure to visit www.OnlyBitters.com/tonics (worldwide shipping) – and in Europe, we are witnessing the emergence of several brands. We assume that this microbe will also take root here in the near future. We have selected a few for you.* For those who like it a bit stronger, there are also tonic bitters available.

* Don't forget: tonic syrups are artisanal and 100% natural, which means they have a limited shelf life. Our message is keep them cooled and use them before their expiry date.

UNITED KINGDOM

BTW BERMONDSEY TONIC SYRUP

BTW Lab created this very first, British, handmade tonic syrup based on a Victorian recipe. The cinchona bark is soaked in purified water in order to draw out the quinine. Afterwards, only sugar and citric acid are added. The producers do not filter the syrup (unlike authentic recipes). This way, the brownish syrup is maintained and it foams nicely when soda water is added. Using the syrup is simple: add 25 ml BTW Tonic Syrup to 50 ml of gin and create your own individual taste with added soda water.

GERMANY

PHENOMENAL TONIC SYRUP

The two German buddies, Peter Hundert and Hendrik Schaulin, wanted something different from the commonly available tonics for mixing their gins. They began experimenting with their own creations until they ultimately devised a recipe based on citrus, ginger, lemon grass and agave nectar. Their syrup was so dead on target that they decided to produce pHenomenal Tonic. This syrup too is easy to use: mix 2 cl of syrup with 10 cl of ice-cold soda water and you have instant tonic.

GERMANY

43 %

THE BITTER TRUTH TONIC BITTERS

The Bitter Truth GmbH is the German jalopy of Stefan Berg, whose image is on the left side of the label. Alexander Hauck is on the right side. They focused primarily on marketing bitters with concentrated alcoholic aromas (for example on the basis of peach, orange, celery, cucumber or even chocolate) that bar professionals like to use to give their cocktails an extra twist. Their range also includes Tonic Bitter. This bitter – only a few drops are sufficient – contains a combination of pomelo, Sicilian lemon, lime, orange (from Seville), juniper berry, orris root and Japanese green tea leaves. The ideal way to give your G&T that extra twist!

GIN:
CATEGORIZATION

Historically, we can divide gin into a number of **classic categories:** Old Tom, London Dry, Distilled, Plymouth and Compound gin.

Because of the recent explosion of new gins, today we go further than these classic divisions and make use of the **flavour cross**, with each of the four arms of the cross representing a different taste: **spicy/complex**, **citrus**, **sweet** and **floral**. This flavour cross first appeared in 2010 in *IMBIBE*, a leading magazine in the bar community.

In 2010, the palette of tastes didn't take into account the explosive rise of gin, or the creativity of the inventors and distillers. Alongside the completely new generation of gins developed in the last few years, totally new taste experiences have also evolved which can be described as **exotic** thanks to the use of eccentric botanicals. It is not easy to allocate a place on the flavour cross for these gins and for this reason we will be dealing with this category separately.

In this categorization we will also be giving you advice as to which tonic – or which type of tonic – you can best combine with which gin. By now, you know that we can divide tonics into three taste groups: neutral, aromatic and fruity/floral. In other words, for every gin, we will also give the category of the tonic taste, from which you can then choose your favourite. We will also be supporting these descriptions by means of a visual aid, the **G&T flavour cross** (the universe of gins combined with the tonic flavours), so you will be able to clearly see how to make these combinations.

For now, we will leave the garnish as it is. The priority is to begin with the basics, and for the moment, to concentrate on the facts of the matter, and so the use of a garnish depends on the analysis of the ingredients of your favourite gin & tonic, nothing more and nothing less. But don't worry; we will come back to this in the next chapter, where we relate the theory into practice.

Further on in the book, in the section on the 19 most remarkable gins, we will give you a few complete gin & tonic recipes, including garnish, as inspiration to start you off in making your own creations.

Anyway, let's start at the beginning...

CLASSIC PRESENTATIONS

OLD TOM GIN

The name Old Tom gin is used for sweet (retro) gins, like those made during the Gin Craze. This type of gin is rarely used now, but due to the revival of classic cocktails, Old Tom gin is once again being produced, and is becoming more readily available. This gin is sweeter than London Dry and a little dryer than jenever, and so is sometimes referred to as the missing link. The name Old Tom most likely has its origins in the 18th century, when various bars mounted a wooden plaque in the form of a black cat – Old Tom – on the outside walls. Thirsty passers-by could throw a penny into the mouth of the cat and the barman would pour a shot of gin through a small tube which came out between the paws of the cat. And so the first automatic drinks dispenser was born! At the time of writing this book there are around five Old Tom gins on the market. Below are four, and you will find the fifth one further on in the section on aged gins.

Old Tom gins are not combined with tonic, but have recently been brought back onto the market to give bartenders the opportunity to revive retro gin cocktails (such as Tom Collins or Martinez) and get them back on the menu. If you do fancy trying these sweet gins, drink them neat.

BOTH'S
BOTH
OLD TOM
GIN
BOTH'S
Alc. 47% vol.
94 Proof
BOTTLED BY
THE BOTH DISTILLERY
ESTD 1886

GERMANY

47 %

BOTH'S OLD TOM GIN

ORIGIN

Both's Old Tom Gin is the only gin of the Both distillery, set up to re-establish the sweet retrogins. The high alcohol content of 47% means that this gin is unique in comparison to other varieties of Old Tom which only manage a lower alcohol percentage. The label on the bottle is made from felt, and is finished with golden decorative details. The look of the bottle immediately invokes the glory days of Old Tom gins anno 1700.

TASTE AND AROMA

Both's has a rather subdued nose, with light sweet and mild flowery notes. In the mouth you get a strong fruity sweetness followed by an intense mix of flowery tones. Strong purple lavender is conspicuous with a mild flavour of juniper in the background. Even though this is a substantial gin, it remains relatively smooth in the finish.

INGREDIENTS

No information available

COMBINE WITH

drink neat or in retro cocktails

UNITED KINGDOM

40 %

HAYMAN'S OLD TOM GIN

ORIGIN

The Hayman family is one of the oldest distilling families in Great Britain. The Hayman's Old Tom Gin recipe was originally produced between the end of the 19th century and the beginning of the 20th century. Hayman's Old Tom was relaunched in 2007 thanks to increasing demand from bartenders and mixologists who wanted to bring body back to their classic gin cocktails, just like in the 'roaring 20s'. In the 19th century, the family business was taken over by James Burrough, the man who also held the recipe for Beefeater Gin.

TASTE AND AROMA

Hayman's Old Tom Gin is an intense botanic and lightly sweetened gin which sets it apart from other gins. This gin is used in recipes for numerous classic cocktails such as the Tom Collins or Martinez.

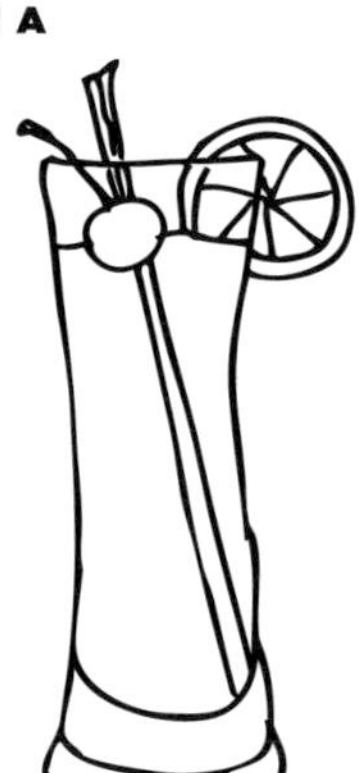

TOM COLLINS

INGREDIENTS

juniper berry
coriander seed
angelica
orange and lemon peel
orris root powder
and others

COMBINE WITH

drink neat, with a neutral tonic or in retro cocktails

OTHER GINCREATIONS

- Hayman's 1820 Gin Liqueur / 40% / citrus
- Hayman's 1850 Reserve Gin / 40% / matured
- Hayman's Sloe Gin / 26% / sloe liqueur
- Hayman's Royal Dock Gin / 57% / extra strong

LD
OM
49
VALLEY

jensen
jensen's
london
distilled
old
tom
gin
bermondsey gin ltd.,se1 3tq
70cl. e 43%vol.
TD12/164

43 %

JENSEN'S OLD TOM GIN

ORIGIN

This Old Tom is a product of Christian Jensen who originally wanted to create a London Dry. When visiting Japan, he was given the chance to taste a selection of old gins, some dating as far back as the 40s. The barman responsible for letting him try these gems, challenged Christian to make his own Old Tom style gin. He took a sample to the Thames Distillers and, after trying out many recipes, they developed Jensen's Bermondsey London Dry Gin. Following the success of this gin, Christian once again directed his energies to the challenge, eventually resulting in the creation of Jensen's Old Tom Gin. Old Tom Gin is based on a recipe from the 1840s, in which emphasis is given to a pure palette of tastes, with the juniper playing the leading role. The sweetness of the gin is not created by adding sugar, but instead by liquorice root.

TASTE AND AROMA

Jensen's Old Tom smells of eucalyptus and juniper berries in combination with liquorice, orange peel and a hint of almond. The tastes are predominantly of eucalyptus, supported by the liquorice. The eucalyptus has a long finish combined with vegetable tints.

INGREDIENTS

juniper berry
liquorice
eucalyptus

COMBINE WITH

drink neat, with a neutral tonic or in retro cocktails

OTHER GINCREATION

- Jensen's Bermondsey Gin / 43% / classic

40 %

SECRET TREASURES
OLD TOM STYLE GIN

ORIGIN

This gin is part of the Secret Treasures collection, an array of premium spirits from the German company Haromex. Only 700 bottles of this gin are produced per year, making it extremely exclusive. Secret Treasures Old Tom Style Gin was first brought to the market in 2007 and was nominated in the same year at the Berlin Bar Show as 'Spirit of the Year'.

TASTE AND AROMA

The aroma of Secret Treasures Old Tom Style Gin is sweet and earthy with a weak juniper berry fragrance which fully explodes in the mouth. A dry and fiery mouth feel with a long finish and subtle sweetness.

INGREDIENTS

ripe juniper berries from the Apennines and other (unlisted) herbs and essences

COMBINE WITH

drink neat or in retro cocktails

The
SECRET TREASURES

LONDON DRY GIN

London Dry is a gin with qualitative ingredients, and can be therefore seen as a quality label. London Dry is, in other words, a qualification, signifying a single distillation process during which all the ingredients are distilled together. The only ingredient that may be added after the distillation process is water. London Dry is the classic style of making gin and is not specifically related to the place, and so therefore does not have to come from London per se. London Dry is made in a traditional still, by re-distilling ethyl alcohol together with all the flavourings.

Conditions with which London Dry gin must comply in order to carry the label (EU regulations):

- *The ethyl alcohol must be of high quality. The methanol level in the alcohol may not exceed the maximum of 5 g per hectolitre in 100% alcohol volume.*
- *The flavourings used must be natural, and must only be used to add flavour during the distillation process.*
- *The use of artificial flavourings is forbidden.*
- *The resulting distillate must have a minimum 70% alcohol content.*
- *More ethyl alcohol may be added after distillation, but it must be of the same quality.*
- *The distillate may be sweetened as long as the sugars do not exceed the maximum level of 0.5 g per litre in the final product.*

- *The only other ingredient that may be added after distillation is water.*
- *In no instance may London Dry be coloured.*

DISTILLED GIN

Distilled gin is characterized by the same process as London Dry, but extra infusions may be added after, or extra ingredients added during, the distillation process. Many of the 'premium gins' fall into this category.

COMPOUND GIN

Compound gin mostly consists of a few added flavourings and extracts, often with no actual distillation of botanicals at all. Frequently all that is mentioned on the label is that it is gin. Mostly supermarket or liquor traders own brands are compound gins.

PLYMOUTH GIN

Plymouth Gin is a one of a kind gin, produced by the Black Friars Distillery inside the walls of what was once a Dominican monastery in the city of, you guessed it, Plymouth. Plymouth Gin gained popularity at the beginning of the 20th century and also has protected geographical indication, which relates to all gins distilled in Plymouth. To this day, there is only one brand of gin with this distinction: Plymouth Gin.

Plymouth Gin should be combined with a neutral tonic.

PLYMOUTH GIN
TRADE
MARK
IN 1620 THE MAYFLOWER SET SAIL FROM PLYMOUTH ON A JOURNEY OF HOPE AND DISCOVERY
41.2% Vol.
70cl
Black Friars Distillery
BLACK FRIARS
DISTILLERY

UNITED KINGDOM

41.2 %

PLYMOUTH GIN

ORIGIN

In 1793, in an old Dominican monastery, Fox and Williamson began distilling the brand, Plymouth. Soon after, Fox & Williamson became known as Coates & Co, and so they remained until March 2004. In 2005, the brand was bought by the Swedish V&S Group. Now however (since 2008), it is owned by the French company Pernod Ricard. The first bottle of Plymouth Gin depicted a monk on the inside of the back label. In 2006, the form of the bottle changed to become more art deco in style with a picture of The Mayflower ship on the front. In 2012, Plymouth Gin once again changed its look, going back to basics with a more classic shaped bottle with green tinted glass. Plymouth Gin is distilled using a unique combination of at least seven different botanical herbs and spices and pure grain alcohol. Between 1999 and 2006, Plymouth Gin took home various awards, from amongst others 'International Spirits Challenge', 'Beverage Testing Institute', 'The International Wine and Spirits Competition' and the 'San Francisco World Spirits Competition'.

TASTE AND AROMA

The aroma of the juniper is clearly present, but is also supported by lavender, camphor, lemon, sage and eucalyptus. The taste is fresh with hints of lemon and orange. The character of this gin is shaped by the subtle addition of coriander and white pepper corns.

INGREDIENTS

juniper berry
cardamom
orris root
coriander
lemon and orange peel

COMBINE WITH

neutral tonic or
classic cocktails

OTHER GINCREATION

- Plymouth Gin Navy Strength / 57% / extra strong

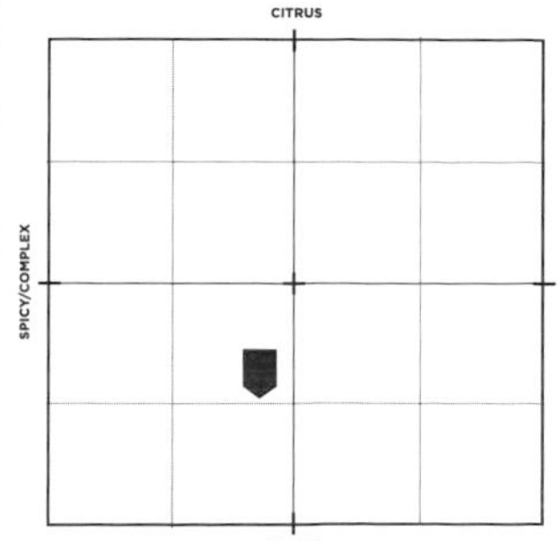

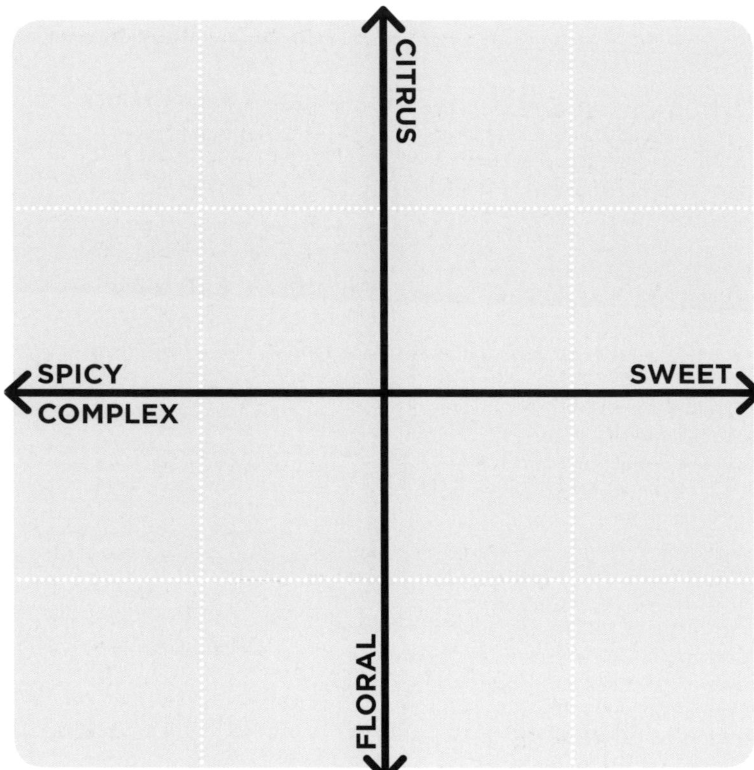
CITRUS
SPICY
COMPLEX
SWEET
FLORAL

CLASSIFICATION ACCORDING TO THE FLAVOUR CROSS

To properly demonstrate the use of the flavour cross we will take a few ambassadors from the new generation of gins and give them a place on the first version of the cross.

Please note: this is not to say that the old guard, like for example Bombay Sapphire, Beefeater Gin, Gordon's Gin, etc., do not warrant a place on the flavour cross. The typical London Dry gins find themselves close to the centre because of their classic gin flavour.

Since we don't want to leave anyone 'thirsty' for too long, we also give the tonics a place on the flavour cross. In this second version, we clarify straight away which tonic should be combined with which gin.

In principal a neutral tonic can be mixed with any gin, however they really come into their own in the centre of the flavour cross with the classic London Dry flavours.

First we will concentrate on the term New Western gin or New Generation gin.

NEW WESTERN GIN OR NEW GENERATION GIN

The new generation of gins date their renaissance from the year 2000 onwards, and have a herby and balanced aroma alongside the dominant juniper berry. The term New Western gin was conceived by Ryan Magarian, an internationally acclaimed bartender from the USA and co-creator of Aviation Gin. The term New Western gin has in the meantime become ingrained in the world of mixology. As authors of this book we also include the previous generation of gins under the heading New Generation gin. Why? The only reason is to make it easier and clearer for you. Are you a professional? Well then you are undoubtedly already familiar with the term New Western gin and you can safely skip over the following comments.

New Western gins stem from the efforts of both big brand producers and regional distilleries and gin adepts. By adepts we mean those passionate believers who knock on the doors of distilleries to get their own gin developed. After casting an eye over the available range of dry gins, they all saw that there was huge potential in creating new gins with more 'freedom of taste'; thus, an opportunity to put other botanicals into the spotlight alongside the juniper berry, which had had the starring role for so many years. Legally speaking the juniper berry has to remain the dominant flavour, but this new generation is not only defined by juniper but also by the careful integration of other supporting flavours.

According to Ryan Magarian, Tanqueray Malacca is one of the first New Western gins ever created. First introduced in 1997, this gin label was quickly taken off the market in 2001 due to limited success. It is possible that ten years ago, the timing was just not right for the new evolution in gin, or perhaps it's better to call it a gin revolution. Today however, it is a different story. In 2013, the label was brought back for the general public and has proved to be a big success. Hendrick's Gin followed suit and brought out a gin with aromas of cucumber and Bulgarian rose. This opened the floodgates, leading to other new artisan gins, only too happy to show off their creativity and regional specialities. The number of New Western gins on offer is on the rise, and keeps rising to this day.

THE FLAVOUR CROSS AND SOME GIN AMBASSADORS

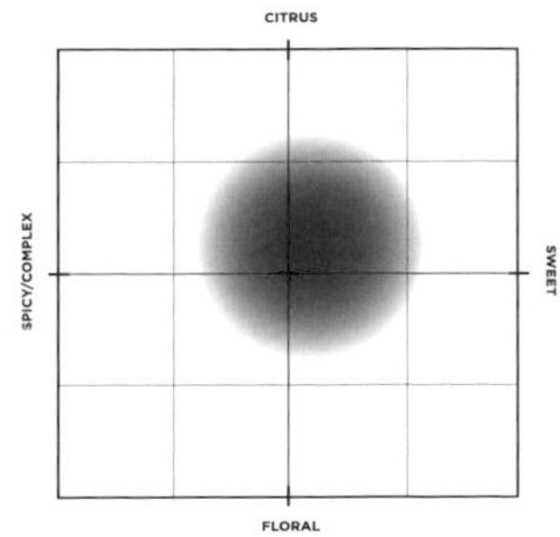

IN THE MIDDLE: CLASSIC LONDON DRY STYLE

COMBINE WITH NEUTRAL TONIC

As mentioned earlier, London Dry is a classic style of creating gin and is a label of quality, which furthermore has nothing to do with the place it is made or the taste of the gin.

It is true that London Dry was (before the 'gin explosion' of the last few years) considered to be the typical gin taste: sharp bitter (sweet), a hint of citrus and a dry finish. Nowadays, gins which carry the label London Dry have very little in common with the Dry gins of the past.

One thing is certain though, to be allowed to carry the label London Dry, the gin must conform to certain EU regulations and conditions (see page 108). There are also many new gins which comply with these regulations, and so likewise belong in this category. These comply with the rules of what a London Dry should be, but introduce new botanicals and distillation techniques, moving further and further away from the centre of the flavour cross. To sum up: a gin that finds itself close to the centre has the classical London Dry taste. The further away it deviates from the centre of the cross, the more different the taste notes are, or to say it in another way, the more the citrus-sweet-floral-spicy/complex taste manifest themselves in the gin.

UNITED KINGDOM

40 %

BEEFEATER GIN

ORIGIN

Beefeater is owned by Pernod Ricard and bottled and distributed by James Burrough Ltd. Beefeater was owned by the Burrough family up until 1987. Named after the 'Yeomen Warders' better known as 'Beefeaters': the ceremonial guards at the Tower of London. A unique feature of Beefeater Gin's production is that the peel from lemons and oranges, the entire juniper berries and other plant botanicals are allowed to steep for 24 hours before they are distilled. This process ensures that the aromas are completely extracted. The distillation itself takes about eight hours and the whole process is closely watched over by master distiller Desmond Payne.

TASTE AND AROMA

One of the classics, and the most recognisable, typical London Dry on the market. On the nose, juniper, black pepper and orange. Beefeater Gin has a sharp and dry taste. On the palate, an explosion of citrus and juniper berry in the finish.

www.beefeatergin.com

INGREDIENTS

juniper berry
angelica
angelica seed
coriander seed
liquorice root
almonds
orris root
Seville oranges
lemon peel

COMBINE WITH

neutral tonic

OTHER GINCREATIONS

- Beefeater24 / 45% / floral
- Beefeater Burrough's Reserve / 43% / matured

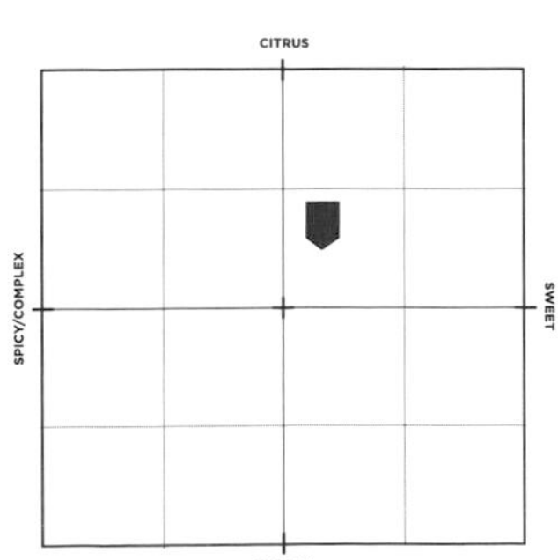

40 %

GREENALL'S LONDON DRY GIN

ORIGIN

Greenall's London Dry Gin was first developed in 1761. Since then, little has changed from the original family recipe. The gin has been distilled in Warrington for the past 250 years. This distillery was set up by Thomas Dakin who, in 1860, sold it to the Greenall family. The craft and expertise of the Greenall family has been passed from generation to generation and today sees the seventh master distiller, Joanne Moore, carefully watching over the quality of Greenall's Gin.

TASTE AND AROMA

A fresh and inspirational gin with hints of juniper berry and citrus fruit in the mouth. A traditional London Dry, well-balanced with a nicely rounded flavour that is not too complex.

INGREDIENTS

No information available

COMBINE WITH

neutral tonic

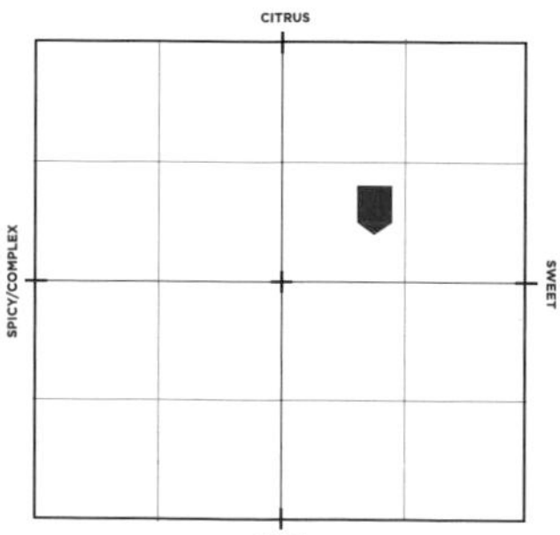

Greenall's

U N I T E D   K I N G D O M

40 %

MARTIN MILLER'S DRY GIN

45 %

MARTIN MILLER'S WESTBOURNE STRENGTH GIN

ORIGIN

'Born of Love, Obsession and Some Degree of Madness' is a wonderful slogan for this exceptional gin. Created in 1997, it was the brainchild of Martin Miller and two friends who sat at a bar sipping a poor gin and tonic. Like many others, they embarked on a quest for the perfect gin. Martin, after all, was convinced that the best gins are made with at least ten botanicals. Martin Miller's is distilled in small quantities in the heart of England, namely in Black Country near Birmingham. Their still even has its own name: Angela. And did you know that their gin once contained a secret ingredient? Cucumber! But that was earlier, because Martin Miller admits that he is not good in keeping secrets (sic). The water for this gin comes from Iceland, because the makers are pledged to use the purest water. The original Martin Miller's with 40% alcohol was launched in 1999, and the Westbourne Strength with 45% alcohol was developed in 2002-2003 upon the demand of barmen and mixologists who wanted a somewhat 'stronger' Martin Miller's. This gin was produced by distilling it twice: The first distillate of juniper berries and earthy botanicals is mixed with a second distillate of bitter oranges, bitter limes and lemon peels.

TASTE AND AROMA

Martin Miller's 40% has a strong citrus aroma (in the bouquet) with hints of juniper berries and a mild and sweet aftertaste. The Westbourne Strength is dominated by juniper berries, but this gin also has a mild aftertaste.

INGREDIENTS IN THE FIRST DISTILLATION

juniper berries ....
coriander ....
angelica ....
liquorice ....
cassia bark ....
orris ....
a small quantity
of lime peels ....

INGREDIENTS IN THE SECOND DISTILLATION

peels of bitter orange ....
lime and lemon peels ....

COMBINE WITH

fruity/floral or neutral tonic

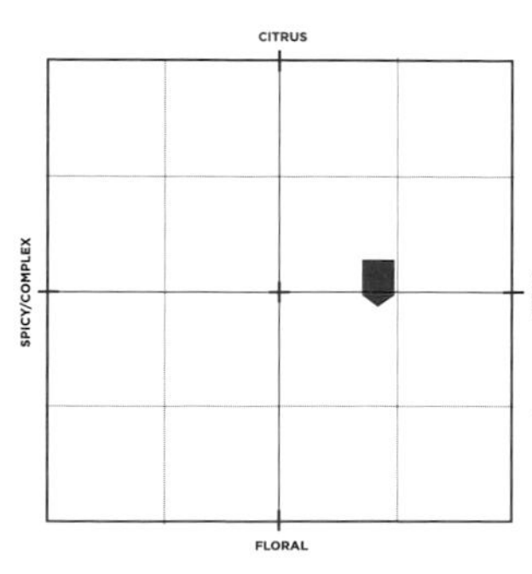

DRY
OXLEY
GIN

47 %

OXLEY COLD DISTILLED LONDON DRY GIN

ORIGIN

This superb premium gin is an outstanding and elegant gin in a simply beautiful bottle. The gin is cold-distilled at 5 °C. Because the molecular structure is not altered at this temperature, the flavours of the botanicals are better preserved. The launch of this gin in 2009 kicked up a storm in the gin world. Oxley Spirits Company, owned by Bacardi-Martini, began developing Oxley gin in 2002. It took eight years and 38 recipes to get the right proportion of ingredients. Oxley Gin contains 14 botanicals and is produced manually and in small volumes – hardly 240 bottles per day – in a special facility at Thames Distillers. That explains the high retail price.

TASTE AND AROMA

A refreshing gin with wonderful grain accents. The juniper berry isn't dominant and the aroma comes from lavender, vanilla and almonds, along with mild citrus.

INGREDIENTS

juniper berry
meadow sweet
pomelo
anise seed
vanilla
orange
lemon
cacao and more

COMBINE WITH

ice, perhaps a zest of pomelo or with neutral tonic

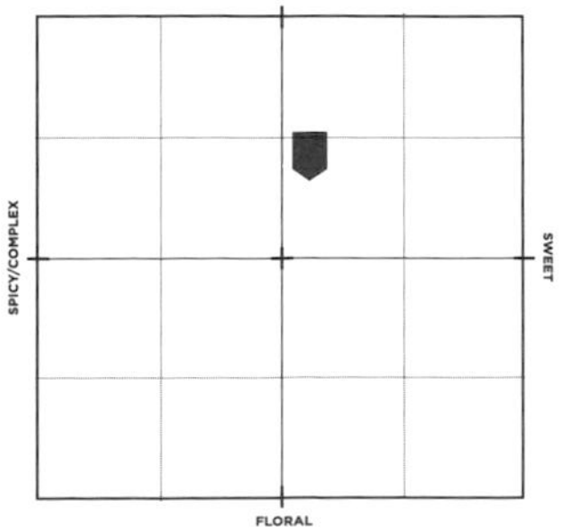

41.6 %

SIPSMITH GIN

ORIGIN

Sipsmith Independent Distillers was set up in London in 2009. After years of gaining experience in the drinks industry, a group of friends made the decision to go into business to brew their own gin and follow their passion for artisan spirits. They call themselves 'sip-smiths'. The smiths still make use of the traditional production processes, the so-called 'one-shot' gin. In this process the botanicals are distilled with the spirit, and the herbs are only used once for one batch only. Aside from the ingredients, this is a really unique London Dry Gin due to the use of vodka as the base for the production. Sipsmith Gin has taken home many awards due to its taste and craftsmanship.

TASTE AND AROMA

On the nose, the flowery tints are reminiscent of summer meadows, filled out with the round fragrance of the juniper berry and the freshness of citrus. Tastes of juniper, lemon tart, and orange marmalade are recognisable in this gin. Sipsmith Gin finishes like any classic London Dry: dry with hints of juniper and lemon.

www.sipsmith.com

INGREDIENTS

juniper berry...............................
Seville orange ....
Spanish lemon peel ....
Bulgarian coriander seed.......
French angelica........................
Spanish liquorice root ....
Italian orris root.......................
cinnamon from Madagascar..
Chinese cassia bark.................
ground almonds from Spain..

COMBINE WITH

neutral tonic

OTHER GINCREATIONS

- Sipsmith Sloe Gin / 29% / sloe liqueur
- Sipsmith Summer Cup Gin / 29% / summer liqueur
- Sipsmith London Dry Gin VJOP / 57.7% / extra strong

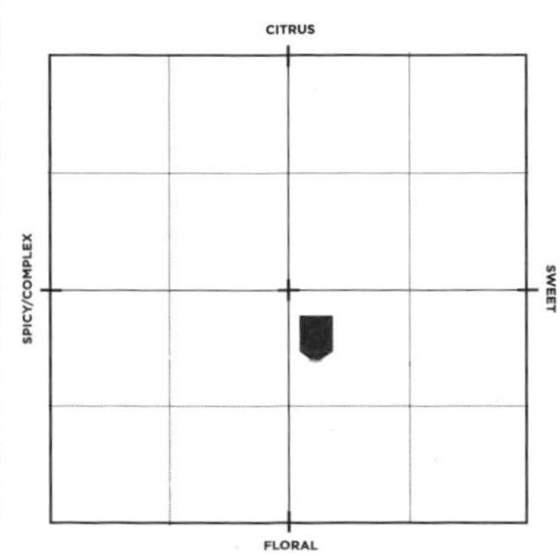

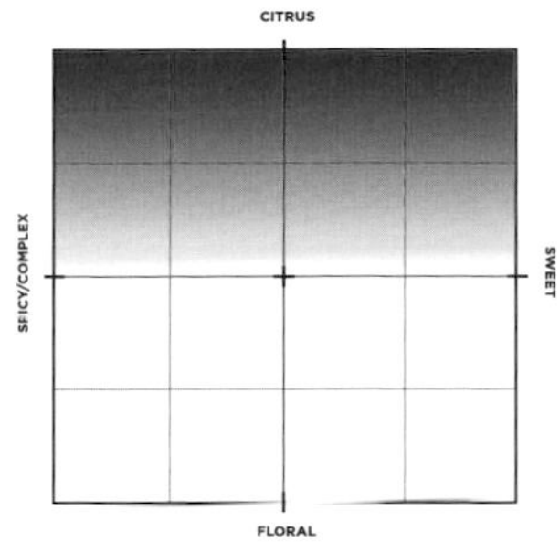

ON THE TOP: CITRUS

COMBINE WITH AROMATIC TONIC
(OR NEUTRAL TONIC)

The gins situated at the top of the flavour cross have an outspoken citrus taste: spicy, sour tones such as bergamot (bitter orange), grapefruit, orange, lemon and lime. This is not to say that you will necessarily find these flavours present, as you will often discover other very different taste accents, but the master distillers or creators of these kinds of gin are certainly of the opinion that citrus is a very important, and above all, delicious ingredient. In summary: the name 'citrus' is a collective name for a mishmash of all sorts of fruit with a peel, meaning you can discover a vast difference from (citrus)gin to (citrus)gin, in this corner of the flavour cross. Something else worthy of note: these gins always offer a certain freshness, especially in a gin & tonic, so come highly recommended for a warm summer's day...

GERMANY

42 %

ADLER GIN

ORIGIN

This gin has been meticulously distilled in a brewery in the Berlin neighbourhood of Wedding ever since 1874. Adler Gin has been translated into English as Eagle Gin, which explains the picture on its label. Adler Gin is based on wheat distillate and botanical herbs, produced by means of vacuum distillation at temperatures under 80°C (similar to Sacred Gin). Before it is bottled, this gin rests for three to eight months in earthenware casks.

TASTE AND AROMA

Very mild and well-balanced gin with hints of citrus, juniper berries, lavender and ginger.

www.psmberlin.de

INGREDIENTS

- juniper berries
- coriander
- lavender
- lemon peels
- ginger

COMBINE WITH

aromatic (or neutral) tonic

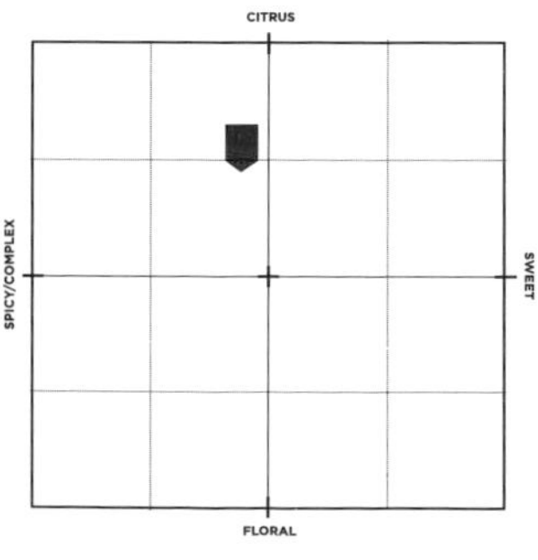

0,7Liter
42 % vol
PREUSSISCHE SPIRITUOSEN MANUFAKTUR

AVIATION
AVIATION
AMERICAN GIN™
BATCH DISTILLED
FROM AN ADVENTUROUS BLEND OF
SPICES FROM AROUND THE WORLD
42% ALC BY VOL · 700 ML

42 %

AVIATION AMERICAN GIN

ORIGIN

Aviation Gin is the outcome of intensive collaboration between mixologist Ryan Magarian and The House of Spirits distillery in Portland, Oregon. This gin was launched in 2002 after more than 30 attempts. The aim was to create a gin that would be perfect for mixing in the well-known Aviation cocktail created by barman Hugo Ensslin about 100 years ago in New York. That also explains the name of the gin. Aviation gin gives the juniper berry a subordinate role. Admittedly, Aviation Gin belongs in a complete new category of dry gins (new generation) that puts an end to the domination of the juniper berry and places the botanicals in the forefront.

TASTE AND AROMA

A smooth and well-balanced gin with a distinct floral aroma. The juniper berry fades into the background to make room for the herbal taste of cardamom and lavender.

INGREDIENTS

juniper berry ....
cardamom ....
lavender ....
sarsaparilla ....
coriander ....
anise seed ....
sweet orange peel ....

COMBINE WITH

neutral or floral/fruity tonic

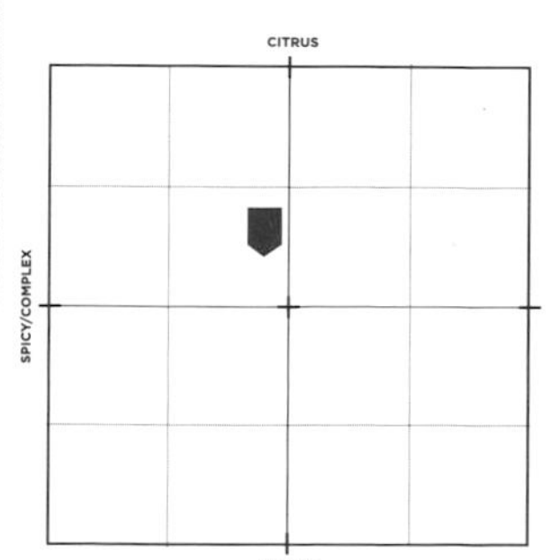

UNITED STATES

47 %

BLUECOAT GIN

ORIGIN

This American gin from Pennsylvania was named after the blue coats worn by the men who fought the British army during the Revolutionary War. The gin is distilled five times and manually bottled one by one in a striking cobalt-blue bottle. Distillation is in a handmade copper pot still and the basis is a four-grain distillate of corn, rye, wheat and barley. Subsequently, the distillery uses the batch system whereby the pot still is slowly heated and the alcohol vapours rise only very gradually, resulting in this fine premium gin.

TASTE AND AROMA

Fragrance of citrus with mild tones of juniper. On the palate mainly touches of citrus that alternate with herbs. A long aftertaste.

INGREDIENTS

organic juniper berry ....
coriander seed ....
citrus peel ....
angelica root and more ....

COMBINE WITH

aromatic or neutral tonic

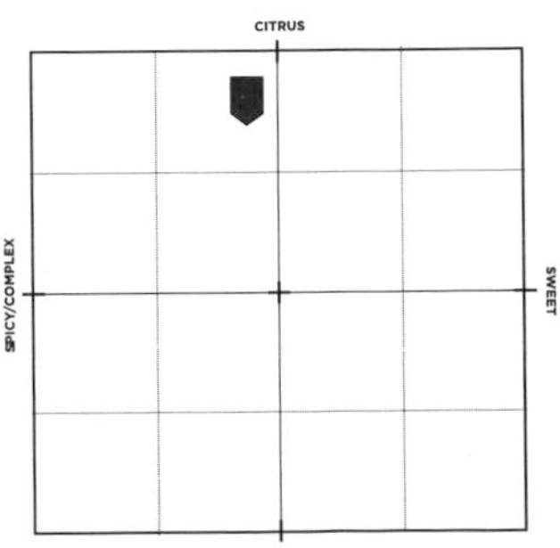

COCK RUSSELL
BOODLES
AND COMPANY
EST. 1845
BRITISH
GIN
LONDON DRY

UNITED KINGDOM

40 %

BOODLES GIN

ORIGIN

Boodles is a classic London Dry Gin, founded in 1845 and one of the fathers of modern London Dry gin. It is still made in England according to the traditional recipe and distilled in a Carter Head pot still. Interestingly enough, there are no citrus fruits processed in this gin.

This was the practical decision of its stubborn producers, because they assumed that the typical consumer would anyway add a slice of lemon to his gin & tonic, and the coriander takes care of the rest. Boodles Gin was named after Boodle's gentlemen's club in London, which was established in 1762 and was originally managed by Edward Boodle. A famous member of the club was Winston Churchill.

TASTE AND AROMA

Dry, fresh and pure with a subdued taste of juniper berries.

INGREDIENTS

juniper berries from Italy .....
sage ....
rosemary ....
nutmeg ....
coriander ....
cassia bark ....
angelica and caraway seeds ..

COMBINE WITH

aromatic or neutral tonic

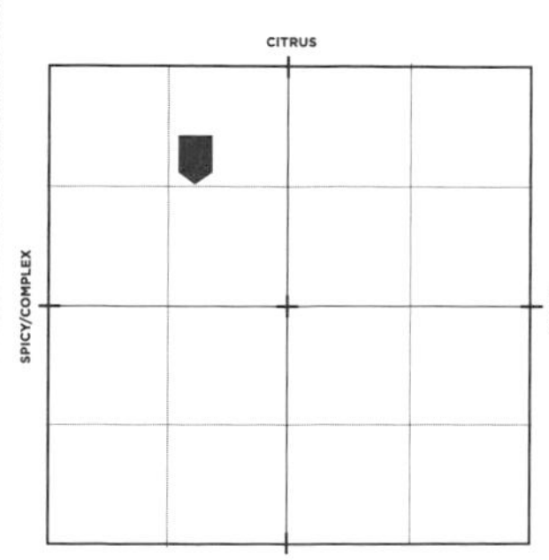

40 %

BOTANIC GIN PREMIUM 1

45 %

BOTANIC GIN ULTRA PREMIUM 2

ORIGIN

Although this gin is produced in Spain, Botanic is a genuine London Dry gin. The reason that we can classify it in this category is that makers use only high quality English grain, which is distilled three times. One of the notable ingredients in Botanic Gin is Buddha's Hand, better known is Japan as bushukan. This extremely fragrant citrus fruit with its finger-like segments is one of the oldest species in the lemon family. The fruit does not have a juicy pulp and it is cultivated primarily for its aromatic peel.

The Botanic Ultra Premium expands the recipe of the real London Dry. This drink is distilled four times in age-old stills according to traditional production methods of the real London Dry, which explains the higher alcohol percentage. This is certainly appealing to seasoned gin lovers. However, the Ultra Premium doesn't deviate from the special ingredient, Buddha's Hand.

TASTE AND AROMA

Botanic is a light, dry gin in which the taste of juniper berry and almond come to the fore. In the aftertaste, you can feel the light citrus touch of Buddha's hand, bergamot and sweet oranges.

INGREDIENTS

- juniper berries
- Buddha's Hand
- mandarin
- thyme
- coriander
- lemon
- cinnamon
- peppermint
- camomile
- anise
- sweet orange
- almonds
- cardamom
- mango

COMBINE WITH

aromatic or neutral tonic

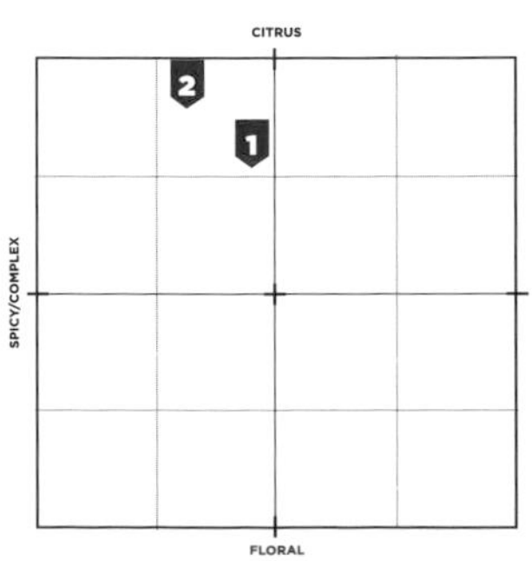

BOTANIC
W&H
LONDON DRY GIN
PREMIUM
Three Times
DISTILLED
TANIC
W&H

BROKEN HEART
GIN
Distilled in the Pure South of New Zealand
BROKEN HEART
GIN
Distilled in the Pure South of New Zealand
40% ALC BY VOL.
700ML | NZ MADE

NEW ZEALAND

40 %

BROKEN HEART GIN

ORIGIN

Broken Heart Gin is distilled in South Island, New Zealand, proving that gin is brewed even in the farthest corners of the earth. The story of Broken Hearts Gin began with two German friends who lived in the Southern Alps of New Zealand. Joerg was an ex-pilot and Bernd an ex-engineer, but both became fully dedicated to distilling fine spirits. They devoted a long period to developing a superb premium gin with 11 botanicals and a twist of orange. But fate had something else in store; Bernd became sick and died. Joerg and Bernd's girlfriend, who were left with a 'broken heart', decided to name the gin Broken Heart. This gin, by the way, won a silver medal at the Wine and Spirits Competition in London in 2013.

TASTE AND AROMA

Elegant and traditional taste with a playful reference to oranges.

INGREDIENTS

juniper berry
coriander
lemon peel
lavender
cinnamon
angelica root and more

COMBINE WITH

aromatic or neutral tonic

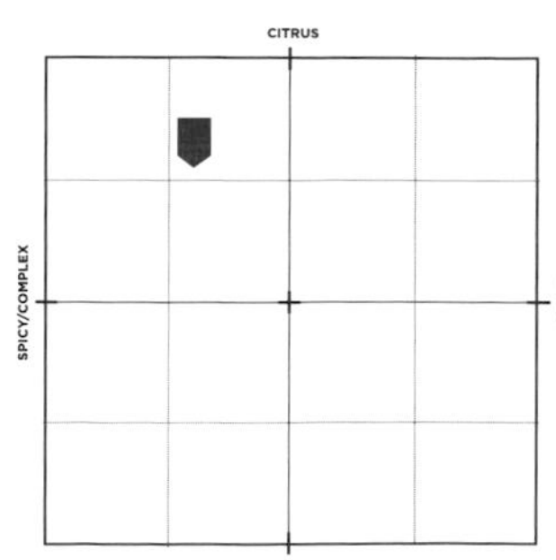

40 %

BROOKLYN GIN

ORIGIN

As the name suggests, this gin comes from New York. Brooklyn Gin is the product of three guys with a passion for gin. The founders of this small company are Joe Santos and Emil Jattne, both former marketers of Bacardi. They distinguish and promote this gin as 'handcrafted small batch gin'. They do everything manually and use fresh botanicals, such as juniper berries and fresh citrus. It takes them three days to make 300 bottles of their gin. During distillation, they use only local fruits and corn from Orange County.

TASTE AND AROMA

Crispy gin with a distinct citrus flavour, reinforced by the taste of juniper berries; a dry aftertaste.

INGREDIENTS

juniper berries

citrus peels

COMBINE WITH

aromatic tonic
or neutral tonic

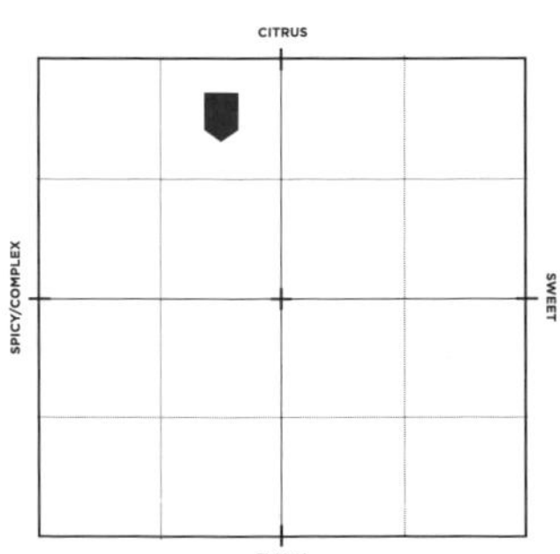

BROOKLYN
GIN

Burleigh's
LONDON DRY
GIN

42 %

BURLEIGH'S LONDON DRY GIN

ORIGIN

It took only eight months before Phil Burey was able to realise his dream: to set up a small distillery in his home town. Together with master distiller, Jamie Baxter, he put this way Leicestershire on the gin map. Their gin is distilled at Bawdon Lodge Farm in Nanpantan. The inspiration came from the woods near the farm, where they found most of the eleven botanicals.

TASTE AND AROMA

The bouquet is refreshing with a hint of eucalyptus and citrus. A robust flavour of eucalyptus and juniper berries. In the background there is a delicate herbal and floral taste. The aftertaste is peppery.

INGREDIENTS

juniper berries ....
white birch ....
dandelions ....
burdock ....
elderberry ....
orris and more ....

COMBINE WITH

aromatic or neutral tonic

OTHER GINCREATIONS

- Burleigh's Distiller's Cut / 47% / spicy
- Burleigh's Navy Strength / 47% / extra strong

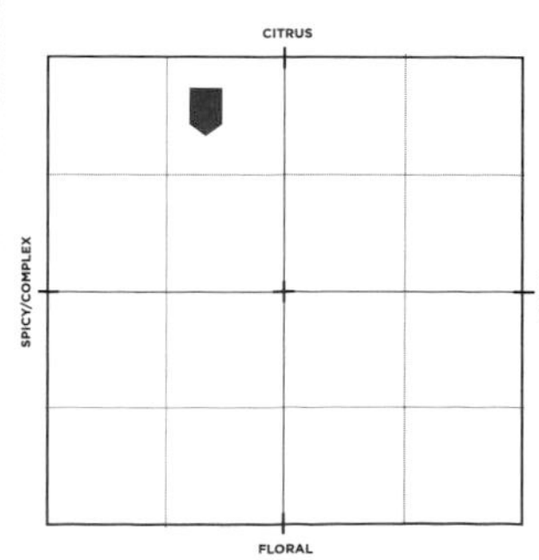

46 %

COTSWOLDS DRY GIN

ORIGIN

The Cotswolds is a jewel in the crown of British heritage. It is considered an 'Area of Outstanding Natural Beauty' and it is where this gin is produced. The Cotswolds Distillery is a relatively new brewery, established by Dan Szor and managed by the young and ambitious head distiller, Alex Davies. In addition to gin, this deeply-rooted local brewery would like to launch rye whisky (first bottles in 2017), eau-de vie and all sorts of liquors. Their gin is brewed with nine carefully selected botanicals in a customised Holstein still with a capacity of 500 litres.

TASTE AND AROMA

In the nose refreshing tones of pomelo, coriander and juniper. The pure taste of pomelo and coriander and the smooth, dry touch of angelica root with a distant taste of pepper and lavender.

www.cotswoldsdistillery.com

INGREDIENTS

- juniper berry
- coriander
- angelica root
- lavender
- laurel
- grapefruit
- lime
- black pepper
- cardamom

COMBINE WITH

aromatic or neutral tonic

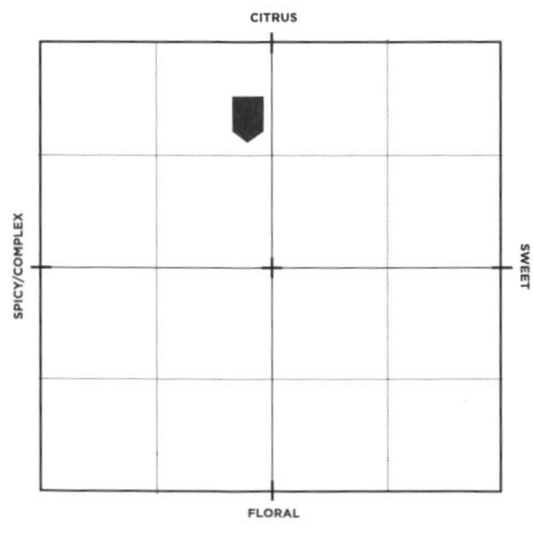

SMALL BATCH RELEASE
Estd 2014
COTSWOLDS
DRY GIN
PRODUCT OF ENGLAND
BATCH No.
01/14
NUMBER OF BOTTLES
6005/7000
THE FOUNDER
INAUGURAL
RELEASE

GIN DESTILADO 40% VOL / 0,70 L. / Servir
Elaborado y Embotellado por R.E. 300/CS para

SPAIN

40 %

GINSELF

ORIGIN

Since 2009, Ginself has been produced in Valencia and you can taste that. Production is limited to a batch of 500 litres, which fills around 715 bottles. The makers use only top quality herbs and fruits since this is the only way to guarantee the highest possible concentration of extracts. The creators of this gin want to offer a true gin lover with a unique experience – solely for him or her. That's why it's called *Ginself*...

TASTE AND AROMA

A well-defined gin with the aroma of juniper berries and citrus aromas; elegant in the mouth with a sweet aftertaste.

INGREDIENTS

- juniper berries
- sweet oranges
- bitter oranges
- orange blossoms
- mandarin
- lemon peels
- angelica root
- angelica seeds
- earth almond

COMBINE WITH

aromatic or neutral tonic

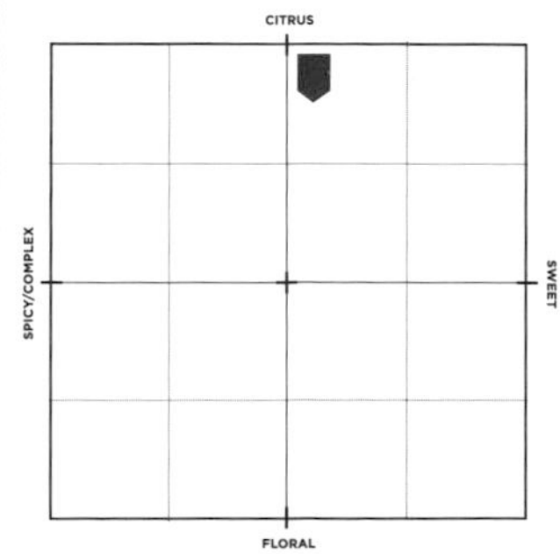

UNITED KINGDOM

47 %

HASWELL GIN

ORIGIN

Haswell London Dry Gin is an award-winning gin, created by Julian Haswell. According to Julian, the three most important ingredients of a classic London Dry gin are the juniper berry, angelica and coriander seed. On this basis Julian creates a gin with the unashamedly citrus flavours of sweet and bitter oranges with just a touch of lemon.

TASTE AND AROMA

The powerful citrus flavours of oranges with a hint of lemon

INGREDIENTS

juniper berry
angelica
coriander seed
savoury
lime peel from Spain
Aframomum melegueta or grains of paradise (a peppery spice from West Africa)
bitter orange peel from Morocco and Haiti
sweet orange peel from Morocco and Spain
liquorice root

COMBINE WITH

aromatic tonic
(or neutral tonic)

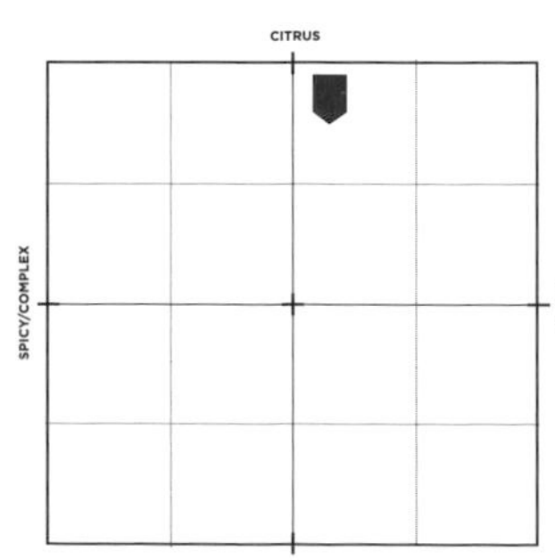

Haswell
LONDON DISTILLED
DRY GIN
70cl. ALC. 47% BY VOL.

UNITED KINGDOM

46 % LONDON N°3

ORIGIN

Despite the British roots of this gin, it is actually distilled in the Netherlands by de Kuyper Royal Distillers. De Kuyper is a 100% family-owned business and is the world's largest producer of cocktail liqueurs. De Kuyper was granted permission to produce London N°3 which is based on a recipe from Berry Bros. & Rudd, London's oldest wine and spirits merchants. Named N°3 after the address in St. James Street in London where the wine and spirit merchants have been based since 1698. With juniper berry as its base, this gin is an ode to the integrity and character of a traditional London Dry Gin. Six perfectly balanced botanicals are distilled in traditional copper pot stills.

TASTE AND AROMA

Because London N°3 is flavoured with three types of spice and three types of fruit, it is perfectly balanced. There are fresh aromas of grapefruit and orange, and a recognisable scent of cardamom. The taste can be perfectly attributed to the use of grapefruit, which is supported by the spicy coriander. An earthy dryness comes through in the finish.

INGREDIENTS

juniper berry from Italy
Spanish orange peel
grapefruit
angelica
Moroccan coriander seed
cardamom

COMBINE WITH

aromatic tonic
(or neutral tonic)

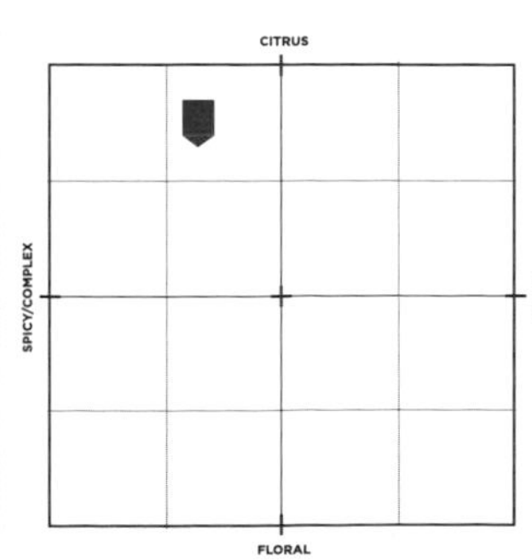

UNITED STATES

46 % N°209

ORIGIN

N°209 is a prestigious, artisan premium gin from San Francisco. The name is due to the fact that this was the 209th distillery registered in the United States. N°209 gin came into being thanks to Leslie Rudd. Leslie was a winemaker producing exclusive wines at his vineyard in the Napa Valley. The distiller, avid amateur cook and saxophonist, Arne Hillesland's creative spirit and love of cuisine proved to be the ideal combination to blend with Leslie's wine expertise. The result is a top quality gin that is soft and memorable.

TASTE AND AROMA

N°209 opens with an aromatic nose of citrus and floral tones with a hint of spiciness. The palette of flavours begins with the high notes of lemon and lime followed by orange. As the gin warms in the mouth, the flowery tones of the coriander and Bergamot are released. This is subtly followed by the warmth of pepper from the cardamom and juniper berry. A surprising twist comes when the 'mint components' of the cardamom are released. N°209 ends with the cassia bark in the finish.

INGREDIENTS

juniper berry
angelica
lemon peel
Bergamot orange peel
coriander
cardamom
cassia bark

COMBINE WITH

aromatic tonic
(or neutral tonic)

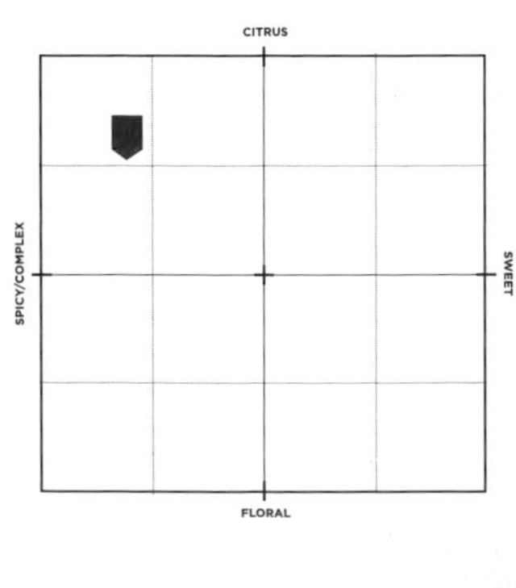

N
GIN VLC
70 CL 39% VOL

SPAIN

39 %

N GIN VLC

ORIGIN

This gin from Valencia is the pride of this sunny municipality and it is produced with the typical Valencia botanicals. The chief role belongs to the orange for which this region is famous. The gin is based on a double distillation in a pot still.

TASTE AND AROMA

A refreshing gin with a distinct reference to oranges and citrus. Smooth and elegant on the palate.

INGREDIENTS

juniper berry
orange
lemon
mandarin
rosemary
liquorice
coriander
cardamom
angelica root
sage
Chardonnay grapes

COMBINE WITH

aromatic or neutral tonic

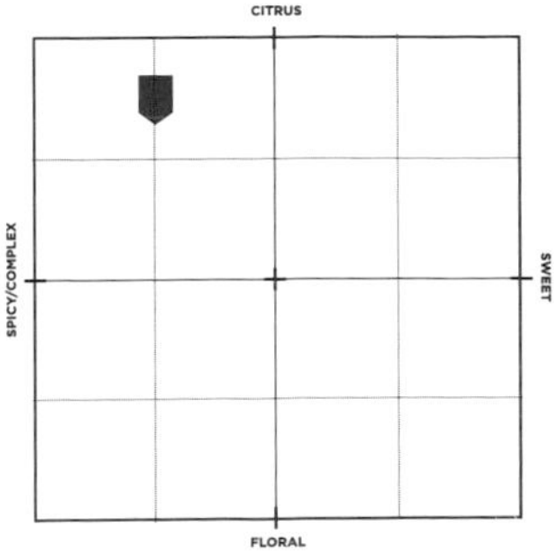

41.3 %

TANQUERAY RANGPUR GIN

ORIGIN

Tanqueray Rangpur Gin was launched in 2006 and perfectly completes the Tanqueray brand range. This gin is part of the new generation which sets itself apart, thanks to the flavouring of Rangpur fruit (a cross between mandarin and lemon) from India.

TASTE AND AROMA

The fragrance of sweet citrus and the soft bouquet of roses invites a long, slow swallow. The botanic aromas greet the tongue subtly and continue through to peak at juniper berry, rounding off with citrus.

INGREDIENTS

juniper berry
Rangpur fruit
coriander
bay leaf
ginger

COMBINE WITH

aromatic tonic
(or neutral tonic)

OTHER GINCREATIONS

- Tanqueray Dry Gin / 43.1% / light citrus
- Tanqueray Ten Gin / 47.3% / floral
- Tanqueray Old Tom Gin / 47.3% / sweet retro gin

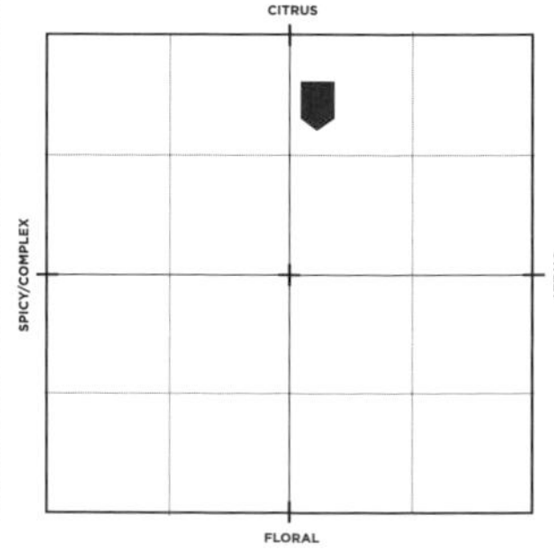

anguera
EXPORT STRENGT
ANGPU
CED AND BOTTLED IN GREAT
OR CHARLES TANQUERAY & C

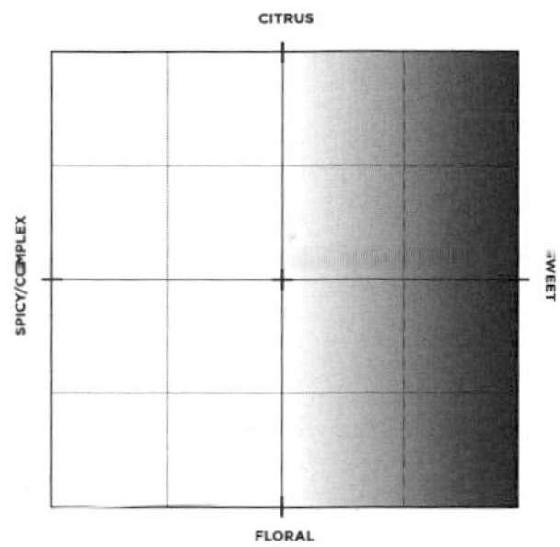

ON THE RIGHT: SWEET
COMBINE WITH FRUITY TONIC
(OR NEUTRAL TONIC)

Gins with a distinctly sweet taste can also include the retro Old Tom gins, whereby extra natural sugars are added, as well as Dry gins where sweet botanicals dominate. Liquorice root is a key ingredient in this case. Liquorice is so to speak the 'candy cane' of the master distiller. The amount of liquorice used will by and large determine whether a gin will tend toward this taste direction.

BATCH Nº 21/12
Fifty Pounds
GIN
RARE and HANDCRAFTED
LONDON DRY GIN
Distilled in London
ORIGINAL RECIPE

UNITED KINGDOM

43.5 %

FIFTY POUNDS GIN

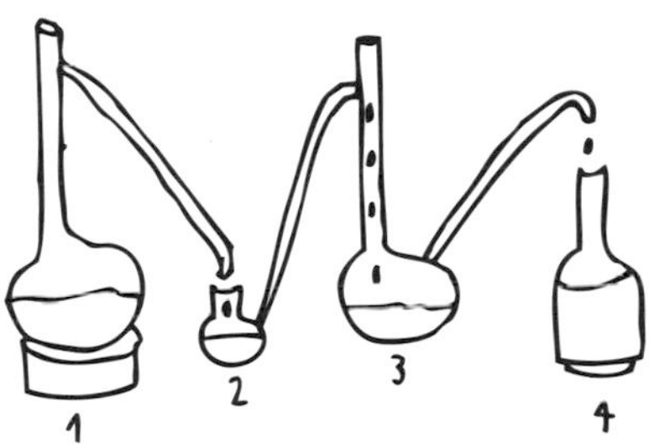

ORIGIN

Fifty Pounds Gin is produced in a small distillery in South East London. This extremely soft London Dry owes its name to the 'tax rise' levied during the time of the Gin Act in 1736. Fifty Pounds is made using traditional methods and uses exclusively natural ingredients. The neutral alcohol is obtained by a fourfold distillation of the wheat. The alcohol is then distilled once again, this time with the addition of herbs and botanicals from all over the world.

TASTE AND AROMA

Fifty Pounds Gin has a heady bouquet, full of citrus, mint, lavender and juniper berry. On tasting, it is mostly the aniseed and pepper flavours that come to the foreground. The coriander seed helps accentuate the sweet taste.

INGREDIENTS

juniper berry from Croatia ....
coriander seed from the Middle East ....
grains of paradise from the Gulf of Guinea ....
savoury from the South of France ....
orange and lemon peel from Spain ....
liquorice from Calabria ....
angelica from Western Europe ....
Other ingredients are also used, but that secret stays in South East London.

COMBINE WITH

fruity tonic
(or neutral tonic)

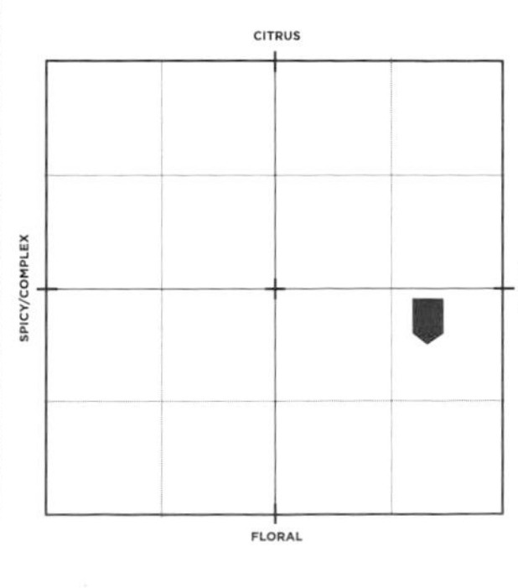

UNITED KINGDOM

44 %

OLD ENGLISH GIN

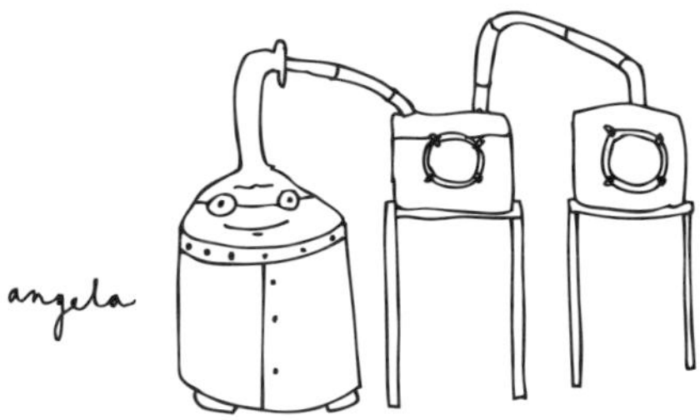

ORIGIN

This gin is made following a recipe from 1783 and continues to be distilled in the oldest pot still in England by the Langley Distillers. The boiler is called Angela or Grandma, after the grandmother of the original distiller. This gin is uniquely bottled in 100% recycled old champagne bottles. Old English Gin was launched in 2012.

TASTE AND AROMA

From the moment you pop the cork you are rewarded with the fresh aroma of juniper berries. This fragrance is quickly followed by a rich earthy complexity of warm hay, black pepper and spices. In the background, hints of basil and mint. The taste is surprising due to the controlled sweetness and a silky soft mouth feel.

INGREDIENTS

juniper berry
coriander
lemon and orange peel
angelica
orris root
cassia
cinnamon
liquorice
nutmeg
cardamom

COMBINE WITH

fruity tonic
(or neutral tonic)

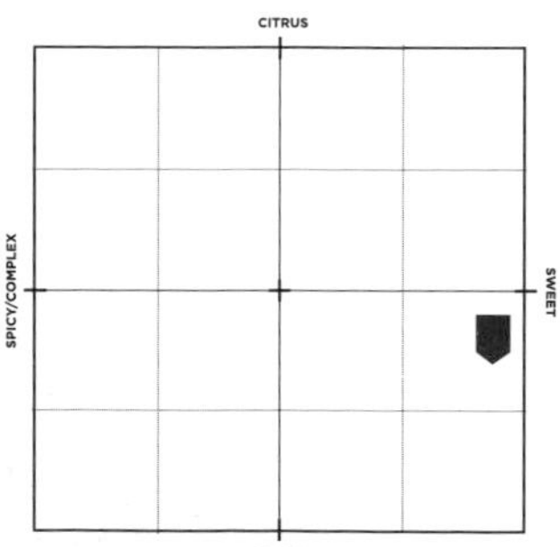

PURE OLD POT STILL
HAMMER
& SON
LTD.
AD ORIGINEM 1783
Old English

SPAIN

40 %

SIKKIM GIN
PRIVÉE [1], BILBERRY [2] & FRAISE [3]

ORIGIN

Sikkim Gin is a Spanish gin, distilled in England in a copper still. Sikkim Gin has three variations: Sikkim Gin Privée, Sikkim Gin Bilberry and Sikkim Gin Fraise. The unique feature of this gin is the combination of British gin and Indian tea. The name Sikkim refers to the small, sparsely-populated state in India located in the Himalayan Mountains. This region produces Temi Tea, a type of Darjeeling tea. This high-quality tea is what you taste in Sikkim Gins. The distilled results are smooth, sweet-floral gins... for the connoisseur!

TASTE AND AROMA
SIKKIM GIN PRIVÉE

Smooth gin with the sweet aroma of red tea.

TASTE AND AROMA
SIKKIM GIN BILBERRY

Sweet and fruity gin with a floral aroma.

TASTE AND AROMA
SIKKIM GIN FRAISE

A full gin with the aromas of strawberries and forest fruits.

INGREDIENTS
SIKKIM GIN PRIVÉE

juniper berries
from the Netherlands ....
red tea from Tibet ....
coriander ....
other fine herbs ....

INGREDIENTS
SIKKIM GIN BILBERRY

juniper berries
from the Netherlands ....
red tea from Tibet ....
orris ....
bilberries ....
coriander ....
sweet flag ....
orange peels ....

INGREDIENTS
SIKKIM GIN FRAISE

juniper berries
from the Netherlands ....
red tea from Tibet ....
floral essences ....
wild strawberries ....
red cranberries ....
coriander ....
orris ....
orange peels ....

COMBINE WITH

fruity/floral or neutral tonic

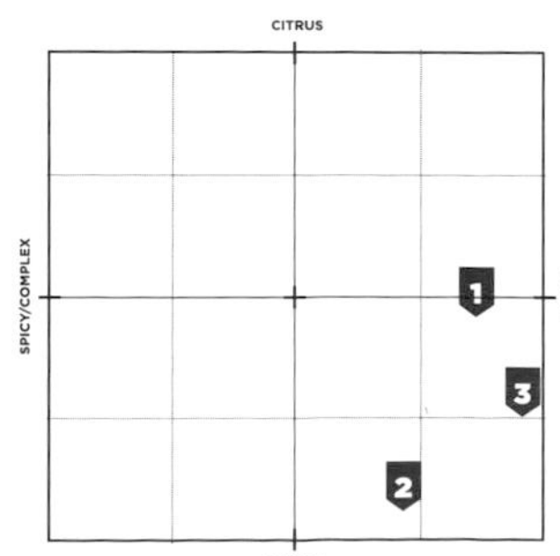

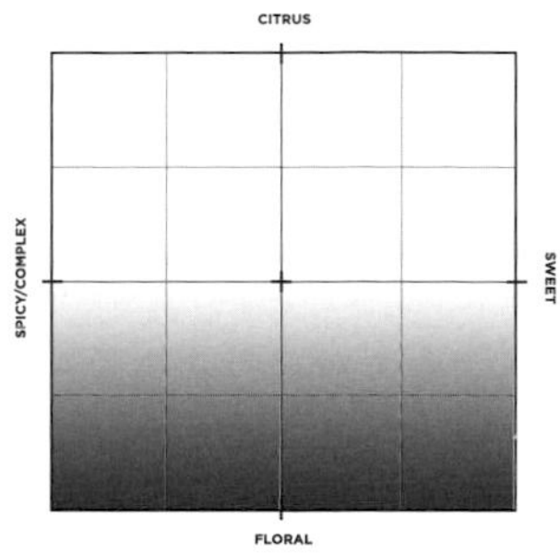

AT THE BOTTOM: FLORAL

COMBINE WITH FRUITY TONIC
(OR NEUTRAL TONIC)

Gins which inhabit the bottom arm of the flavour cross are notably floral in character. Summery tastes such as elderflower and honeysuckle are clearly present. The floral tints appear thanks to the use of an assortment of flower-like products (editor's note: not the most obvious botanicals to begin with) and tea extracts. This corner of the flavour cross is where the gins with predominantly fruity tones can be located.

40 %

BLOOM PREMIUM LONDON DRY GIN

ORIGIN

BLOOM Gin, produced by G & J Greenall, one of Great Britain's largest distilleries, aims at people who don't like the distinct taste of juniper. Instead, the leading role is played by Bach flower, pomelo and chamomile. The distiller in charge of this gin is Joanne Moore, one of the few female master distillers active in the gin-business and also an internationally respected expert in the jenever industry. Joanne supervises every stage of the gin process from concept to creation. Her desire for innovation and her passion for the product led to the unforeseen creation of BLOOM, the super-premium gin among Greenall's range of gins.

TASTE AND AROMA

Extremely delicate gin that starts with the floral tones of Bach flower. The citrus taste of the pomelo gives it a perfect finish.

INGREDIENTS

juniper berries
Bach flower
pomelo
chamomile and more

COMBINE WITH

fruity or neutral tonic

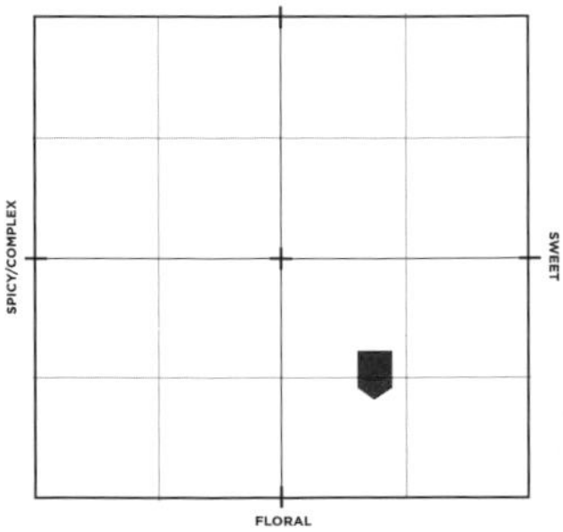

BLOOM
PREMIUM
LONDON DRY GIN
A delicate floral
gin inspired by the true
beauty of nature

44 %

CITADELLE GIN

ORIGIN

Citadelle Gin is originally a French gin with 19 different herbal ingredients, distilled three times. The brand was first brought to market in 1998 and is produced in Cognac by Gabriel & Andreu. Citadelle is distributed by Cognac-Ferrand and is named after an 18th century distillery in Dunkirk. This gin has won countless awards, far too many to list here. No expense has been spared for the botanicals, with a seemingly worldwide hunt to gather this treasure trove of spices.

TASTE AND AROMA

The taste is unusual in comparison with other gins, due to its pleasant and aromatic character, amidst beautiful undertones of fresh flowers, jasmine, honeysuckle and cinnamon. It is a gin with an unusually broad spectrum of flavours, but little else is expected from 19 different botanicals. The longer the gin stays in the mouth, the more the palette of flavours changes in character, and the ingredients such as the aniseed, grain and cinnamon come to the fore. A lively gin with a distinctly floral character.

OTHER GINCREATION

- Citadelle Réserve Gin / 44.7% / matured

INGREDIENTS

juniper berry from France
Moroccan coriander
orange peel from Mexico
cardamom from India
liquorice from China
cubeb pepper from Java
French flavourings
Mediterranean fennel
Italian orris root
cinnamon from Sri Lanka
French violets
almonds from Spain
cassia from Indochina
German angelica
grains of paradise (a sort of pepper) from West Africa
Dutch cumin
nutmeg from India
Spanish lemons
star anise from France

COMBINE WITH

fruity tonic (or neutral tonic)

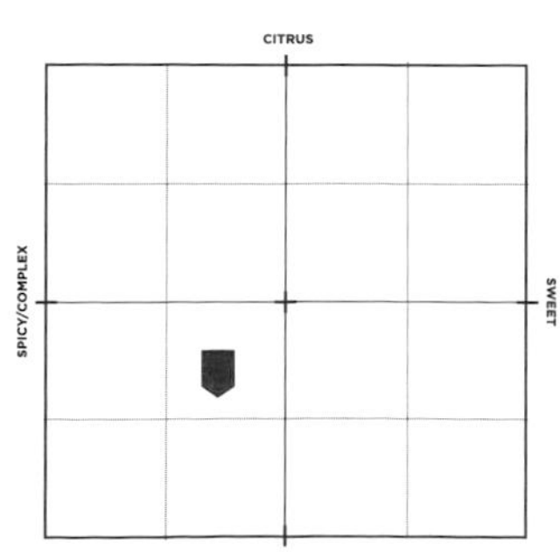

DENMARK

44 % GERANIUM GIN

ORIGIN

Geranium Gin is a creation by a father-son team looking for the perfect gin. Dane Henrik Hammer and his father have crafted a gin that is both dry and floral in flavour. This London Dry gin combines juniper berry with the oil of Danish geranium plants. This Geranium Gin is distilled in the traditional way but with the addition of a few new techniques. Henrik's father, a chemist by trade, has succeeded in extracting the oils from the geranium plant, and we can see – or rather drink – the results.

TASTE AND AROMA

Geranium Gin has a slightly spicy and a definite floral taste, held up by the London Dry character.

INGREDIENTS

juniper berry
oil of the Danish geranium plant
coriander
lemon peel
angelica
orris root
aniseed
cinnamon
and other unnamed ingredients

COMBINE WITH

fruity tonic
(or neutral tonic)

OTHER GINCREATION

- Geranium 55 Gin / 55% / extra strong

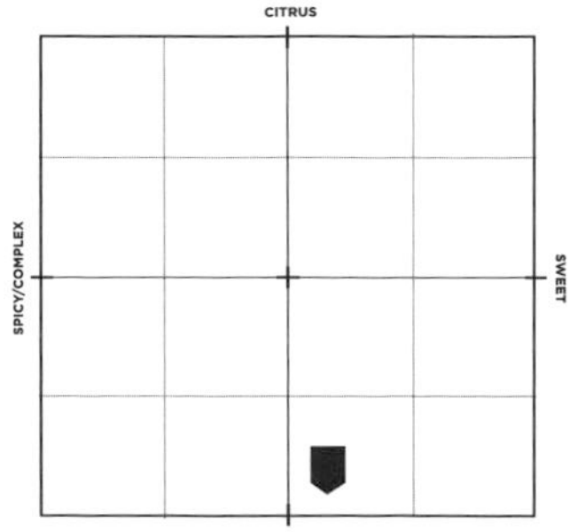

Geranium
Premium
London Dry Gin
by Hammer & Son

700ml
Gin Gold
99,9

40 %

GOLD 999,9 DISTILLED GIN

ORIGIN

The history (albeit the alleged one) of Gold 999,9 Gin starts with the discovery of a gilded still in the Alsace region of France at the beginning of the 20th century. This apparently dated to the time of the French-Prussian wars. The current distiller purchased the still and wanted to brew a 'golden' spirit. That's how the gin got its name: Gold 999,9 or pure gold. Gold 999,9 Finest Blend is distilled nowadays in Fougerolles by The Water Company. In several African countries, this gin is an outright hit due to its *bling-bling* packaging.

TASTE AND AROMA

The initial aroma comes undoubtedly from the juniper berries, followed immediately by a touch of mandarin and ends with an explosive fragrance of floral notes, caused mainly by gentian, violet and Papaver.

INGREDIENTS

juniper berry ....
mandarin ....
ginger ....
violet ....
field poppy ....
coriander ....
angelica root ....
cinnamon ....
gentian ....
Papaver ....

COMBINE WITH

fruity or neutral tonic

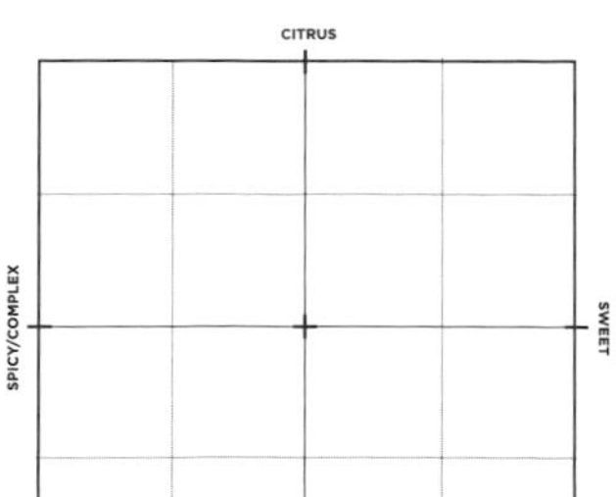

40 %

G'VINE FLORAISON

ORIGIN

G'Vine Gin is produced by EuroWineGate, a French company set up in 2001 and located in the Cognac region of France. The founders are oenologists and have 45 years of collective knowhow in the production and selling of wines and spirits. A daring ultra-premium gin based on the highly prized Ugni Blanc grape, this gin bridges the gap between a flavoured vodka and gin. Floraison is French for blossom time: when the fruit on the grapevines is just starting to grow (setting) which takes place once a year in mid-June. G'Vine Gin has also won many awards.

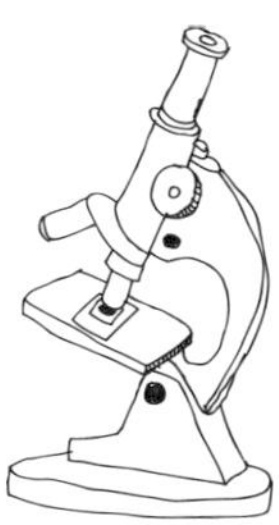

TASTE AND AROMA

The taste of G'Vine is soft with an undertone of flowers and grass. The spectrum of flavours in G'Vine is broad: velvety, full, soft and exuberant spice, strong, intense and audacious. We get an alcohol which is softer and stronger than a classic grain-based gin. Amongst the palette of flavours of the other aromatic plants is also the soft note of vine blossom.

INGREDIENTS

- juniper berry
- Ugni Blanc grape
- coriander
- pepper berries
- ginger
- liquorice
- cardamom
- cassia
- lime

COMBINE WITH

1724 Tonic Water or Fever-Tree Tonic

OTHER GINCREATION

- G'Vine Nouaison / 43.9% / complex

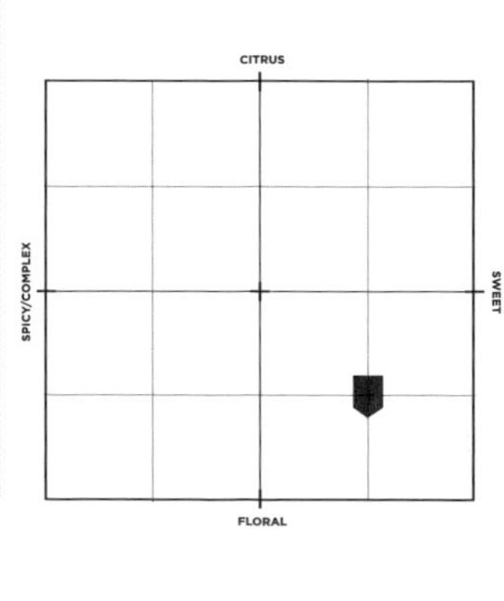

I N

hernö
swedish excellenc

40.5 %

HERNÖ SWEDISH EXCELLENCE GIN

ORIGIN

Hernö Gin comes from the most northerly distillery in the world, situated in the north of Sweden, in Dala. The gin is distilled in a German-made, hand-beaten copper boiler, which can hold 250 litres. The copper boiler is named 'Kierstin' and was fitted in 2012. The complete production process is artisanal and only natural botanicals and homemade grain alcohol is used. The eight botanicals macerate for at least 18 hours in the grain alcohol before the distillation process begins. This is a gin with a distinct personality, reflecting the individuality of the distillery and the master distiller.

TASTE AND AROMA

The taste begins with juniper berry, before revealing a jam-like combination of flowery aromas. The finish is long and lingering, with plenty of citrus and nuttiness thanks to the use of almond and nutmeg.

www.hernogin.com

INGREDIENTS

juniper berry
coriander
meadowsweet
cassia
black pepper
vanilla
lingonberry
lemon peel

COMBINE WITH

fruity tonic (or neutral tonic)

OTHER GINCREATIONS

- Hernö Navy Strength Gin / 57% / extra strong
- Hernö Old Tom Gin / 43% / sweet retro gin
- Hernö Juniper Cask Gin / 47% / matured

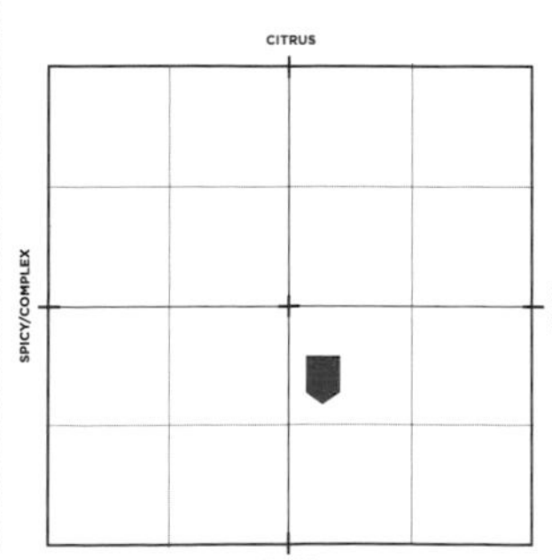

40 %

MAYFAIR LONDON DRY GIN

ORIGIN

Mayfair Gin originates from the spirit of four entrepreneurs who wanted to capture the wealth and elegancy of their neighbourhood– the Mayfair district in Westminster, London. The prestigiousness of this district is emphasised by the presence of many embassies, five-star hotels and reputed culinary establishments. The gin is brewed locally at Thames Distillers, which has been operating in London for more than 300 years by the same family. Charles Maxwell, its current CEO, belongs to the eighth generation of the family. The distillery uses a copper brewing still named Thumbelina. The limited production volume of Mayfair Dry Gin and the several hand-picked ingredients, contribute to its exceptional character.

TASTE AND AROMA

The overflowing presence of herbs is brilliant on the palate and the aftertaste is floral.

INGREDIENTS

juniper berries ....
coriander seeds ....
angelica root ....
savory ....
orris root and more ....

COMBINE WITH

fruity tonic
(or neutral tonic)

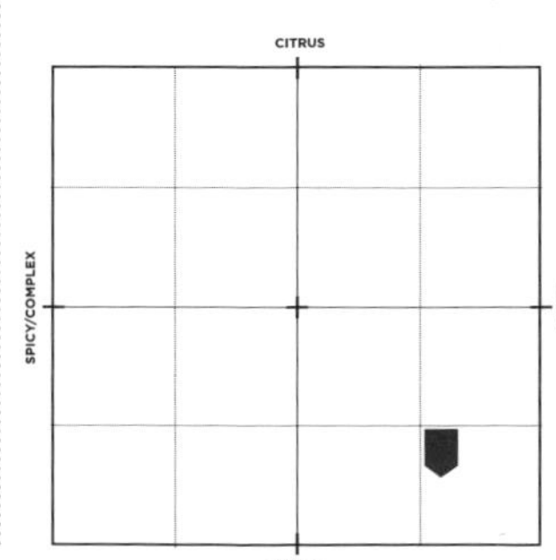

MAYFAIR
LONDON DRY GIN

NOLET'S®
DRY GIN
NOLET DISTILLERY
SILVER
IMPORTED
SCHIEDAM · HOLLAND
C.H.J. NOLET 10th GENERATION
NOLET DISTILLERY
47.6% Alc/Vol 700ml / 47.6% vol 70cl ℮

THE NETHERLANDS

47.6 % NOLET'S DRY GIN

ORIGIN

In 1691, Joannes Nolet set up his distillery in the Dutch town of Schiedam. He chose the location as it was close to the North Sea and the big grain auctions. The Nolet Distillery in Schiedam has now been producing high quality spirits for ten generations. It is the oldest surviving distillery in the Netherlands which is still owned by the family who started it. Nolet's Silver Dry Gin uses a distinctive combination of botanicals never before used in gin, such as Turkish rose, peach and raspberry. The basis of the gin is distilled in pot stills. The extracts of the roses, peaches and raspberries are distilled separately and then combined with the juniper base. Afterwards, the blend is allowed to rest so as to reach the perfect balance.

TASTE AND AROMA

This ultra-premium gin is a good example of a fruity-floral gin with the aromas of roses, peaches and blackberry. The taste is, at the very least, surprising for a gin and deviates from the traditional juniper berry. Despite the high alcohol content, this gin is very soft.

www.ketel1.nl

INGREDIENTS

juniper berry
wheat
lime
orris root
liquorice
peaches
raspberries
Turkish roses

COMBINE WITH

fruity tonic
(or neutral tonic)

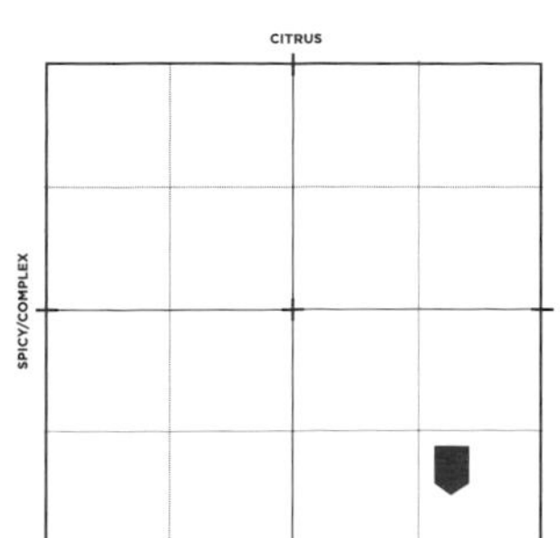

SPAIN

40 %

TANN'S GIN

ORIGIN

Tann's gin has been on the market since 1977–which makes it a veteran gin. It originates from the region of Barcelona. It is produced by Destilerias Campeny by means of a three-step infusion process. With an eye on South European markets, the company strove to put more emphasis on the refreshing, fruity and floral aspects during the distillation process that changed the gin taste slightly over the years. Tip: To get a good first impression of this gin, try tasting it with natural lemonade. Incidentally, the gin won various awards in recent years: bronze medal in the IWSC, silver at the Spirit Award in Brussels, silver at the Spirits Challenge and furthermore, a gold recognition at the Spirits Business Award.

TASTE AND AROMA

Dry yet floral gin with a perfumed aroma; pure aftertaste.

INGREDIENTS

juniper berries
coriander seeds
cucumber
rose petals
cardamom
mandarin peel
orange blossoms
lemon peel
liquorice
raspberry

COMBINE WITH

fruity tonic (or neutral tonic)

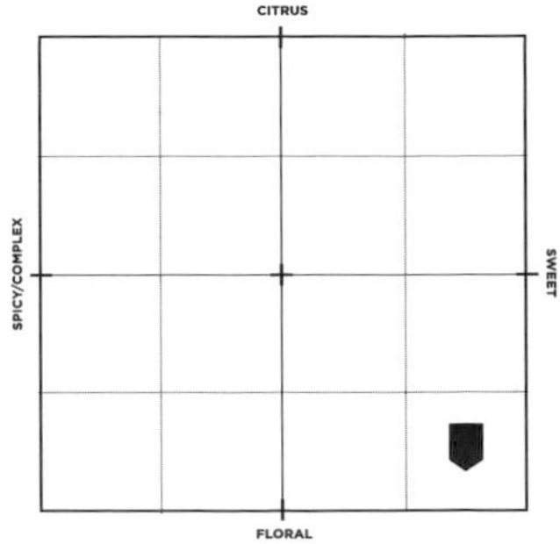

ARTISAN SPIR
SOUTHWESTER
DISTILLERY
EST. 2012
HANDCRAFTED IN CORNWA
TARQUINS
GIN

42 %

TARQUIN'S HANDCRAFTED CORNISH DRY GIN

ORIGIN

Tarquin's Handcrafted Gin originated in the wild Atlantic coast of North Cornwall, where it is still produced in small batches in North Cornwall by Southwestern Distillery and is signed off by Tarquin, its founder and master distiller. In addition to gin, the family business also produces pastis. The heart of the distillery is the copper still called Tamara. Tarquin's Gin won a gold award during IWSC 2014. Part of the ingredients, such as the Devon violets can be found in the family's garden. The other botanicals come from around the globe.

TASTE AND AROMA

Its scent is reminiscent of the sweet breeze of orange blossoms. The taste is sweetly fresh with exotic touches. The aftertaste is rather herbal (predominantly of cardamom).

INGREDIENTS

juniper berries from Kosovo
Devon violets from North Cornwall
coriander seeds from Bulgaria
sweet orange peels
lemon peels
grapefruit peels
angelica root from Poland
orris root from Morocco
green cardamom seeds from Guatemala
bitter almonds from Morocco
cinnamon from Madagascar
liquorice from Uzbekistan

COMBINE WITH

neutral or fruity tonic

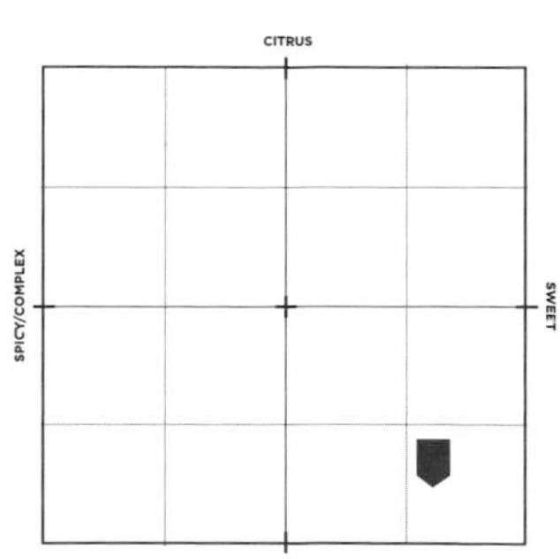

45 %

THE DUKE MUNICH DRY GIN

ORIGIN

The name of this gin refers to Franz Bonaventura Adalbert Maria Herzog von Bayern, or in short the Duke of Bavaria. This duke stood at the head of the House of Wittelsbach, which used to rule the Kingdom of Bavaria. To this very day, Franz still holds his royal title. Duke Gin is produced in Munich using 13 botanicals, including two typical beer flavourings: hop and malt. All the herbs are organic. The untreated juniper berries are mainly responsible for the character of Duke Gin. Before bottling, the gin is carefully filtered again to guarantee the purity of the gin.

TASTE AND AROMA

Juniper berries are felt in the nose and on the palate, yet coriander is also clearly noticeable when tasting the gin. A strong floral taste and creamy aftertaste with hints of chocolate and coffee.

INGREDIENTS

juniper berry
coriander
lemon peel
lavender
ginger
orange blossoms
hop
malt
cinnamon bark
cranberries
caraway
a secret ingredient

COMBINE WITH

neutral or aromatic tonic

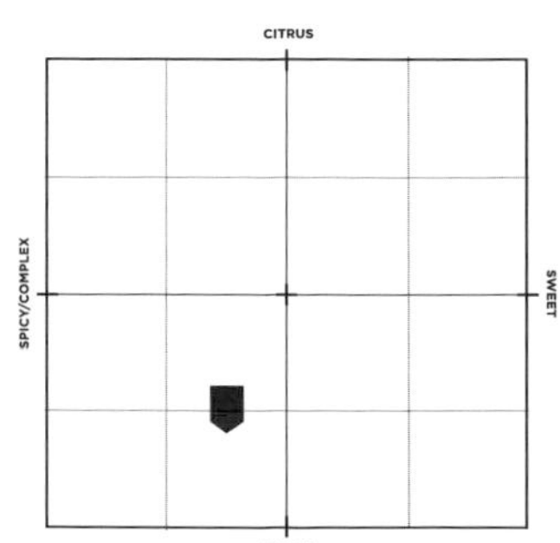

THE DUKE
THE DUKE
Handcrafted in Bavaria
Munich Dry
45% vol
GIN
70 cl

PRODUCT OF
LONDON N°1®
ORIGINAL BLUE GIN
personal supervision of our master distiller.
DISTILLED GIN • 47% VOL

47 %

THE LONDON N°1 GIN

ORIGIN

London N°1 is distilled four times in small batches under the watchful eyes of master distiller, Charles Maxwell. This gin has a very distinct colour, which also gives it its appropriate name: The Original Blue Gin. This striking blue colour derives from maceration with gardenia flowers (many men use this in their lapels). This ultra-premium gin has four distinguishing features: the use of North London spring water, processing the best Suffolk and Norfolk grains, a meticulously implemented distillation process, and the use of a dozen herbs and spices from around the world. London N°1 belongs to a select group of gins that are distilled in London.

TASTE AND AROMA

The gardenias leave their mark on this gin and that is what you smell the minute you open the bottle. The taste is rather sweet, but with herbal accents.

INGREDIENTS

juniper berries from Croatia ....
blackcurrant from Hong Kong ....
anise from Turkey ....
cinnamon from Sri Lanka .....
coriander from Morocco ....
orris root from Italy ....
peel of lemons and oranges from Italy ....
savory from the French Alps
almonds from Greece ....
gardenias ....
bergamot oil ....

COMBINE WITH

fruity tonic
(or neutral tonic)

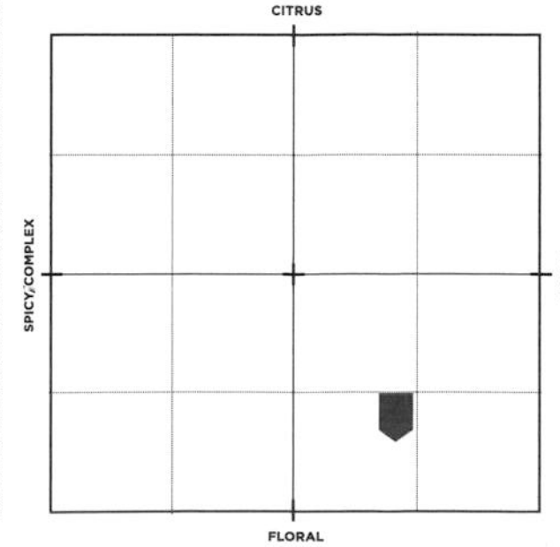

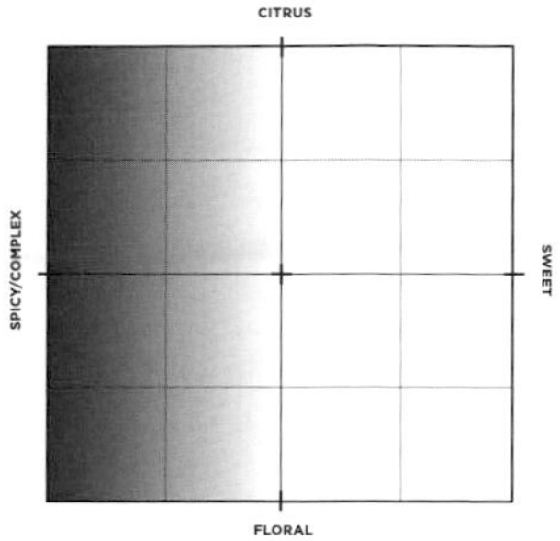

ON THE LEFT: SPICY/COMPLEX
COMBINE WITH AROMATIC TONIC
(OR NEUTRAL TONIC)

Complex flavours and spicy tones predominate. Think of earthy tastes, pepper and hints of herbs and spices, such as fennel and ginger, but also chocolate, apples and wood. Gins which find themselves in this corner of our taste spectrum are a real joyride for the gin lover. Whereas in the other corners of our flavour cross we can speak of monotone flavours – and that is certainly not to say 'boring', but more a sign of quality of content – with this type of gin the drinker will enjoy a roller-coaster ride of taste impressions. When trying a spicy/complex gin neat, you will discover that the first, typical flavours of gin are often next replaced by new nuances in the body of the drink. On the finish, even more taste sensations come peeping around the corner. It is precisely this multifaceted nature which acts as the power (and definition) behind complex gins. And yes indeed, we are getting more daring by choosing these kinds of gin more regularly. The adventurous type always does prefer the roller-coaster at the funfair. Would you rather play it safe? In that case, it is perhaps wise to leave this area of the flavour cross well alone.

SCOTLAND

40 %

BLACKWOODS VINTAGE DRY GIN

ORIGIN

Blackwoods Gin is a Scottish Premium Dry gin that uses herbs from the Shetland Islands, an archipelago northeast of the Scottish mainland. Although the Shetland Islands have been part of Scotland since 1472, geographically they are situated closer to Bergen (Norway) than to Edinburgh. The Shetland's climate greatly resembles that of Scandinavia: long winters and short summers. On nice days, the islands are truly idyllic; spectacular vistas flaunt the beauty of the islands. Also the storms that sometimes rage over Shetland are breathtaking. Although beautiful flowers grow on the difficult-to-reach cliffs, only some hundred flora species are found there due to the extreme weather conditions. To make Blackwoods gin, which is based on a local Scandinavian recipe, the producers wait every year for the perfect weather conditions to harvest their botanicals by hand. The year on the bottle indicates the year in which the botanicals were picked, which produces slight deviations in taste. In addition to the 40% version, there is also a 60% gin. The latter was developed specifically for experienced mixologists. Only 22,000 bottles are produced annually, just as many as the number of residents on the Shetland Islands.

INGREDIENTS

juniper berry ....
sea pink ....
marsh marigold ....
meadow sweet ....
coriander ....
lemon peel ....
cinnamon ....
liquorice ....
nutmeg ....

TASTE AND AROMA

Abundant citrus and orange fragrance in the nose. Smooth on the palate, yet crisp with the definite reference to juniper. A plant-based gin that pays homage the Shetland Islands.

COMBINE WITH

neutral or aromatic tonic

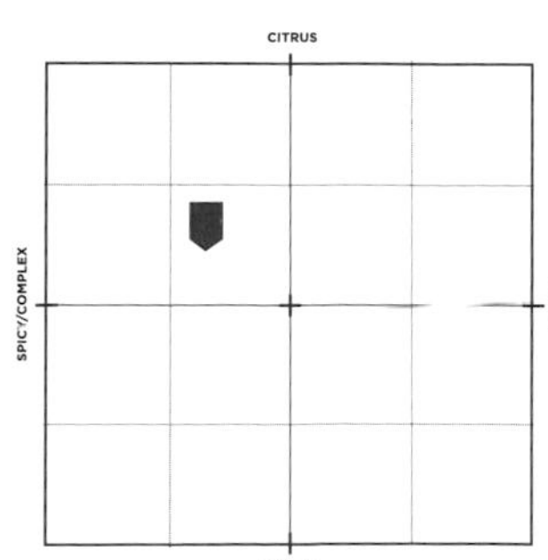

D DRY
Reisetbauer
BLUE GIN
PREMIUM
AUSTRIAN
QUALITY
VINTAGE
DISTILLED
DRY GIN
SMALL BATCH
43% VOL e 70CL

40 % BLUE GIN

ORIGIN

Blue Gin is from the hands of the Austrian distillers Hans Reisetbauer, who brought this surprising gin to the market place in 2006. The distillation process is unusual to say the least. Small copper boilers, each with a 300-litre capacity, are used to first distill the raw materials such as the grain type 'Mulan' and corn, using the 'pot still' method with a basic distillate of 40% alcohol. The second distillation uses 96% alcohol and more than 27 botanicals sourced from no less than ten different countries such as Spain, Vietnam, Egypt, Romania, China, Indonesia, The Netherlands, Turkey and America. During the three day fermentation period, the mixture is processed again using the pot still method, followed by splitting the botanicals and the alcohol. Blue Gin is then diluted with crystal clear water from the 'Alm' mountain river.

TASTE AND AROMA

The flavour is fresh, elegant and spicy, with the typical tastes of juniper berry filled out with hints of citrus. The spicy finish with its surprising earthy taste certainly makes this a gin worth investigating.

INGREDIENTS

juniper berry
grated lemon peel
angelica
coriander seed
turmeric
liquorice

COMBINE WITH

aromatic tonic
(or neutral tonic)

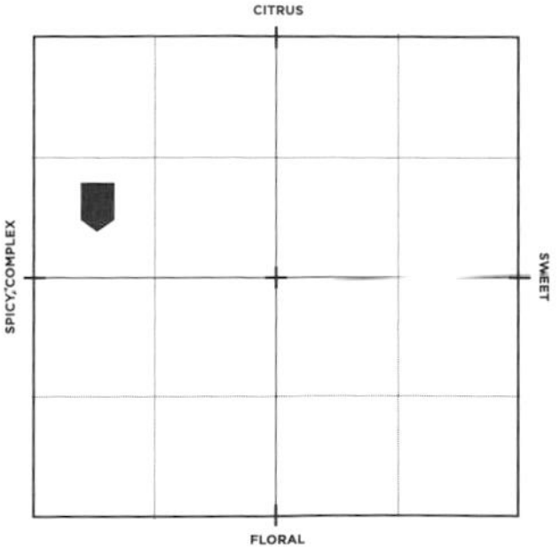

40 %

BULLDOG GIN

ORIGIN

A really butch gin from London, launched in 2007 by a former investment banker. The twelve botanicals in the gin represent the brand's worldwide trip. The bottle has a rugged-looking studded dog collar illustrating its domineering character. The gin is distilled four times and has received worldwide acclaim. Bulldog Gin is perfect to drink 'on the rocks', but can also hold its own in any number of cocktails.

TASTE AND AROMA

Once you have dared to open the bottle, the very flowery bouquet of coriander and citrus becomes immediately apparent. Very dry and soft on the palate, where the juniper plays a dominant role. Bulldog Gin is brought into balance by the botanical elements.

INGREDIENTS

juniper berry
almonds
lavender
cassia bark
coriander seed
dragon eye (a type of lychee)
liquorice
poppy
lotus leaves

COMBINE WITH

aromatic tonic
(or neutral tonic)

OTHER GINCREATION

- Bulldog Gin Extra Bold / 47% / extra strong

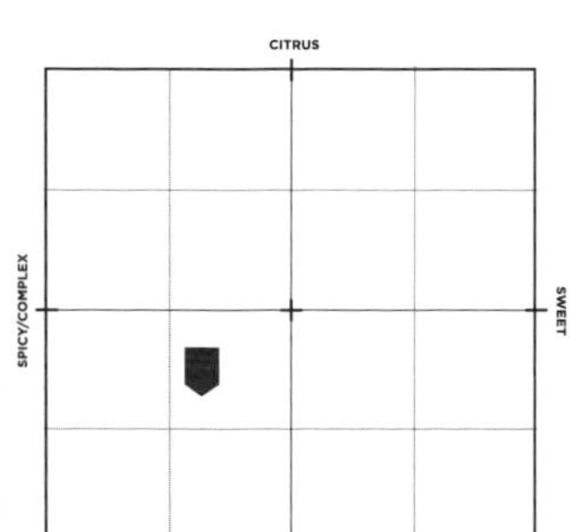

BULLDOG
A Brazen
Perfectly
Natural
And
Bulldog

RALPH
DODD'S
GIN
GIN
CRAFTED
BY
SEASON
SMALL BATCH
SMALL BATCH
D
R
LONDON
ENGLAND
GIN
GIN
GENUINE BRITISH SPIRITS
CORDIALS & COMPOUNDS

49.9 %

DODD'S GIN

ORIGIN

Dodd's Gin is the first gin (alongside whisky) made by The London Distillery Company, which was established in 2011 via crowdfunding. It is housed – along with other businesses, such as a bar, a boxing club, an art gallery, a design studio and a food truck business – in an old milk factory in Battersea in London.

Nowadays the chemist, Andrew MacLeod Smith, is in charge of distillation. The striking thing about this gin is the fact that it consists of two separately distilled gins that are blended to make Dodd's Gin. Firstly, a London Dry gin is produced and afterwards a second distillate of botanicals is brewed. A few weeks later, these two distillates are mixed together and bottled at 49.9% alcohol. Just as unique in this gin is the use of honey! And now Graham Michie, a colleague who also contributes to the gin production, creates his own tonic syrups. What a creative bunch of people!

TASTE AND AROMA

Smooth and perfectly balanced gin with a hint of honing on the tongue.

INGREDIENTS

juniper berry ...
cardamom ...
angelica root ...
fresh lime peel ...
red raspberry ...
laurel ...
bay leaf ...
honey from The London Honey Company and more ...

COMBINE WITH

neutral tonic
or aromatic tonic

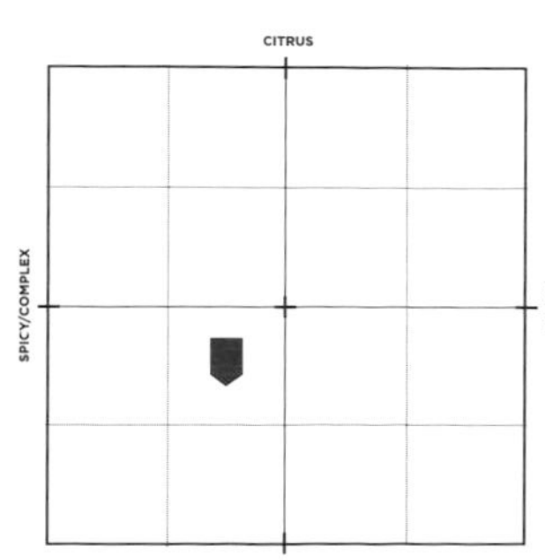

44 % FERDINAND'S SAAR DRY GIN 1
30 % FERDINAND'S SAAR QUINCE GIN 2

ORIGIN

Ferdinand's Saar Dry Gin is produced from Riesling grapes that are carefully hand-picked from the steep, shale slopes of the Zilliken estate at the Saarburger Rausch. The craftsmanship of master distiller, Andreas Vallendar, and the more than 30 well-balanced botanicals – some that originate from the vineyard and others that are cultivated on the estate – guarantee a gin of exceptional quality. Ferndinand's Saar Dry Gin owes its name to the Royal Prussian District Forester, Ferdinand Geltz. This historical figure was the co-founder of the VDP Mosel-Saar-Ruwer Zilliken estate, one of the most beautiful vineyards in Germany. Ferdinand's Quince gin is made from freshly picked quinces, which are grown near the distillery. Like Ferdinand's Saar Gin, this gin also gets infused with Riesling Rausch Kabinett (wine) after the distillation process.

TASTE AND AROMA FERDINAND'S SAAR DRY GIN

The aroma has floral and grassy notes with a hint of citrus, while the grapes and juniper berries are also recognisable. The lavender and rose petals make the complexity in taste come alive, followed by the taste of the Riesling.

TASTE AND AROMA FERDINAND'S SAAR QUINCE GIN

A wonderful balance between sweet and bitter. The low alcohol content also makes it perfect for drinking pure.

INGREDIENTS FERDINAND'S SAAR DRY GIN

juniper berry ....
thyme ....
lavender ....
sloe ....
rose hip ....
angelica root ....
hop blossom ....
rose ....
almond ....
coriander ....
ginger ....

INGREDIENTS FERDINAND'S SAAR QUINCE GIN

juniper berry ....
thyme ....
lavender ....
sloe ....
rose hip ....
angelica root ....
hop blossom ....
rose ....
almond ....
coriander ....
ginger ....
quinces ....

COMBINE WITH

aromatic tonic
or neutral tonic

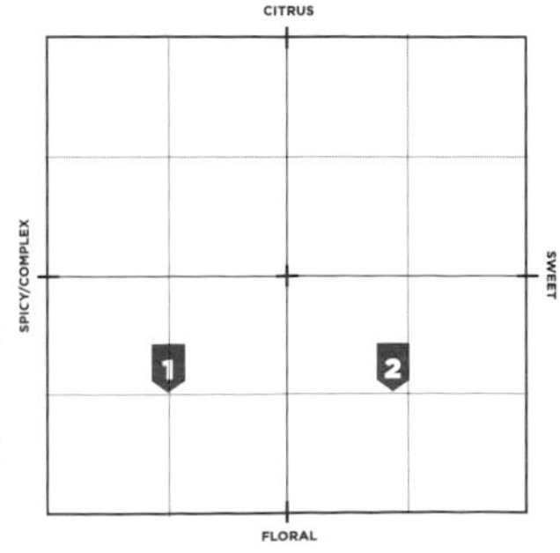

43 %

INVERROCHE CLASSIC GIN

ORIGIN

Inverroche Gin is the first gin that comes from South Africa and a clear sign of the global ascendancy of distilled gin. Inverroche Distillery is a limited distillery, carachterised by authenticity, limited volumes and exceptional quality. The city of Inverroche is located where the Goukou River flows into the Indian Ocean, close to Stilbaai. It is a region exceedingly rich in natural beauty with sloping hills, dunes, fynbos and renosterveld flora, with mountains and indigenous forests in the background. The distillery is surrounded by vineyards, olive groves and fynbos. The name Inverroche comes from a combination of French and Celtic words. Many ancient languages combine words to indicate the names of places. 'Inver' refers to the merging of bodies of water, 'Roche' is the French word for cliffs and refers to the limestone cliffs on which the unique fynbos vegetation thrives so successfully. The buildings of the distillery are also constructed from limestone. The logo is a geometric flower design that symbolizes the interaction between water and rocks. Inverroche Gin Classic is distilled twice and after the juniper berry, the fynbos plays a major role.

TASTE AND AROMA

An elegant, refreshing and complex gin made from a tasteful mix of African and traditional herbs. Refreshing and dry on the palate with top notes of juniper and citrus followed by the taste of herbs. The subtle undertone of fynbos gives the gin a smooth finish.

INGREDIENTS

juniper berry
fynbos
cassia bark
cinnamon
anise seed
liquorice
sweet orange peel
lemon peel
ginger root
angelica root
fennel seed
coriander seed
star anise
cardamom
orris root
lime peel
grains of paradise
nutmeg
sweet flag root and more

COMBINE WITH

aromatic tonic
(or neutral tonic)

OTHER GINCREATIONS

- Inverroche Gin Amber / 43% / matured
- Inverroche Gin Verdant / 43% / floral

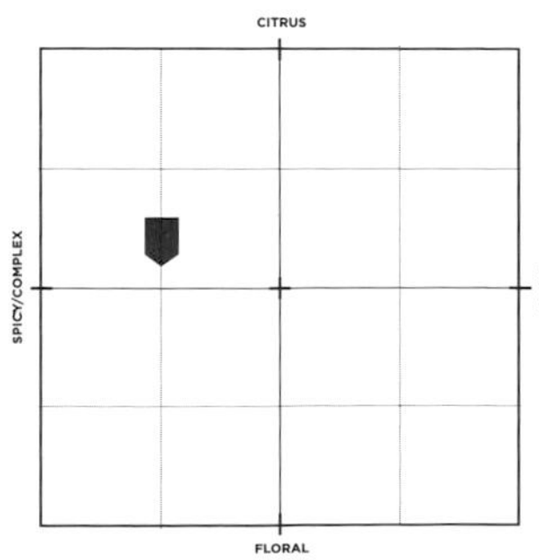

41.5 %

MOMBASA CLUB GIN

ORIGIN

Mombasa Club Gin is an archetypal retro gin, made following a 19th century recipe which was originally intended for the British colonists in Mombasa (Kenya). These colonists founded the first exclusive club — you guessed it — the legendary Mombasa Club. Some of the Mombasa Club members — naturally only English — were privileged enough to enjoy this gin. Nowadays, this spirit is crafted from carefully selected aromatic herbs and spices and new life has been breathed into the authentic flavours of this exclusive recipe.

TASTE AND AROMA

Mombasa Club Gin smells exotic and tastes sweet but, at the same time, fresh. In one word: elegant. Overall it is pretty spicy, and the lime and aniseed tints contribute to the complete package. The finish is an elongated bitterness. Mombasa Club Gin lends itself wonderfully to being served 'on the rocks'.

INGREDIENTS

juniper berry
cassia bark
cumin
coriander
cloves
exotic angelica

COMBINE WITH

aromatic tonic
(or neutral tonic)

OTHER GINCREATION

- Mombasa Colonel's Reserve / 43.5% / spicy

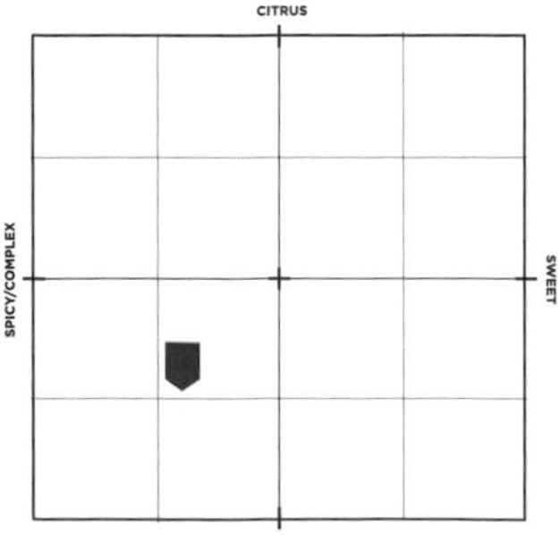

London Dry Gin
100% Pure Grain Spirit
MO

MONKEY 47
47%VOL
500ML
HANDCRAFTED
UNFILTERED
SCHWARZWALD DRY GIN

GERMANY

47 %

MONKEY 47

ORIGIN

Monkey 47 is a complex, full-flavoured gin from the Black Forest. The name gives you a clue as to both the number of botanicals used (47), as well as the alcohol content (47%). Before bottling, Monkey 47 is left to mature for about 100 days in earthenware vats. The label marks not only the date of bottling, but also the vat and bottle number. The character of Monkey 47 is determined by the traditional British recipe, combined with botanicals from the Black Forest and India. Today, this gin is produced by Black Forest Distillers.

TASTE AND AROMA

Monkey 47 is a highly unusual gin with a clean flavour. The taste of the juniper berry and citrus is complemented by sweet and floral aromas, giving the gin a spicy 'bite'. Peppery spices and bitter fruits complete the picture.

INGREDIENTS

47 botanicals including
juniper berry
cranberries
pine needles
lavender
peppers
cloves
Approximately half of the botanicals originate from the Black Forest.

COMBINE WITH

aromatic tonic
(or neutral tonic)

OTHER GINCREATIONS

- Monkey 47 Distiller's Cut / 47% / complex
- Monkey 47 Sloe Gin / 29% / sloe liqueur

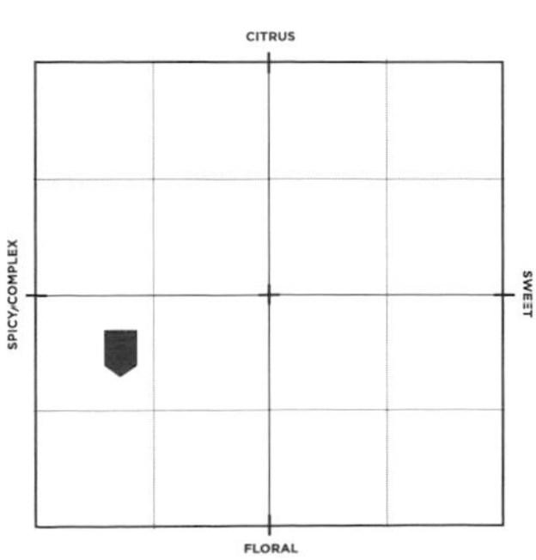

40 %

OPIHR ORIENTAL SPICED LONDON DRY GIN

ORIGIN

Opihr Oriental Spiced London Dry Gin is made in the United Kingdom, but seasoned with ingredients found along the Spice Route. Scroll through their lovely website that tells you in an original way where all the botanicals come from. The gin is distilled in the oldest distillery in England: G&J Greenall.

TASTE AND AROMA

Exotic and complex gin with the delicate perfume of cumin, cardamom and citrus. The peppery touches perfectly complement the taste of herbs.

INGREDIENTS

juniper berries from Venice
cubeb berries from Malaysia
black pepper and cardamom from India
cumin seeds from Turkey
coriander from Morocco
oranges from Spain

COMBINE WITH

aromatic tonic
(or neutral tonic)

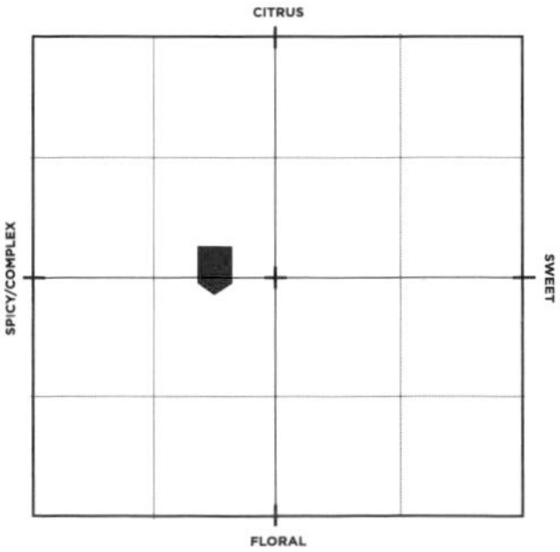

SINCE 1761
OPIHR
ORIENTAL SPICED
London Dry Gin

45 %

ST. GEORGE
TERROIR GIN [1], BOTANIVORE GIN [2] & DRY RYE GIN [3]

ORIGIN

St. George Spirits was founded in 1982 by Hörg Rupf as an artisanal distillery. Nowadays, St. George Spirits has expanded from a one-man business to a company spread over 65,000 m^2 with a complete team of distillers, yet it still upholds its authentic values. The distillery is located in the historical Alameda Naval Air Station in California and it currently has three gins in its range. The various botanicals in Terroir Gin include three that pay tribute to The Golden State of California, namely the Douglas spruce, laurel and sage. Terroir is actually used metaphorically because it refers to the geographical area where the ingredients grow. St. George Botaniver or the 'botanical eater' owes it name to the 19 botanicals in the gin. The third one, St. George Dry Rye Gin, is actually a maverick gin, because it is made with rye, which gives this gin its warm and malty signature. In addition, the Dry Rye Gin has 50% more juniper berries than the other two St. George gins.

www.stgeorgespirits.com

TASTE AND AROMA ST. GEORGE TERROIR GIN

The juniper berry almost plays a subordinate role here and is dominated by laurel and spruce.

TASTE AND AROMA ST. GEORGE BOTANIVORE GIN

Simultaneously refreshing, elegant and spicy.

TASTE AND AROMA ST. GEORGE DRY RYE GIN

The fragrance of nutmeg and fresh juniper berries. The juniper berry also plays a dominant role in the taste, accompanied by the touch of spicy pepper, lavender and other herbs.

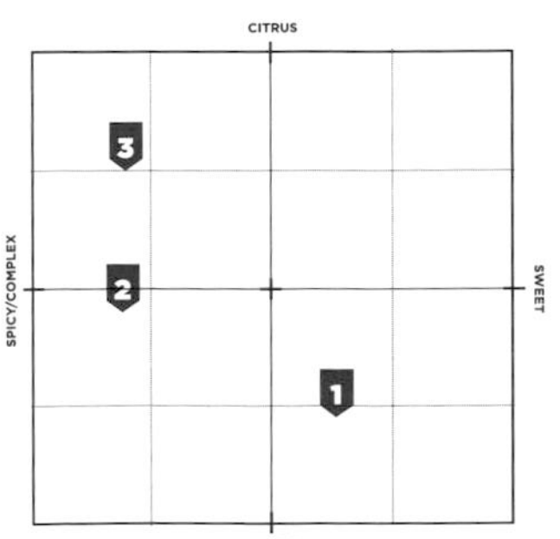

INGREDIENTS ST. GEORGE TERROIR GIN

- juniper berry
- coriander seed
- Douglas spruce
- laurel
- sage and more

INGREDIENTS ST. GEORGE BOTANIVORE GIN

- juniper berry
- angelica root
- laurel
- bergamot peel
- black pepper
- cumin
- cardamom
- coriander
- cinnamon
- hop
- dill seed
- fennel
- ginger
- lemon peel
- lime peel
- orris root
- orange peel
- star anise

INGREDIENTS ST. GEORGE DRY RYE GIN

- juniper berry
- black pepper
- cumin
- coriander
- grapefruit peel
- lime peel

COMBINE WITH

neutral tonic

46 %

THE BOTANIST ISLAY DRY GIN

ORIGIN

The Botanist is a creation of the Bruichladdich Distillery, known for its quality single malt whiskeys. The Botanist is a small batch gin made from 9 basic aromas and 22 local, hand-picked, botanicals that grow wild on the Isle of Islay, known for its excellent peated whiskeys. The gin is distilled in a unique and famous still named Ugly Betty. Betty lets no one rush her and works under low pressure, which helps release the subtle aromas.

www.thebotanist.com

TASTE AND AROMA

A tingling aroma with tones of pine resin, juniper berries, eucalyptus and refined ginger. A spicy complexity softened by the presence of liquorice. In the finish, once more the taste of juniper, parma violets.

INGREDIENTS

juniper berry
cassia bark
cinnamon bark
coriander seed
liquorice
orris root
elderberry wine
ferns
hawthorn
rhubarb
nettle syrup
syrup of violets
heather
spring flowers
Cicely seeds
seaweed
moss
pear
angelica root
nettle syrup
lime
apple mint leaves
camomile
peppermint leaves
thyme
myrtle and more

COMBINE WITH

aromatic tonic
(or neutral tonic)

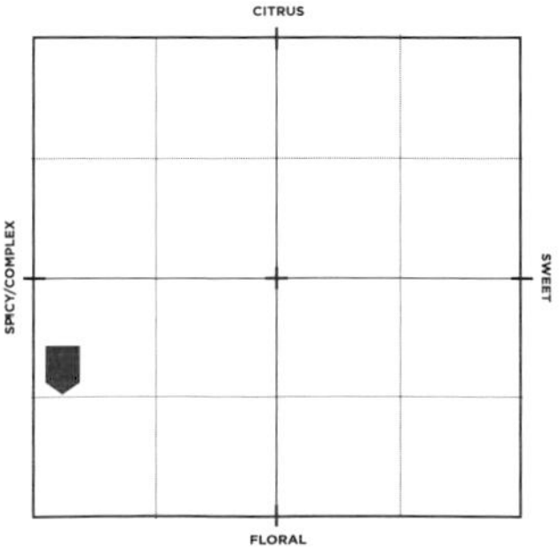

ungava
PREMIUM GIN

43.1 %

UNGAVA CANADIAN PREMIUM GIN

ORIGIN

Ungava Gin is the brainchild of Susan and Charles Crawford. The couple lives at Domaine Pinnacle, between the apple orchards of Frelighsburg in the southern part of Québec. They initially focused on making cider, but very quickly took it a step further and started making their first gin: Ungava, which in the Inuit language means 'to the open sea'. The yellow colour of this gin derives from the specific tea blends used in the production. The six botanicals that give Ungava gin its taste are picked during the short summer season.

TASTE AND AROMA

Spicy gin with 100% natural ingredients, powerful aroma and mild in taste.

INGREDIENTS

Nordic juniper
wild rose hips
cloudberry
crowberry
Labrador tea
Arctic Blend (type of tea)

COMBINE WITH

neutral tonic, preferably

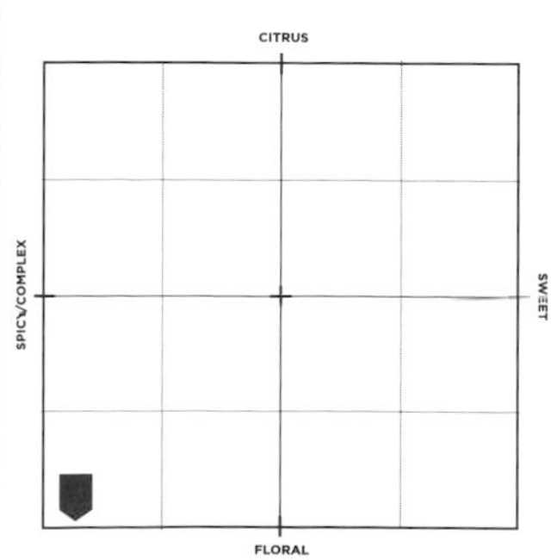

UNITED KINDOM

42 %

WHITLEY NEILL HANDCRAFTED GIN

ORIGIN

Neill Handcrafted Gin-United Kindom-42% Origin: Whitley Neill is a hand-crafted gin of exceptional quality, inspired by the vivid beauty of Africa, but produced in England. The gin is distilled in small batches by Johnny Neill, a direct descendant of Thomas Greenall and the last in a long line of distillers. Whitley Neill combines eight generations of expertise with a lifelong love for adventure. The result is an unparalleled, award-winning gin that skilfully combines rare, African flora and unusual aromas with an exotic experience. Like a good wine, this gin coats the sides of the glass.

TASTE AND AROMA

Intense aroma from the herbs and the taste is also spicy with hints of citrus.

INGREDIENTS

juniper berry
coriander seed
golden berry
Baobab fruit
sweet lemon peel
sweet orange peel
Angelica root
cassia bark
orris root

COMBINE WITH

aromatic or neutral tonic

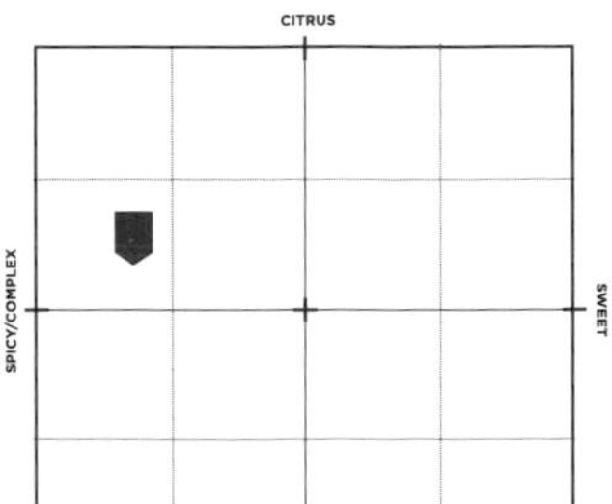

Inspired by Africa
TRADE MARK
WHITLEY NEILL
HANDCRAFTED DRY GIN
BATCH
Distilling gin for 8 generations SINCE 1762
GIN of exceptional quality,
flavours of AFRICA. Fresh
aromatic CAPE GOOSEBERRIES
TRADITIONAL BOTANICALS
COPPER STILL to produce a
TRUE AFRICAN SPIRIT.
JOHNNY NEILL
Batch No. 002
42%VOL 70CL e

KORIGUER

38 %

XORIGUER GIN

ORIGIN

Xoriguer Gin originates from Menorca (Mahon) and was established by Miguel Pons Justo. The name Xoriguer comes from the old windmill built in 1784 that belongs to the Pons family. People have been producing gin in Menorca since the British occupation in the 18th century. Like Plymouth, it is one of the few gins in the world that is named after a geographical location. During distillation, wine alcohol is used instead of the commonly used grain distillate. Before bottling, the gin is first ripened in American oak casks. The most important ingredient is, of course, the juniper berry, while the names of the other botanicals are a carefully guarded secret.

TASTE AND AROMA

A light aroma of fresh flowers and vanilla. The taste has juniper and floral touches (violets) with a warm-spicy aftertaste.

INGREDIENTS

juniper berries and other secret ingredients ....

COMBINE WITH

neutral tonic, preferably

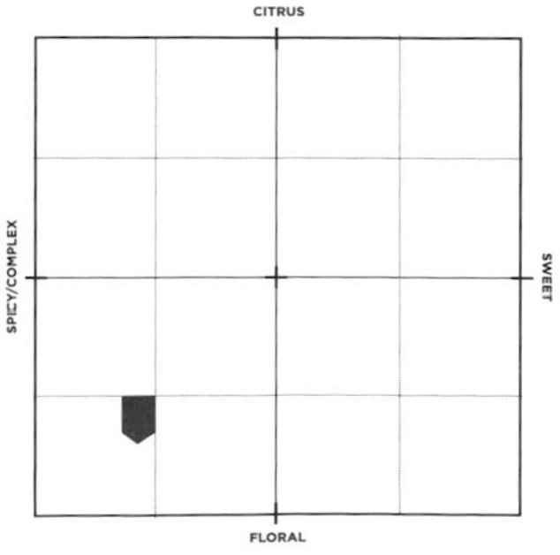

EXOTIC GINS

The flavour cross is our guide to the categorization of gins. Due to recent developments in flavours, there are some gins that we cannot equivocally place on the flavour cross. Therefore we define these gins as exotic. Just as a few years ago in the world of whisky, the producers shifted the boundaries with regards to taste, and so completely new taste experiences are also manifesting in the gin universe.

Let's give you an example to clarify. The word 'finishers' has recently started popping up in connection with whisky. Big brands have been trying to maintain the perception of whisky as a sexy product by offering new patterns of taste. Instead of maturing the whisky in classic wooden barrels, the producers are now also making use of old wine vats, old port vats or old Madeira vats. This leads to totally new flavour variations. The same phenomenon is also occurring with gin. Producers are breaking through the so called 'flavour boundary' and are experimenting with new ingredients and working methods. So for instance, Hoxton Gin uses coconut as an ingredient and Gin Mare, amongst others, creatively uses Arbequina olives. New methods of finishing are being established, with some gins left to mature in vats, such as Ransom Old Tom Gin, Columbian Aged Gin and Citadelle Réserve Gin.

In support of our convictions we will be discussing some of the exotic gins on the basis of their ingredients. Aged gins will come later and have a place in our section on mavericks.

At this exotic level of gins, our tonic categorization as we discussed earlier is not applicable, and therefore it is necessary to assess each gin individually.

HAND CRAFTED
LONDON
DRY GIN
GREAT NAMAQUA LAND
CAPE TOWN
CAPE COLONY
ELEPHANT GIN
BATCH NAME (1)
Mazithe
BOTTLE No
171
45% VOL
(1) EACH BATCH IS NAMED AFTER PAST GREAT TUSKERS OR ELEPHANTS WE CURRENTLY PROTECT.

GERMANY

45 %

ELEPHANT GIN

ORIGIN

Elephant Gin is a gin with social responsibilty, to say the least. The German master distillers, Robin Gerlach, Tessa Wienker and Henry Palmer, are devoted to protecting elephants and believe that the current generation is responsible for the survival of African wildlife. 15% of their profit goes to the Big Life Foundation and Space for Elephants. They produce only 800 bottles per batch and every batch is named after an elephant supported by this good cause. Elephant Gin undergoes a one-shot distillation in Hamburg (Germany) but the intention of its producers is for the gin to be associated with exotic Africa. They do that by using typical African botanicals: Baobab fruit, Buchu plant, lion's tail and devil's claw.

TASTE AND AROMA

This gin has the aroma of pinewood, brine, a touch of ginger and fruit. The first sip feels exotic and spicy. The end is somewhat flowery due to the elderflower.

INGREDIENTS

- juniper berry
- cassia bark
- orange peel
- ginger
- lavender
- elderflower
- pimento berries
- fresh apples
- pine needles
- Baobab fruit
- Buchu plant
- lion's tale
- devil's claw

COMBINE WITH

neutral tonic

JUNIPER BERRY

SPAIN

42.7 %

GIN MARE

ORIGIN

Gin Mare is made with the highest quality botanical herbs and spices, predominantly selected from the Mediterranean region. These are separately distilled in Vilanova i la Geltrú, a village on the Costa Dorada – and just to it make even more idyllic – in a picturesque old chapel. The domain is a former refuge for monks. In 1950, the terrain was purchased by the Giro Ribot family to accommodate their growing business. Launched in 1940, their MG Gin was a big hit in Spain. Later, in 2007, they made the decision to join Global Premium Brands – who had much more marketing experience than the Ribot brothers – and began developing a new gin. Gin Mare came to light in 2008 after much experimentation with a variety of herbs and spices. In 2012, the brand launched a new bottle.

TASTE AND AROMA

A herby nose, reminiscent of a damp forest full of tomato plants, alongside subtle aromas of rosemary and black olives. A full taste which bursts open with the juniper berries and coriander before switching over to the bitter, herby tones of thyme, rosemary and basil. The light bitter finish has notes of green olive, cardamom and basil. This super-premium gin has a character all of its own and a balance that is unlike any other gin on the market.

INGREDIENTS

hand-picked juniper berry.....
Arbequina olives ....
rosemary from Greece ....
Italian basil...............................
Turkish thyme ....
coriander from Morocco........
cardamom from Sri Lanka.....
bitter oranges from Seville ....
sweet oranges
from Valencia............................
lemons from Lleida ....

COMBINE WITH

1724 Tonic Water or
Fever-Tree Mediterranean
Tonic Water

MEDITERRANEAN GIN
Colección de autor.
GIN MARE
DISTILLED FROM OLIVES, THYME, ROSEMARY AND BASIL
700 ml. Alc. 42,7 % vol.

10 Botanicals
GIN SEA
18 90
LONDON DRY GIN
100% Grain Neutral Spirits
BY MANUEL BARRIENTOS
70 Cl.e
5
DISTILLATIONS
40% Vol.

40 %

GIN SEA

ORIGIN

Gin Sea is owned by one of the most famous sommeliers in Spain, Manuel Barrientos, but it was a collaboration of more than 100 professionals who developed the recipe. Gin Sea uses a 100% grain distillate from London which has been distilled five times. Ten different botanicals are used for the formula. Each ingredient is steeped separately and then distilled in an old still from Herve & Moulin (Bordeaux), which has been in service since 1890. Hence the reference to 1890 on the label.

TASTE AND AROMA

Delicate flavours with a touch of spice. Pleasantly fresh from the mint. In turn, the citrus in turn ensures a certain crispness.

INGREDIENTS

- juniper berry
- cardamom
- coriander
- thyme
- bitter chamomile
- liquorice
- peppermint
- lemon peel
- the peel of sweet and bitter oranges

COMBINE WITH

Thomas Henry Tonic Water

41.9 % MADAME GENEVA GIN ROUGE
44.4 % MADAME GENEVA GIN BLANC

ORIGIN

Madame Geneva is a revolution in the traditional gin market. The combination of the typical taste of juniper berries and the fruitiness of a red wine give it a complete new spirit. The bitter, yet refreshing gin consists of 46 botanicals combined with an intensive and aromatic red wine. The red wine is made from Primitivo grapes grown in Apulia, Italy. The grapevines are more than 60 years old and are famous for their Rubin red wine. The gin is distilled by Kreuzritter GmbH & Co. KG in a former farm called Meyerhof, surrounded by a beautiful park. The name of the gin refers to the nickname that gin acquired in the middle of the 18th century during the Gin Craze in England.

Its sister, Madame Geneva Gin Blanc, is just the opposite of the red version: a classic 'retro gin' with only three ingredients. If you want to know how gin tasted 100 years ago, Madame Geneva Gin Blanc has the answer. Both gins are presented in an opaque, black wine bottle. You can only see the difference in the white or red dot. So pay attention when you buy this gin!

TASTE AND AROMA
MADAME GENEVA GIN ROUGE

A mild and fine gin that does not overlook the contribution of juniper, yet with 46 botanicals it is considered a complex gin. Madame Geneva Rouge succeeds in perfectly combining the refreshing character of gin with the fruitiness of a concentrated red wine.

INGREDIENTS
MADAME GENEVA GIN ROUGE

juniper berry ....
red wine ....
a large number
of secret botanicals ....

COMBINE WITH

neutral tonic

TASTE AND AROMA
MADAME GENEVA GIN BLANC

Pure, classic gin with aromatic and slightly piquant tones.

INGREDIENTS
MADAME GENEVA GIN BLANC

juniper berry ....
coriander ....
ginger ....

COMBINE WITH

neutral or aromatic tonic

N
NORDÉS
ATLANTIC GALICIAN GIN

SPAIN

40 %

NORDÉS ATLANTIC GALICIAN GIN

ORIGIN

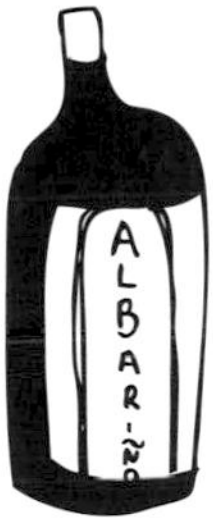

Nordés is a Spanish gin from Galicia. The remarkable characteristic of this gin is that in addition to 15 botanicals, the makers have added a distillate of Albariño wine. Albariño is the grape species grown in the Galician region of Rías Baixas, located in the northwestern corner of Spain. Nordés owes its name to the fresh northern wind that blows in that region. Albariño wines are considered to be among Spain's premier quality wines. They are characterised as floral with a flavour of peach, apricot and other tropical fruits.

TASTE AND AROMA

A defiant gin, which thanks to the eucalyptus and Albariño, has a unique perfumed aroma. The taste is on the sweeter side, but not too sweet. Glasswort and lemon help Nordés retain its refreshing character. In terms of taste and aroma, nothing comes close to Nordés gin.

INGREDIENTS

juniper berry ....
glasswort ....
lemon grass ....
lemon peel ....
eucalyptus leaves ....
sage ....
mint ....
cardamom ....
quinine ....
ginger ....
hibiscus ....
liquorice ....
tea ....

COMBINE WITH

neutral tonic

FRANCE

40 %

SAFFRON GIN

ORIGIN

Saffron Gin is based on a recipe that was once lost but then rediscovered, originating from the French colonists in India. Given its new lease of life, the recipe is brewed in the microdistillery belonging to Gabriel Boudier. The recipe is characteristic of colonial times: a gin with exotic botanical ingredients, bursting with flavour and intense aromas. Saffron Gin is made by hand in small batches using saffron. In our opinion, this is a gin you do not come across every day.

TASTE AND AROMA

Saffron Gin has a deep, orange colour and the aroma of orange and mandarin with subtle notes of the juniper berry. A soft mouth feel and a restrained and slightly delayed saffron taste.

INGREDIENTS

juniper berry............................
coriander ....
lemon...
orange peel...............................
angelica ....
orris root..................................
fennel..
saffron ....

COMBINE WITH

don't, drink neat (with a couple of coffee beans). Or, even better, neutral tonic and a slice of orange.

SAFFRON GIN
IMPORTED
GABRIEL BOUDIER
DIJON
e 70 cl
40% vol.
- Since 1874 -

SKIN
GIN

GERMANY

42 % SKIN GIN

ORIGIN

Skin Gin is a recent gin, developed as the result of a friendship between the Dane Martin Birk Jensen and the German Mathias Rüsch. Not only does the packaging catch the imagination, but also its primary ingredient: Moroccan mint. Inspired by the world of skin and tattoos (the stylistic anchor on the bottle), this gin is also marketed in various packaging: sometimes with a leather look, sometimes in an imitation snakeskin, but always with an extraordinary taste. The packaging is always done by hand, a painstaking job.

TASTE AND AROMA

A distinct hint of mint, wonderfully embraced by many citrus tones in the distillate. When tasting this gin, its ability to retain a perfect balance is very noticeable.

INGREDIENTS

juniper berry ....
coriander ....
Moroccan mint ....
lime ....
lemon ....
pomelo ....
orange ....

COMBINE WITH

1724 tonic or neutral tonic

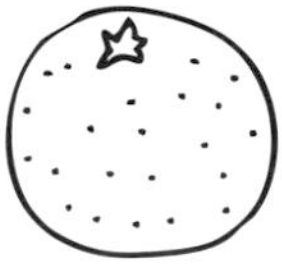

SPAIN

40 % TIDES GIN

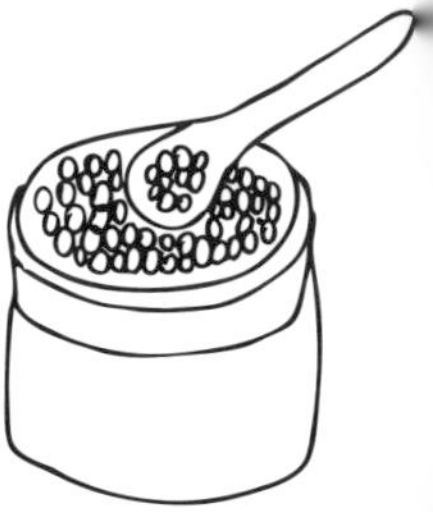

ORIGIN

Tides gin is produced by Blanc Luxury Gastronomy in Cadiz in sunny Andalusia, which has a long tradition of exceptional and luxurious food products including Las Perlas de Afrodita caviar. The same finesse and know-how is embedded in their gin. Tides Gin is one of the few gins distilled according to the au-bain-marie method in which the makers keep the temperature at a constant level. This of course results in a much longer distillation process, but it also means that the distillate better absorbs the flavour of the botanicals. The gin is distilled three times in copper stills.

TASTE AND AROMA

A very fine and intense aroma; exotic in taste with notes of citrus and a salty aftertaste from glasswort.

INGREDIENTS

juniper berry ....
glasswort ....
coriander ....
angelical root ....
verbena ....
cinnamon ....
orange ....
lime ....
lemon ....
bergamot ....

COMBINE WITH

neutral tonic

Catavinum World Wine & Spirits Competition
Gold
- Spain 2014 -
blanc
salicornia
premium collection

MAVERICKS

There is indeed such a thing as a gin with a temporary character, gins that are created for or during a particular season. We will cover all of them, so allow yourself to be pleasantly surprised by the diversity of gin!

SLOE (BERRY) GIN

DRINK NEAT OR COMBINE
WITH NEUTRAL TONIC

Sloe gin is a red liqueur which is made by macerating (steeping or infusing) sloe berries in gin, and sometimes also by adding sloe berry juice. The juice can be extracted by adding sugar to the sloe berries. Natural flavourings may also be added to the liqueur. The alcohol content of sloe gin is at least 25 %. Sloe gin is an infusion of fruit with a minimum amount of sugar added. Today, there are several commercial sloe gins which are produced by adding flavourings to cheap, neutral grain alcohol, but there are also producers using the traditional methods, with the recipes for sloe gin varying depending on the distiller. The taste can still be adjusted at the end, but in any case sufficient sugar must be used to ensure the complete extraction of the flavour from the sloe berries. When the sloe gin is properly produced, the alcohol also absorbs an almond-like flavour from the pit of the berry, which gives sloe gin its characteristic taste. Some creators use a shorter steeping time and will instead add almond essence afterwards. Another commonly seen variation adds cinnamon. Sloe gin is perfect on its own, on a cold winter's evening, but it is also excellent when it is mixed in many sorts of cocktail, for example a gin fizz, or try it in wine or champagne. Sloe gin can also give an extra dimension to your gin & tonic.

Sloe (berry) gin can thus either be consumed neat or with a neutral tonic. And to add just a touch of distinction you can also include a little of the original gin from the same makers.

UNITED KINGDOM

26 %

GORDON'S SLOE GIN

Gordon's Sloe Gin is made with ripe, hand-picked sloe berries, which are brought into balance with a select amount of herbs and spices. Gordon's Sloe Gin has a deep red colour.

TASTE AND AROMA

The nose of this gin is floral, with a hint of juniper berry and herbs. The taste is well-balanced, with an even-handed fruitiness and an intriguing tone of Earl Grey tea.

COMBINE WITH

drink neat or with neutral tonic

GERMANY

29 % MONKEY 47 SLOE GIN

Monkey 47 Sloe Gin is a traditional winter gin, distilled by Christoph Keller for Alexander Stein of the Black Forest Distillers.

THE BLACK FOREST DISTILLERS

TASTE AND AROMA

Very fresh and fruity, with touches of juniper and almonds. A very high-level sloe gin. The gin is distilled in small batches with 47 botanicals, with the addition of hand-picked wild sloe berries from the Black Forest.

COMBINE WITH

drink neat or with neutral tonic

CAUTION
WILD ANIMAL

TRADITIONAL SLOE GIN
1883 RECIPE

26 %

PLYMOUTH SLOE GIN

Plymouth Sloe Gin is a quintessentially English liqueur based on a recipe from 1883. This gin is the result of using Plymouth Gin which manages to get the most out of the sloe berry extract. The majority of the sloe berries used grow wild on Dartmoor, not far from Plymouth.

TASTE AND AROMA

Plymouth Sloe Gin has a rich red colour, a result of steeping the sloe berries in strong Plymouth Gin and soft Dartmoor water. The end product is a smooth liqueur taste with a good balance between sweet and bitter fruit flavours, complemented by a hint of almond from the pit of the fruit.

www.booking.plymouthgin.com

COMBINE WITH

drink neat or with neutral tonic

29 %

SIPSMITH SLOE GIN

The Sloe Gin from Sipsmith is made using frozen, freshly-picked sloe berries to macerate in the gin. The result is beyond compare: silky smooth, blackcurrant, ripe winter fruit and naturally the dominant sloe berry. Sipsmith Sloe Gin is only available in winter months.

TASTE AND AROMA

The nose offers berries with winter fruit and almonds. On the palate, a strong flavour of blackcurrant with subtle hints of cherry. A velvety finish of balanced sweetness from the berries and sugars complete this cosy gin.

COMBINE WITH

drink neat or with neutral tonic

SIPSMITH
independent spirits
LIMITED EDITION SERIES
Sloe Gin 2011
Hand crafted by master distiller:
50cl e
29%vol

FRUIT/SUMMER CUP

COMBINE WITH NEUTRAL TONIC OR A GOOD QUALITY LEMONADE SUCH AS FEVER-TREE LEMONADE

A fruit cup or summer cup is a traditional English drink, specially created to be mixed as a long drink with a soft drink or mixer. Most fruit cups are developed on a gin base, but there are also vodka-based fruit cups available. As this book is about gin & tonic we will stick to the gin-based varieties here. The gin base is flavoured with various herbs, spices, fruit and botanicals. Fruit cups or summer cups are most popular in the summer months as the name suggests. Manufacturers recommend garnishing the fruit cup with a variety of fruits, vegetables and herbs such as: apple, orange, strawberry, lemon, lime, cucumber, mint, borage and so on. You can certainly allow your creativity to run wild.

UNITED KINGDOM

20 %

CHASE SUMMER FRUIT CUP

Chase Summer Fruit Cup is based on Chase Vodka. The distillers begin by warming the vodka in the gin still in order to allow it to pass through the vaporization chamber and mix with 17 botanicals. The distillate is then combined with naturally purified water from the aquifer (an underground water bearing rock layer) which runs underneath the distillery's apple orchard. Following this, a carefully selected blend of elderflower, locally grown raspberries and blackcurrants are added to the gin in varying ratios.

TASTE AND AROMA

Earl Grey tea, rosemary and thyme in the nose, which is followed by the floral aromas of raspberry, elderflower and lavender. In the mouth, ripe and juicy blackcurrant and raspberry. In the background, tones of star anise and ginger. To finish, the fruit cup surprises you with the flavours of rosemary and thyme again, rounded off with lemon.

COMBINE WITH

neutral tonic or a good quality lemonade

OTHER GINCREATIONS

- Chase Extra Dry Gin / 40% / extra juniper berries
- Chase Junipero Vodka/ Single Botanical Gin / 40% / only juniper berries
- Chase Elegant Crisp / 48% / classic
- Chase Seville Orange Gin / 40% / citrus

29 %

SIPSMITH SUMMER CUP

This fruit cup is based on Sipsmith London Dry which is blended with an array of carefully selected summer ingredients, including an infusion of Earl Grey tea, lemon verbena and cucumber. Aromatic but surprisingly dry, this fruit cup lends itself well to the addition of fruit and lemonade.

TASTE AND AROMA

The nose is reminiscent of fresh oranges and fresh cucumber, underpinned by the delicate tones of tea. The juniper berry and the citrus are clearly present in a taste which is enriched with herbs and hints of cherry. The finish is complex but still refreshing.

COMBINE WITH

neutral tonic or good quality lemonade

SEASONAL GIN

A seasonal gin is literally named: a limited edition gin launched for a particular summer or winter season.

The flavours are so diverse so that each case has to be assessed individually when it comes to combining with tonic.

BEEFEATER®
LONDON DRY GIN
LONDON MARKET
Limited Edition
A VIBRANT GIN WITH
POMEGRANATE, CARDAMOM
& KAFFIR LIME LEAF
POMEGRANATE
KAFFIR LIME

40 %

BEEFEATER LONDON MARKET LIMITED EDITION

BEEFEATERS · DESMOND PAYNE ·

This limited edition was brought out in 2011 and developed by Beefeater's master distiller, Desmond Payne. London Market Gin is based on the original Beefeater Gin but enjoys the addition of extra botanicals such as pomegranate, kaffir lime leaves and cardamom.

TASTE AND AROMA

The aroma of redcurrants, vanilla and lime greets your nose. The classic juniper berry, citrus and subtle spices are also clearly present. The taste of the lime and orange peels are complemented by the juniper and bitter orange. The pomegranate is much more subtle in the mouth than on the nose, while the cardamom and the well-thought-out spicing adds to the flavour. The finish is citrusy with tones of bitter herbs, liquorice and peppery spices.

COMBINE WITH

neutral tonic

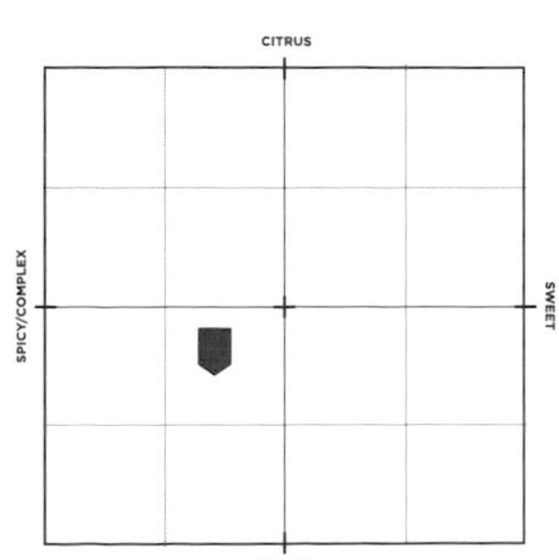

46 %

FILLIERS TANGERINE SEASONAL EDITION

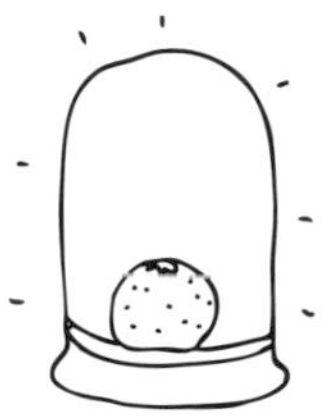

For the summer of 2013, master distiller Pedro Saez Del Burgo created this special seasonal edition with one unusual ingredient (which also happens to be Pedro's favourite fruit), the tangerine. Pedro chose quality tangerines from Valencia in Spain, which are harvested between November and January. During the cold Belgian winter months, the tangerines are brought to the fifth generation Filliers distillery. Filliers Tangerine Seasonal Edition is available from May until the 2013 stock sells out.

TASTE AND AROMA

Filliers Tangerine Seasonal Edition is a perfect base to use in cocktails or long drinks. It has a soft, fruity taste with clear accents of fresh orange and tangerine, interwoven with a mixture of herbs. The juniper berry is clearly present, filled out with cardamom giving a full, warm flavour. Notes of coriander and pepper make the gin surprisingly spicy, while the Belgian hops contribute a hint of bitterness. This Filliers Tangerine Seasonal Edition brings Spanish temperament to your glass, offering the mood of a sultry summer evening.

COMBINE WITH

aromatic tonic

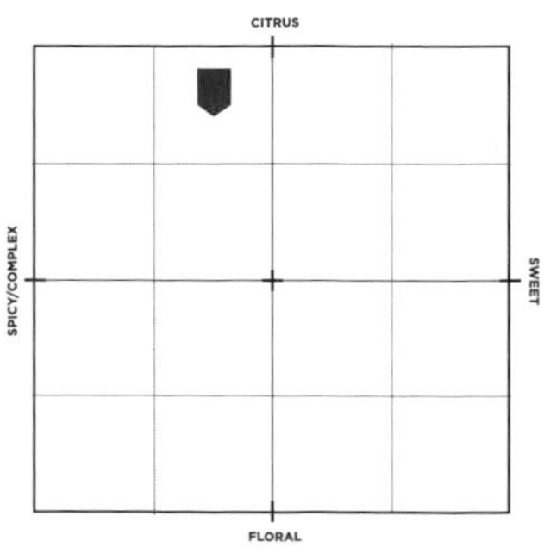

SMALL BATCH
Filliers
Gin

PLYMOUTH GIN
TM
TRADE
MARK
57% IS THE BENCHMARK STRENGTH AT
WHICH A SPIRIT IGNITES GUNPOWDER.
FOR ALMOST 200 YEARS, THE NAVY
NEVER LEFT PORT WITHOUT IT.
COATES & CO.

NAVY STRENGTH GIN

COMBINE WITH NEUTRAL TONIC,
BUT EASY ON THE GIN!

Navy Strength gin is a gin which is bottled with an alcohol percentage of 57%. Navy Strength gin grew from the idea of 'proof spirits' (literally meaning proved spirits). The term proof spirits began in the 18th century when rum was dished out to British soldiers. To be sure of the quality of the rum, gunpowder was added and then the mixture was ignited. If it didn't catch fire, it meant that the rum contained too much water and was therefore marked as being 'under proof'.

Navy Strength gins have a higher alcohol percentage than the original versions and therefore prove their value in mixing present-day cocktails. So be careful with the amount of gin that goes into your 'strong' gin & tonic.

hernö
navy strength
SWEDISH NAVY

SWEDEN

57 %

HERNÖ NAVY STRENGTH

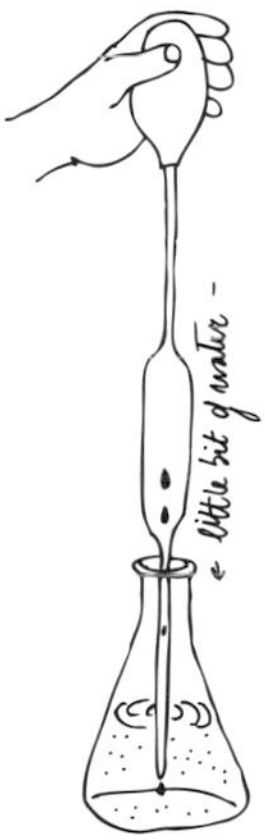

Hernö Navy Strength is manufactured in the same way as Hernö Swedish Excellence Gin. The only difference is in the water content. While thc original Hernö is diluted to a 40.5% alcohol percentage, the navy strength version is diluted to 57%. The difference in taste and feel is very noticeable: the character of the botanicals come more strongly to the fore due to the high alcohol content.

TASTE AND AROMA

Perfectly balanced with the aromas of fennel, coriander, dry pine, beeswax and citrus. There are also some lighter flowery notes.

COMBINE WITH

neutral tonic

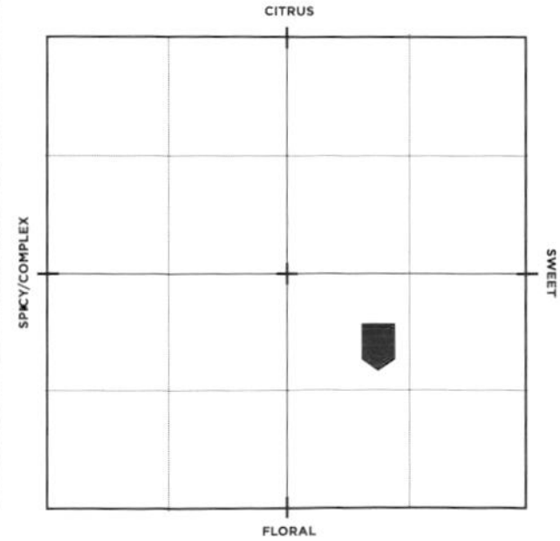

UNITED KINGDOM

57 % PLYMOUTH NAVY STRENGTH

For almost two centuries, the Royal Navy has never left port without a bottle of Plymouth Navy Strength on board. Plymouth Navy Strength Gin is made in the same way as the classic Plymouth Gin, with the same combination of botanicals distilled in a copper, pot still and a neutral grain alcohol. The only difference is that Navy Strength is bottled with an alcohol content of 57%.

TASTE AND AROMA

For some, Plymouth Navy Strength is the ultimate gin with a rich yet wonderfully balanced taste, which can elevate a Martini or gin & tonic to a higher level. Perfect for the demands of today's more adventurous drinkers and mixologists. The high alcohol content strengthens the flavours and aromas of the herbs, but maintains the supple and balanced character for which Plymouth Gin is so famous.

COMBINE WITH

neutral tonic

Other available brands offering a Navy Strength version are: Pimlico (United Kingdom), Leopolds Navy (United States), FEW Standard Issue (United States), Hayman's Royal Dock (United Kingdom), Perry's Tot (United States) and Bathtub Gin Navy Strength (United Kingdom).

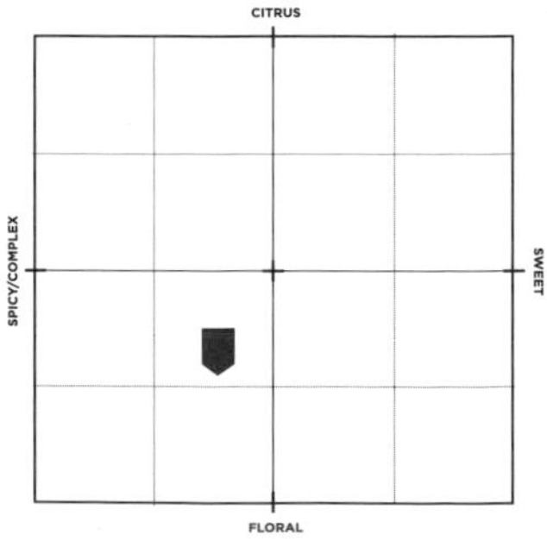

57%Vol

EY 47
500 ML
DISTILLER'S
CUT

DISTILLER'S CUT

COMBINE WITH NEUTRAL TONIC
OR DRINK NEAT

A Distiller's Cut gin is a unique version of the standard gin; whereby the master distiller creates a 'no holds barred' variety.

Due to the intense flavour sensations, we recommend drinking it neat. If however, you do want to mix these gins we suggest choosing a neutral tonic.

GERMANY

60 % BLACK GIN DISTILLER'S CUT

Black Gin Distiller's Cut has, just like its brothers, no less than 74 botanicals from 19 different countries, and is produced by the Gansloser Distillery. This version is extra spicy thanks to the increased alcohol content.

TASTE AND AROMA

The contents are not to be outdone by the design of this mysterious bottle. A combination of aromas immediately greets the nose. On the palate a whole host of ingredients play with each other. The finish is spicy, sometimes referred to as medicinal.

COMBINE WITH

drink neat or with neutral tonic

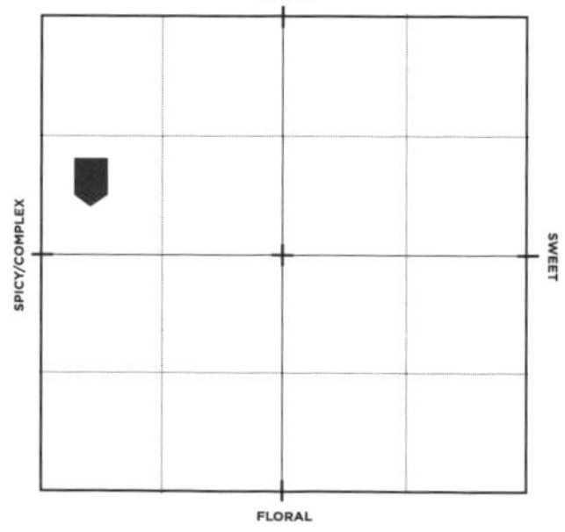

Pink
GIN

MONKEY 47
47%VOL
500 ML
HANDCRAFTED
UNFILTERED
SCHWARZWALD DRY GIN

47 %

MONKEY 47 DISTILLER'S CUT

This special limited edition from Monkey 47 gin is a more complex and fuller-flavoured variety than the standard version. The Distiller's Cut has been left to mature for longer in earthenware vats which allow the flavours to become more refined. This version of Monkey 47 is the personal creation of master distiller Christoph Keller. It is a complex gin, distilled three times and not cool filtered. There are only 2,500 bottles of this gin produced per year.

TASTE AND AROMA

An appealing and complex nose with the typical characteristics of a London Dry: juniper berry and peppery notes. In the nose as well as in the mouth, the Distiller's Cut is crisp, fresh and fruity. The lengthy maturing process ensures a good balance of all the components. An extremely complex and full-bodied gin.

COMBINE WITH

drink neat or with neutral tonic

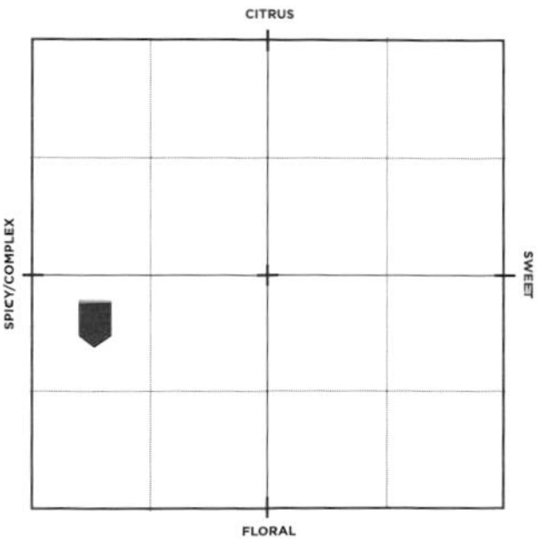

BELGIUM

48.8 %

SPRING GIN GENTLEMAN'S CUT

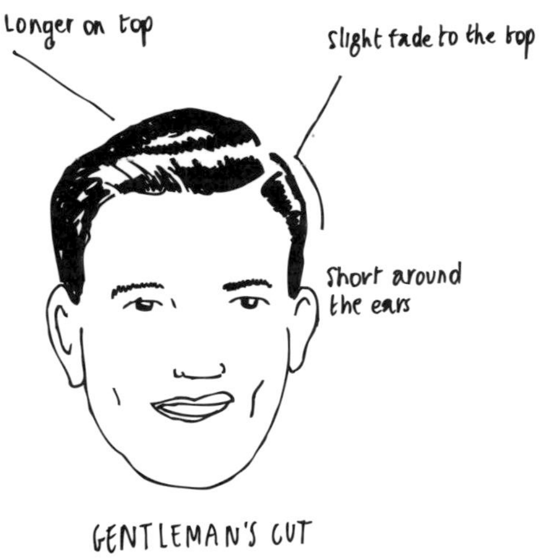

The Gentleman's Cut is the jewel in the crown of Spring Gin and contains the same ingredients as the classic version, but with an extra punch. Spring Gin was launched by Manuel Wouters, owner of the SIPS cocktail bar in Antwerp.

TASTE AND AROMA

This gin is extremely clean-tasting, guaranteeing the freshness of the citrus flavours. A richer mouth feel than the original version. Very delicate in taste with hints of aniseed and coriander.

COMBINE WITH

drink neat or with neutral tonic

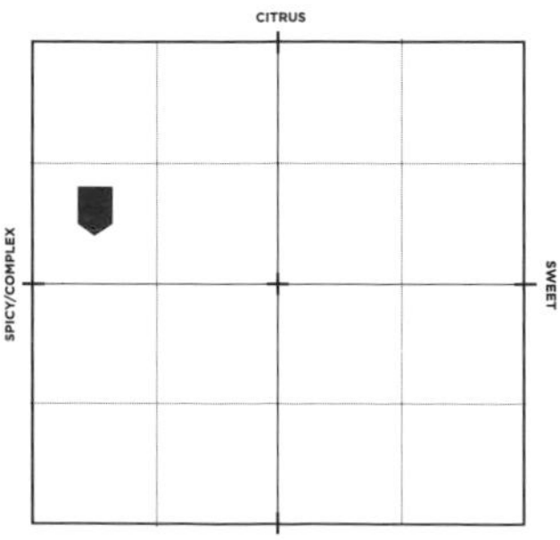

The
ORIGINAL
·BRAND·
SPRING
GIN
Gentleman's Cut
DRINK NEVER TASTE THIN WITH SPRING GIN
A Handcrafted Limited Run
Bottles of which this is
No. 725
DISTILLED IN FLANDERS
48.8% Vol (97.6 Proof), ℮500ML

PINK GIN

COMBINE WITH
NEUTRAL TONIC

Pink gin is based on the cocktail popular in 19th century Britain when a few drops of angostura bitters were added to gin. Angostura bitters is a drink which was first made in 1824 by Dr J. Siegert as a remedy to reduce the symptoms of fatigue and stomach complaints. Angostura is made from more than forty tropical herbs and plant extracts and has a spicy taste. The name derives from the harbour town Ciudad Bolívar in Venezuela, which used to be called Angostura.

Pink
GIN
BOTTLED

UNITED KINGDOM

47 %

EDGERTON PINK GIN

Edgerton Pink Gin has pomegranate to thank for its seductive blush, and is London's first Pink gin. This super-premium gin is distilled in London and sources its ingredients from all over the world: juniper berries, coriander, angelica, orris root, sweet orange peel, cassia bark and nutmeg are all left to infuse together for 24 hours.

TASTE AND AROMA

The first thing you notice is the scent of the sweet pomegranate which is added after distillation. The sweetness disappears almost immediately as you take your first sip and is replaced by an explosion of warmth. Sour and not too complex. Maybe one for the ladies?

COMBINE WITH

neutral tonic

GERMANY

43 %

LEBENSSTERN PINK GIN

Lebensstern Pink Gin is a premium gin specially developed for the Bar Lebensstern in Berlin. The gin is flavoured with the fresh aromatic bitters from 'The Bitter Truth'.

TASTE AND AROMA

Lebensstern Pink Gin has a rich, spicy taste, with just a touch of sweetness. Complex and intense.

COMBINE WITH

neutral tonic

OTHER GINCREATION

- Lebensstern Dry Gin / 43% / spicy

LEBENSSTERN
Bar im Einstein
PINK GIN
℮700 ml
Contains certified color E 129
43 % vol.

PINK GIN

40 %

THE BITTER TRUTH
PINK GIN

The Bitter Truth Pink Gin is a delicious mix of traditionally crafted gin and aromatic bitters. Designed to suit modern tastes, it enjoys a soft and friendly mouth feel alongside delicate, complex flavours.

TASTE AND AROMA

The nose of this fragrant gin is dominated by complex fruity and flowery aromas. The taste is very supple with the distinctive flavours of juniper in the foreground, surrounded by the spicy aromas of liquorice, caraway and fennel.

COMBINE WITH

aromatic tonic
(or neutral tonic)

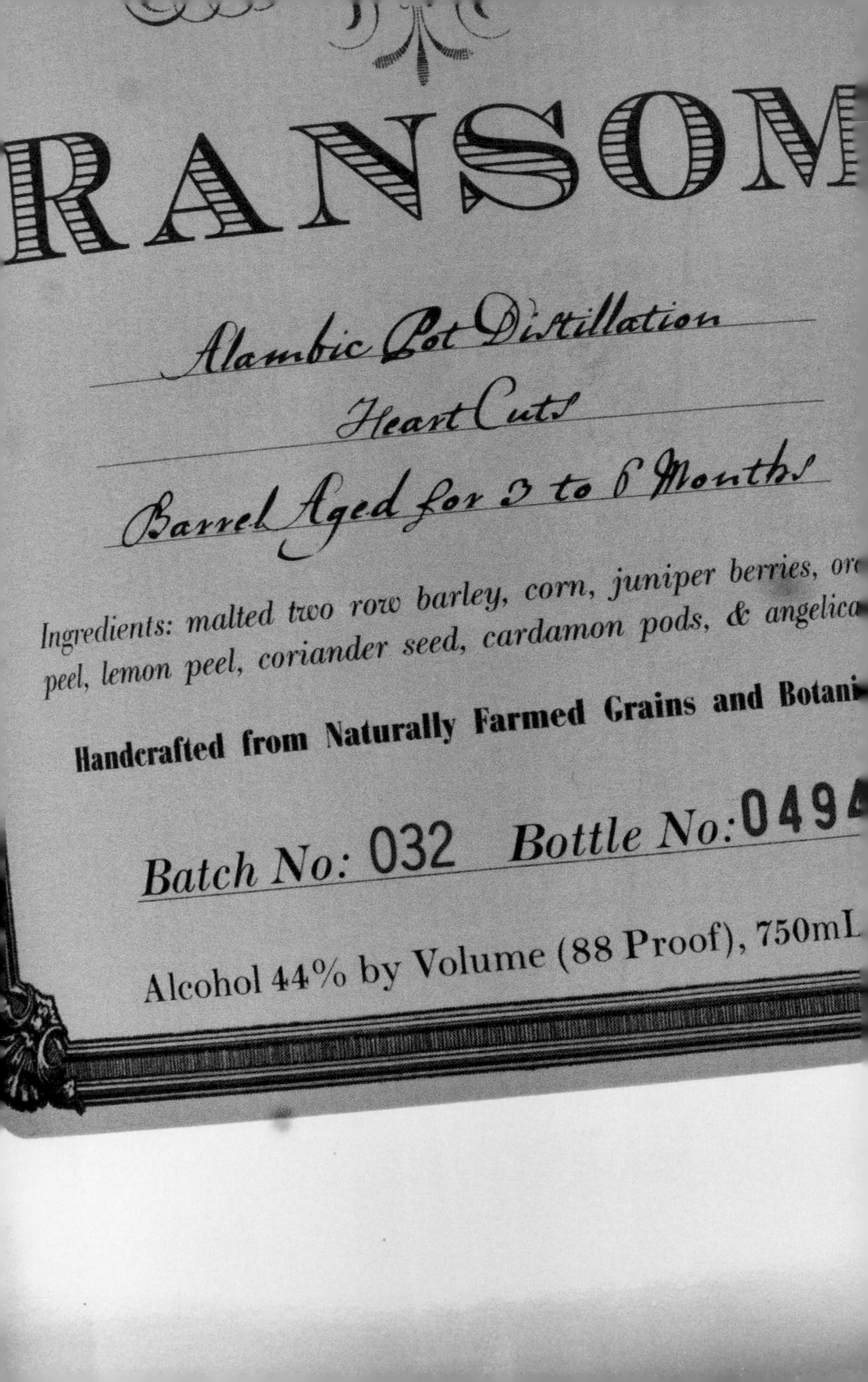
RANSOM
Alambic Pot Distillation
Heart Cuts
Barrel Aged for 3 to 6 Months
Ingredients: malted two row barley, corn, juniper berries,
peel, lemon peel, coriander seed, cardamon pods, & angelica
Handcrafted from Naturally Farmed Grains and
Batch No: 032 Bottle No:
Alcohol 44% by Volume (88 Proof), 750mL

AGED GIN

DRINK NEAT

It may come as a surprise, but there are indeed a few aged gins. Some are left to rest for a short period while others are matured for years in wooden vats. The colours are as varied and stimulating as the tastes. Here we pick out three.

Citadelle
Réserve
GIN

FRANCE

44 %

CITADELLE RÉSERVE GIN

ORIGIN

Citadelle Gin, as cited before, is a French gin from the Cognac region which uses 19 different types of herbs and spices, and is distilled three times. The original Citadelle Gin is officially a London Dry, but makes a few adjustments in the production process. Unusually small boilers are used, heated by a 'naked' flame, signifying that no steam is released during the process. The Reserve is made in batches of only 21 barrels and then matured for two years in Limousin oak vats.

TASTE AND AROMA

The fragrance is light and elegant and very appealing. Mild notes of juniper berry and lemon followed by the woodiness from the Limousin oak vats. Lightly sweet in taste with the trio of juniper berry, oak and citrus. Followed by a mild but solid spiciness which is complemented by a light earthiness.

INGREDIENTS

juniper berry from France
Moroccan coriander
orange peel from Mexico
cardamom from India
liquorice from China
cubeb pepper from Java
French flavourings
Mediterranean fennel
Italian orris root
cinnamon from Sri Lanka
French violets
almonds from Spain
kassia from Indochina
German angelica
grains of paradise from West Africa
Dutch cumin
nutmeg from India
Spanish lemons
star anise from France

COMBINE WITH

don't, drink neat!

43 %

COLOMBIAN AGED GIN

ORIGIN

This gin comes from the makers of Dictator Rum and is left to mature for six months in the Dictator Rum vats. The gin is distilled five times.

TASTE AND AROMA

Golden in colour and full-flavoured with woody tones, vanilla, spices and dried fruit.

INGREDIENTS

juniper berry
berries
spices
botanicals
tropical citrus peel
and others

COMBINE WITH

don't, drink neat!

OTHER GINCREATION

- Colombian White Gin 'Orthodoxy' / 43%

Aged Gin
AGED IN RUM BARRELS BY

Old Tom
Gin
RANSOM
Alambic Pot Distillation
Heart Cuts
Barrel Aged for 3 to 6 Months
Ingredients: malted two row barley, corn, juniper berries, orange peel, lemon peel, coriander seed, cardamon pods, & angelica root.
Handcrafted from Naturally Farmed Grains and Botanicals
Batch No: 032 Bottle No: 0494
Alcohol 44% by Volume (88 Proof), 750mL

UNITED STATES

44 % RANSOM OLD TOM GIN

ORIGIN

Ransom Old Tom Gin is manufactured by the Ransom Wine Company in Oregon (USA). The pharmacy-style bottle invokes the Wild West and cowboys and Indians. This Old Tom Gin is a blend of two distillations which are then combined to give one batch. This batch is then distilled again. One distillate consists of a malted grain mash (similar to whisky) and the other is a neutral grain distillate to which herbs are added. The blend is then allowed to lay in cleaned Oregon Pinot Noir vats for six months. This maturing process gives the gin its beautiful straw colour, making it soft and full of character. Ransom Old Tom Gin is absolutely one of a kind.

Batch No: 001
Bottle No: 0001

TASTE AND AROMA

In the nose, a soft whisky or a dynamic gin. The subtle mouth feel is a result of the use of a malted barley base, combined with an infusion of corn alcohol. You taste, amongst others, mint, pimento berries, cardamom and a light hint of juniper berry.

INGREDIENTS

juniper berry
orange
lemon
coriander
cardamom
angelica

COMBINE WITH

don't, drink neat!

DAMSON GIN

COMBINE WITH NEUTRAL
TONIC OR DRINK NEAT

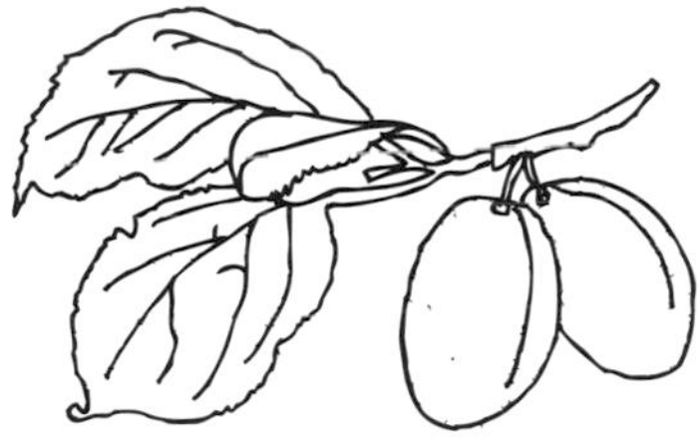

Damson gin is actually a liqueur which bears a strong similarity to sloe gin, in both the idea and how it is produced. In this case a few whole Damson fruits are allowed to macerate for at least eight weeks in sugar, to form a syrup. Damson gin is popular particularly in Great Britain, and is often just made at home and drunk around Christmas.

OUR 19 MOST REMARKABLE GINS

The history of gin spans several centuries, yet the craziest evolutions have occurred only in recent years. That is why our choice of the most remarkable gins reflects our personal way of interpreting this evolution, without denigrating any other brands, but rather with the profound respect for all gin producers. You are free to feel irritated, exulted or amazed by our selection or you might actually decide – as the ultimate tribute – to look for, taste or collect these selected gins. It's entirely up to you! Here too, with every gin, you will find our suggestion for a complete gin & tonic with garnish.

ORIGIN GIN

THE BASIC ONE

A basic gin could not be more basic: only differentiated by the juniper berry and local waters. To understand gin in its purest form, it is perhaps necessary that we take a moment to go a little deeper into the basic ingredient, the juniper berry. Basic but oh so important. The juniper berry is not only the key ingredient, and the most important botanical, but its presence is actually a legal requirement. The aroma and taste of the juniper berry should at the very least be the signature of every gin, both in the nose as well as in the mouth. Even the name of gin itself is derived from the juniper berry. Therefore, allow us a moment to pay homage to the juniper berry, as without it, gin would not even exist.

The juniper is a small evergreen tree or bush which can grow to a height of nine metres. It takes about two years before the berries are properly matured. There are around sixty or so different species and they grow in the majority of countries in the northern hemisphere. They can even be found growing at a height of 3,500 metres. If the juniper berry was a grape, winemakers would certainly be jumping for joy. As we all know, the soil, the climate and the growing conditions all have an impact on grapes. The term 'terroir' is used to denominate vineyards, and is moreover the first feature of a good wine. Following this logic, the provenance of the juniper is also significant when it comes to judging a gin.

It is interesting to know that the juniper tree is dioecious, meaning there are both male and female plants. An individual plant can only produce male or female berries, and you will never find both male and female berries on the same tree.

We can safely say that the uses for juniper vary widely: from bath oil to flavourings, and from spice to natural medicine for all sorts of ailments. The Egyptians, the Romans, the Greeks... all used juniper for something. The wood of the tree was also utilized although not as widely as the berries, mostly for its smoke and the aroma that is given off when the wood is burned.

The aroma of the juniper berry itself also has a big impact on our perception of the taste and varies from region to region, bringing us back to our terroir...

So there are – just as with wine, coffee and chocolate – origins of single estate gin distillates available, each with their own taste and character. We will describe four of these below, but due to the unsurpassed popularity of gin there are already several single origins available and it is highly likely that even more are being made at this very moment.

ORIGI

46 %

ITALY

ORIGIN AREZZO LONDON DRY GIN

This Italian juniper features a clean nose of soft pine needles. Creamy and with a hint of citrus. When other botanicals are added to the distillate, together they form a beautifully rounded gin: warm with a mildly spicy conclusion.

COMBINE WITH
Fever-Tree Tonic Water and juniper berry

46 %

THE NETHERLANDS

ORIGIN MEPPEL LONDON DRY GIN

The juniper from the Netherlands has an almost woody, earthy taste. Hints of tobacco and a slightly longer finish than the Italian juniper. Creamy, but complemented by a note of sweetness. The finish is more complex than the Italian distillate.

COMBINE WITH
Fever-Tree Tonic Water and juniper berry

46 %

ALBANIA

ORIGIN VALBONE LONDON DRY GIN

The juniper from Albania is a special case and clearly demonstrates how the origins of the berry can determine the taste. Red fruits, cocoa, dry. When other botanicals are added, the distillate maintains its character but then with a lively sweetness.

COMBINE WITH
Fever-Tree Tonic Water and juniper berry

46 %

BULGARIA

ORIGIN VELIKI PRESLAV LONDON DRY GIN

The distinctive flavour of the juniper dominates even when other botanicals are added. The sharp perception of alcohol both in the nose and in the mouth is featured.

COMBINE WITH
Fever-Tree Tonic Water and juniper berry

LONDON DRY GIN
GIN, HAPPY PRODUCT OF OUR CITY, CAN SINEWY
AND WEARIED WITH FATIGUE AND TOIL, CAN
LABOUR AND ART UPHELD BY THEE,
GENIUS LIQUID, THY
AND WARMS EACH ENGLISH BREAST

UNITED KINGDOM

46 %

7 DIALS GIN

THE COMMUNITIES ONE

ORIGIN

This London Dry Gin is named after the famous crossroads in the St. Giles district of London. Seven Dials is between St. Giles and Soho. In the late 1600s, seven streets were laid, converging at this point to make a star. During the 1700s, this area was the base for tens of gin shops. 7 Dials Gin is produced by the London Gin Club and makes use of seven botanicals.

TASTE AND AROMA

On the nose, a fresh pine and light floral hint. The taste begins with spice and a strong dose of cardamom, expanded with juniper berry and coriander.

INGREDIENTS

- juniper berry
- coriander
- angelica
- marshmallow root
- clementine peel
- cardamom
- almonds

COMBINE WITH

Schweppes Premium Mixer Original Tonic and zest of lemon and lime

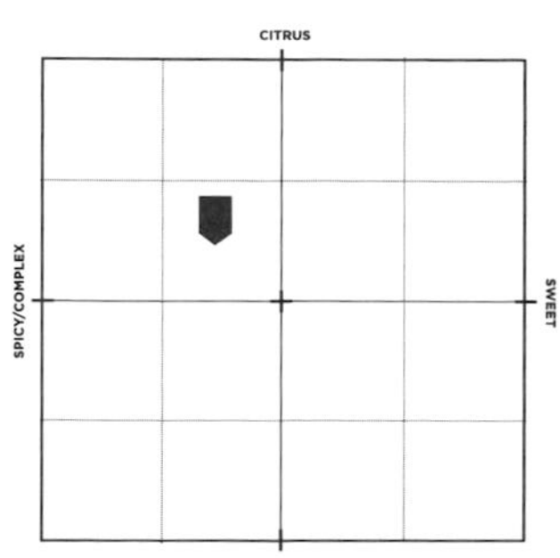

UNITED KINGDOM

43.3 %

BATHTUB GIN

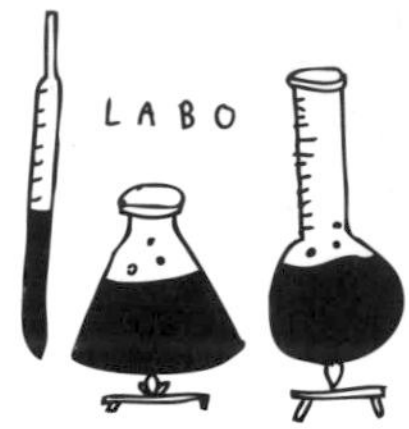

THE MYTHICAL ONE

ORIGIN

An unusual gin created by the enigmatic Professor Cornelius Ampleforth. Shortly before he gained the title of Professor, Cornelius, a mad inventor, dreamed of running a big laboratory full of botanical spirits, bubbling beakers and miles of glass bottles filled with rare ingredients. His dreams came true at the end of 2011, with the release of his already infamous Bathtub Gin. The name is a nod to the gin that people enjoyed during prohibition in the 1920s. Bathtub Gin is only produced in very small quantities of thirty to sixty bottles each time. The brown paper packaging of the gin catapults the drinker back in time to the Victorian chemists.

TASTE AND AROMA

Initially a full bouquet of juniper in the nose, which is complemented by rich grain alcohol. Notes of cardamom and orange blossom and a hint of cinnamon fill out the flavour. The focus of the taste is the juniper berry, but the earthy botanic spices stimulate the palate. The mouth feel is syrupy and, towards the finish, the juniper makes way for the cardamom and cinnamon.

INGREDIENTS

juniper berry ....
orange peel ....
coriander ....
cinnamon ....
cardamom ....
cloves ....

COMBINE WITH

Schweppes Premium Mixer Original Tonic and a cinnamon stick

OTHER GINCREATIONS

- Navy Strength Gin / 57.7% / extra strong
- Cask-Aged Gin / 43.3% / matured
- Old Tom Gin / 42.4% / sweet retrogin

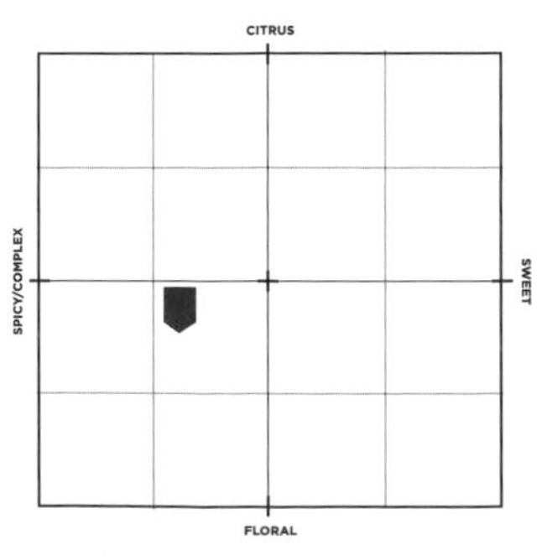

Professor Cornelius
Ampleforth's
athtub

SPAIN

40 %

BCN GIN

THE WINE MAKER'S ONE

ORIGIN

BCN gin is produced in the magical mountains of Priorat. The Priorat region is famous for its complex and powerful wines that come from its shale-flecked soil and abundant sunlight. The vines here must produce their best if they want to survive the poor substrate and the very dry climate. The unique taste of this gin is due to the artisanal distillation from the wine lees of world-famous Spanish Priorat wines in an Arnold Holstein distillation unit. The producers use only natural spring water from the Font del Mas Petit, a spring sunk deep in the Priorate licorella stone. The ingredients and the entire production process are 100% natural. Wine makers extract the essence from the botanicals from the mountains of Priorat and combine these with lemon rinds from South Catalonia. The local Carinyena and Garnatxa grapes are distilled to produce the basic alcohol of BCN Gin. The unique result is obtained through time, effort, craftsmanship, respect and a meticulous selection. BCN gin is distilled in the lovely hills of Reus, near Barcelona.

BCN gin connects the mountains with the sea, nature with the city, and traditions with modernism. Also the bottle refers to Barcelona with a traditional tile motif. In 1916, the design of Escofet Tejera & Co was selected by the Council of Barcelona for tiling the pavements of the city. Ever since, anyone who walks along the Barcelona streets immediately recognises the typical tile motif.

TASTE AND AROMA

A richly perfumed aroma with a background of figs and citrus; a strong gin with a long aftertaste.

INGREDIENTS

juniper berries ....
grapes ....
rosemary ....
fennel ....
pine shoots ....
lemon rind ....
figs ....

COMBINE WITH

Fever-Tree Tonic Water, two halves of dark grapes, lime zest and a sprig of rosemary

GIN

GERMANY

45 % BLACK GIN

THE COMPLEX ONE

ORIGIN

Black Gin is produced at the Gansloser Distillery and is the most complex of gins on the market, with no less than 74 botanicals from 19 different countries such as Germany, Italy, Spain, India, Madagascar and Romania. Of the 74 botanicals, 68 are distilled in a macerate which is inky black in colour, hence the name. An absolutely unique gin with a limited issue.

INGREDIENTS

juniper berry ....
lemon peel ....
orange peel ....
ginger ....
coriander ....
bay ....
and 68 other botanic ingredients we can only guess at

COMBINE WITH

Original Premium Tonic Water Classic and zest of lime

OTHER GINCREATIONS

- Black Gin Distiller's Cut / 60% / spicy
- Black Gin Edition 1905 / 45% / winteraromas

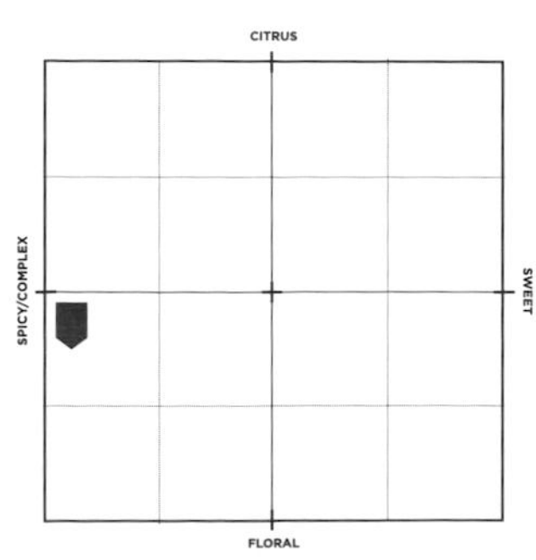

UNITED KINGDOM

40 %

BOMBAY SAPPHIRE

THE REVOLUTIONARY ONE

ORIGIN

Bombay is a light London Dry Gin which was brought out from under the dust covers of London gin in the late 80s – 1987 to be precise. Now distributed by Bacardi, the recipe has been used by the Bombay Spirits Company since 1761 and makes use of ten different botanicals. Revolutionary to its very core and maybe one of the reasons for today's craze for gin, with its fashionable looks and image giving a boost to the dowdy perception of gin. The character of Bombay Sapphire is a perfect way to attract vodka drinkers, and to entice them into the world of gin. The juniper berry is less dominant in this aromatic gin compared with other more classic styles. Bombay is set apart by the distillation methods used in the Carter head still. The herbs and spices are not distilled directly in the still itself, but are instead placed in a basket in the neck of the boiler. This allows for the flavours to be gently absorbed by the alcohol vapours. It is thanks to this method, which creates the delicate and light palate that is so appreciated by vodka drinkers. This gin is still popular in night clubs, and will certainly remain so.

TASTE AND AROMA

An aroma of juniper berry and citrus, but also pepper and spices are clearly present. On the palate, this gin tastes delicate, lightly fruity with the different herbs and spices slowly coming through when holding the gin longer in your mouth. The finish is short.

INGREDIENTS

Italian juniper berry ....
orris root ....
Spanish almonds ....
Spanish limes ....
grains of paradise from
West Africa ....
Moroccan coriander ....
Chinese liquorice ....
cassia bark ....
angelica from Saxony ....
tailed pepper from Java ....

COMBINE WITH

Fever-Tree Tonic Water and lime zest and flaked almonds

OTHER GINCREATIONS

- Bombay Dry / 40% / classic
- Bombay Sapphire East / 42% / spicy
- Bombay Sapphire Star of Bombay / 47.5% / smooth

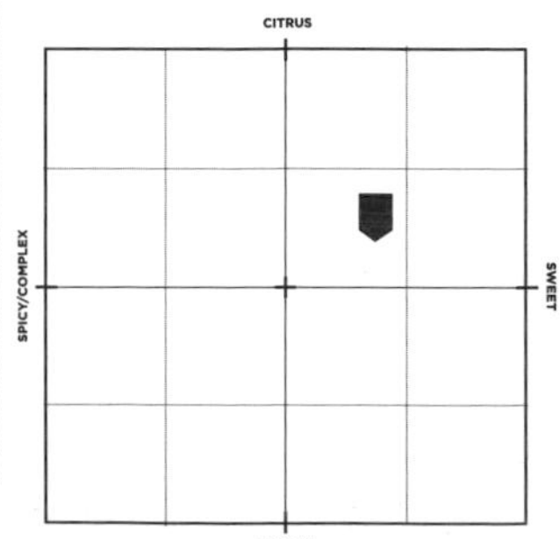

BOMBAY
SAPPHIRE

WASHINGTON ISLAND
WISCONSIN
EST.
DEATH'S DOOR
2005
MADE WITH ORGANIC HARD RED WINTER WHEAT FROM WASHINGTON ISLAND, WI.
SIMPLE ◇ LOCAL ◇ EXCEPTIONAL
Crafted with wild juniper berries
& VARIOUS ORGANIC BOTANICALS
GIN
WASHINGTON ISLAND
Green Bay
Lake Michigan
Deaths Door Passage
DOOR COUNTY
70CL • 47% ALC. BY VOL.

UNITED STATES

47.3 %

DEATH'S DOOR GIN

THE SIMPLE ONE

ORIGIN

Washington Island in Wisconsin is the beating heart of Death's Door Gin. The name is inspired by the notorious water way Death's Door between Washington Island and the Door County Peninsula. Death's Door Spirits work with local farmers whose produce is of exceptionally good quality. The distillery was founded in 2005 by Brian Ellison, and this gin is a perfect example of beautiful simplicity. It is remarkable that Death's Door Gin can draw out so much flavour from just three botanicals: juniper berry, coriander and fennel seed. The juniper berries are picked on the island with the other ingredients carefully selected from the state of Wisconsin. The grain alcohol used is wheat-based and is also grown on the island: after more than 35 years with no agriculture on the island, brothers Tom and Ken Koyen began cultivating wheat again in 2005. A good decision, in our opinion.

TASTE AND AROMA

Death's Door Gin is characterised by the spicy taste and aroma. The juniper berry takes the upper hand, but at the same time is complemented by a warm and peppery deepness.

INGREDIENTS

juniper berry ....
coriander ....
fennel seed ....

COMBINE WITH

Abbondio Tonica Vintage Edition and a marshmallow

BRIAN ELLISON

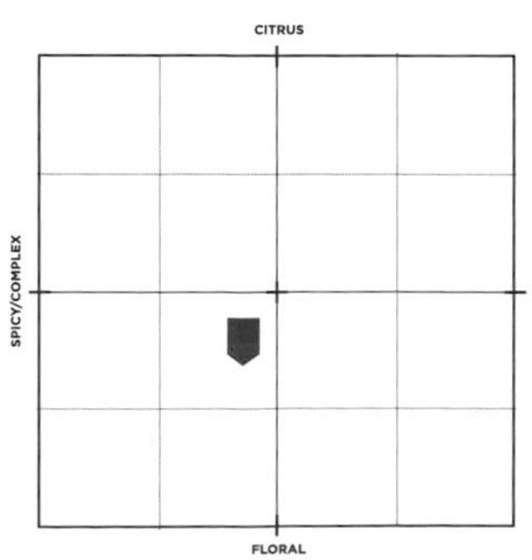

40 %

GILT SINGLE MALT SCOTTISH GIN

THE WHISKY BASE ONE

ORIGIN

Gilt is produced by Valt Vodka Company Limited, a tiny distillery in Scotland, from 100% malted barley and Spey water. The gin is based on a single malt spirit, which is distilled five times from malted barley. That is also its link to whisky. This is the same malt used for making Valt Vodka. The story of Gilt Vodka begins, like so many others, at a bar when two friends launch the idea of creating the first Scottish vodka made from just Scottish spring water; a vodka that's so refined and pure that it requires a brand new distillery process: a five-step micro-distilled technique. Gilt Gin is produced with the same values, passions and love for the profession. It is a London dry gin, but the malt distillate makes it just a touch different.

TASTE AND AROMA

The bouquet is like a fragrant meadow and a touch of anise. The juniper berry is prominent with the first gulp, but then it makes room for the sweet aroma of caramelised sugar. An aftertaste of anise, coriander and orris root.

INGREDIENTS

- juniper berries
- coriander
- cardamom
- lemon
- cassia bark
- liquorice
- orange
- orris root
- angelica root

COMBINE WITH

Fever-Tree Tonic Water and a piece of Chinese anise or some cardamom

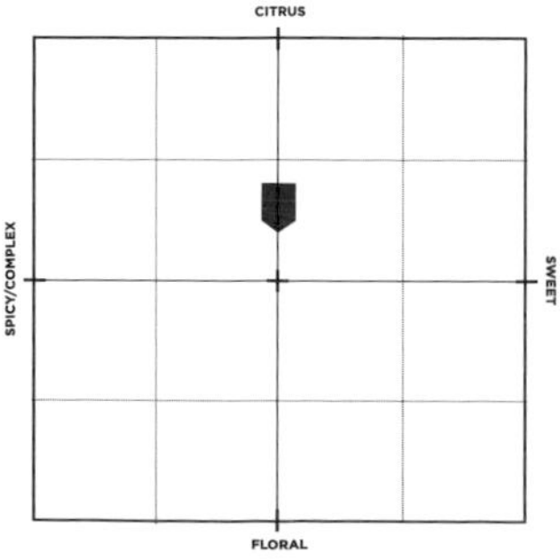

GIL

SMALL BATCH
HANDCRAFTED
NDRIC
GIN

UNITED KINGDOM

41.4 %

HENDRICK'S GIN

THE MARKETING ONE

ORIGIN

Hendrick's Gin is popular, very popular. They call themselves the Monty Python of gins: full of humour and fun. Hendrick's is a super-premium gin with an unusual twist. Hendrick's is distilled in Ayrshire, Scotland, which boasts centuries of distilling expertise, as well as soft Scottish water from the local Penwhapple Burn. Hendrick's Gin is made using eleven botanical ingredients, including Belgian and Dutch cucumbers and Bulgarian rose. The cucumber and rose petal flavours are in fact added afterwards as an infusion. The new apothecary-style bottle and the innovative way of serving with cucumber was ground-breaking and gave the entire gin sector a serious boost when it was launched in 2000. The gin is made in two different distillation vessels: one a Carter-Head and the other a copper Bennet still. This delivers two different spirits which are then blended together: one, a soft citrus spirit, the other, full of character, making Hendrick's a crisp gin with a flowery aroma. Hendrick's is crafted using traditional methods through which the distillation process can be carefully fine-tuned. In 2003, *The Wall Street Journal* named it the best gin in the world.

TASTE AND AROMA

A refreshing gin with a strong character, subtle flavours and a delightful aroma. This is due, amongst other things, to the essence of Dutch cucumbers and the oils of Bulgarian rose petals.

INGREDIENTS

juniper berry ....
chamomile ....
caraway seeds ....
elderflower ....
meadowsweet
(North-American flower) ......
orange peel ....
coriander ....
orris root ....
angelica ....
lemon peel ....
cubeb berries (a sort of pepper)

COMBINE WITH

Fentimans Tonic Water
and cucumber

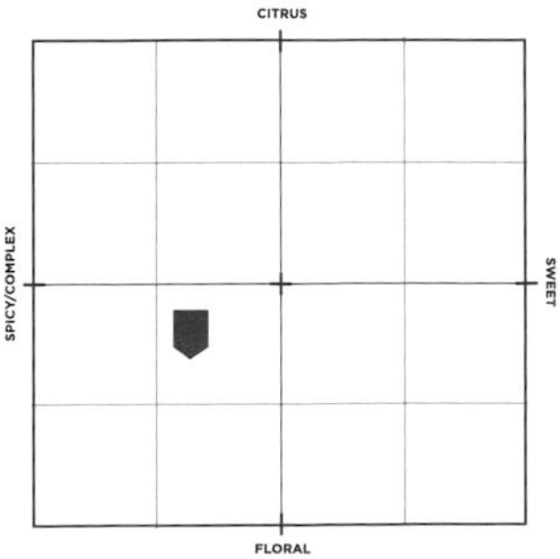

43 % HOXTON GIN

THE EXTREME ONE

BARTENDER SALVATORE CALABRESE

ORIGIN

Developed by the son of the famous barman Salvatore Calabrese in Hoxton – the creative centre of London – it can be described as unique for its kind. The gin is made using alcohol obtained from French summer wheat and a medley of natural ingredients. The botanicals are steeped for five days before they are distilled in 150-year-old copper pot stills. After completion, Hoxton Gin rests for two months in steel tanks. A truly surprising gin with the taste of coconut and grapefruit. Amongst purists there is much discussion as to whether it can even be classed as a gin at all. Taste it and decide for yourself.

TASTE AND AROMA

Coconut and grapefruit predominate in the nose, although the ginger, juniper berry and tarragon are also discernible in the background. The taste is also dominated by the coconut and grapefruit. Here, the juniper plays second fiddle.

INGREDIENTS

juniper berry ....
coconut ....
grapefruit ....
orris root ....
tarragon ....
ginger ....

COMBINE WITH

J.Gasco Indian Tonic and a piece of coconut

HOXTON
GIN
WARNING!
GRAPEFRUIT
AND
COCONUT

-ish
LONDON DRY GIN
Irresistible Scandalous Hallma
MADE BY THE POSHMAKERS
with an extra shot of
Juniper

UNITED KINGDOM

41 %

ISH GIN

THE DRY ONE

Irresistible
Scandalous
Hallmark

ORIGIN

Irresistible Scandalous Hallmark is represented by the initials ISH in this premium gin. Ish Gin is a traditional London Dry style gin, but with a little something extra: a double shot of juniper which makes it the driest of London Dry gins. Ish Gin was thought up by Ellen Baker and is Spanish-inspired, via her 'Bristol Bar' in Madrid. A perfectly balanced recipe that provides a distinctive flavour profile without the use of artificial additives. Ish Gin is distilled five times in a traditional pot still, in the heart of London.

TASTE AND AROMA

A definite juniper berry aroma with coriander and refreshing citrus. On tasting this gin, the orange is immediately noticeable, followed by a harmony of other botanicals.

INGREDIENTS

juniper berry ....
coriander seed ....
angelica ....
almonds ....
orris root ....
nutmeg ....
cinnamon ....
cassia ....
liquorice ....
lemon peel ....
orange peel ....

COMBINE WITH

1724 Tonic Water and dried juniper berries

OTHER GINCREATION

- Ish Limed London Dry Gin / 41% / citrus

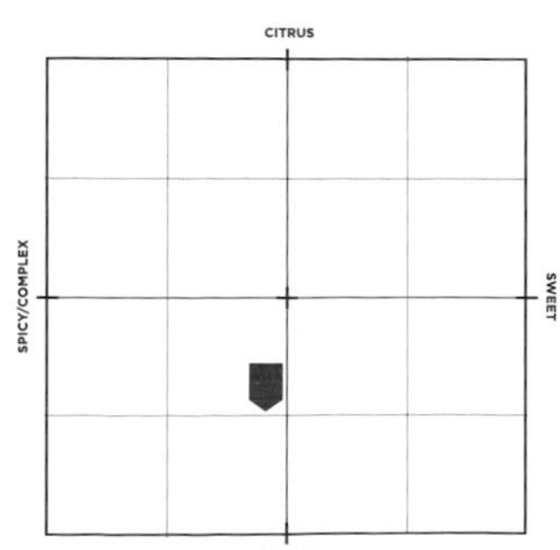

UNITED STATES

49.3 %

JUNIPERO GIN

THE BEER BREWER'S ONE

ORIGIN

Junipero Gin is produced by Anchor Distillery, a micro-distillery on one of the many hills of San Francisco and a part of the Anchor Brewing Company. Anchor Distillery was founded in 1993 by Fritz Maytag, the same man with a vision who bought Anchor Brewing in 1965 and breathed new life into traditional beer. By buying it, Fritz saved this brewery and its iconic Steam Beer and also tapped into new markets by producing all sorts of innovative beers. Nowadays, Anchor Distillery – which moved into a remote corner of the large beer brewery – along with its wonderful single malt rye whiskey, *Old Portrero*, also produces Junipero Gin, a gin with a very strong character and 49.3% alcohol. This gin is the American answer to the traditional London Dry Gin and is very popular in the cocktail scene.

It definitely contains lots of juniper berries, but this immediately converts into a spicy mix. Justifiably, the gin has already snapped up many international prizes.

TASTE AND AROMA

A rich pallet, followed by juniper berries, coriander and liquorice; a formidable cracker, but with sufficient freshness and a light hint of soil.

INGREDIENTS

juniper berries ....
coriander ....
lemon ....
liquorice and more ....

COMBINE WITH

J.Gasco Tonic and a large portion of juniper berries

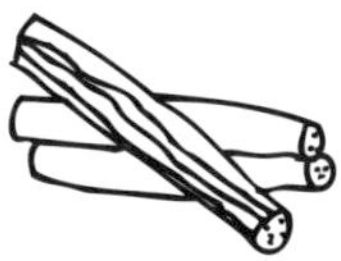

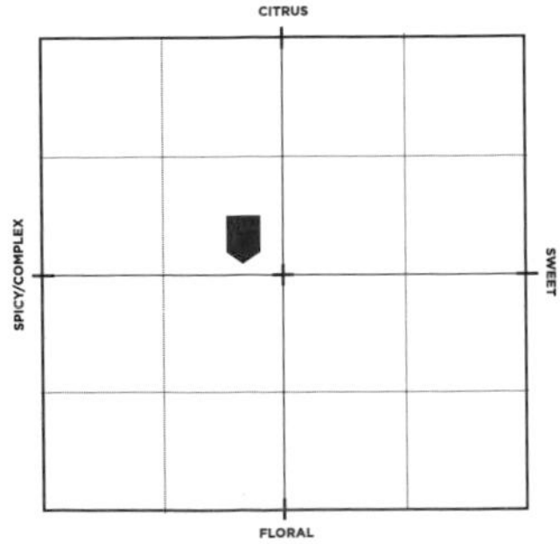

ESSAY
7·DDG·GNS·1
Junípero

SWISS BLEN

43 %

NGINIOUS! COCCHI VERMOUTH CASK FINISH GIN

THE VERMOUTH ONE

ORIGIN

No matter how crazy the idea, logic always wins in the end. That was probably the intention of two Swiss fellows, Oliver Ullrich and Ralph Villiger, with their unshakeable logic of a Swiss clock. Gin is not very suitable for classic aging in wooden barrels because of the risk of rapidly losing its rich and delicate aroma during the process. On the other hand, the world's most well-known cocktail – the Martini – is actually a combination of gin and vermouth. So what if...?

The quest for a high calibre vermouth producer brought them to Roberto Bava Cocchi who – after their stubborn insistence – agreed to this crazy experiment and placed a couple of his reputable Cocchi Vermouth di Torino at their disposal. This led to the world's first vermouth cask aged gin, or better still, the first barrel-aged Martini. The very limited production editions, the leather wrapping and the individually numbered bottles, truly make this gin unique!

TASTE AND AROMA

Citrus and fruit tones in perfect harmony with the typical sweet herbal vermouth accents.

INGREDIENTS

juniper berry
barberry
lemon
orange
fresh pomelo
hay flower
cardamom
clover
camomile
verbena
liquorice

COMBINE WITH

Enjoy this delicacy mainly pure... or with ice, a dash of neutral tonic and a zest of orange.

OTHER GINCREATION

- Nginious! Swiss Blend Gin / 45% / complex

THE NETHERLANDS

52.3 %

NOLET'S RESERVE

THE EXPENSIVE ONE

ORIGIN

With a yearly production of only a few hundred bottles, an extremely careful selection procedure and the application of four generations of production knowhow via Carolus Nolet Senior, this Nolet's Reserve is one of the most exclusive, rarest and most expensive gins ever made. The Nolet distillery is still brewing in Schiedam, and still in its original location. The gin has a recommended retail price of 650 euro, so there really is only one way to enjoy this gin: sip slowly, to comprehend its full complexity. An exclusivity to be proud of, and to give the whole experience a touch more flair, each bottle is numbered and signed by Mr Nolet himself.

TASTE AND AROMA

Strawberries and flowers in the nose. Warm and complex on the palate where a whole host of flavours are slowly revealed: saffron, peach, raspberry, citrus and, of course, juniper berry. A warm and lightly spicy glow of saffron (the most expensive spice) and subtle delicate lemon verbena feature in this gin.

INGREDIENTS

juniper berry ....
saffron ....
lemon verbena ....
and other botanicals

COMBINE WITH

don't, drink neat!

- 100 BOTTLES MAX -

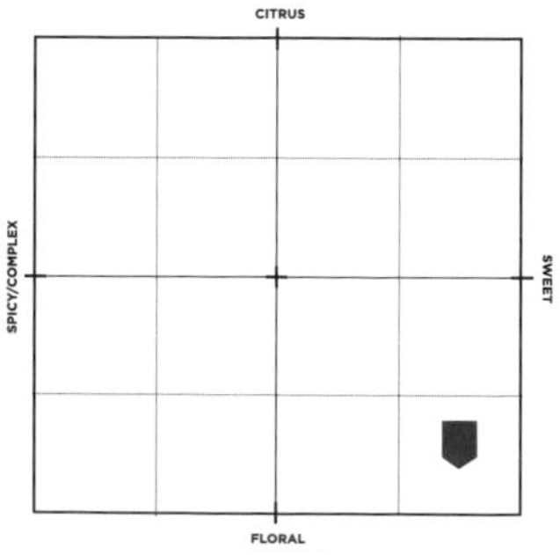

NOLET'S
DRY GIN
THE
RESERVE
IMPORTED

ONE KEY

SLOVENIA

40 %

ONE KEY GIN

THE DESIGN ONE

ORIGIN

One Key is produced by Abnormal Group Singapore. The idea of gin saw the light of day in 2009 and had only one purpose: to introduce something totally different and innovative to the gin landscape. One Key Gin has therefore become a unique gin, mainly due to its special handmade design packaging. This gin can only be opened with an accompanying key – which gave the gin its name. Thus the One Key motto: 'One key opens all the doors!' The packaging is handmade white glass with a deep-blue shine. In 2011, One Key Gin won the IF Packaging Award.

TASTE AND AROMA

With specially selected grains, coriander, juniper berries and a touch of ginger, this is a rich and balanced gin with exotic tones and which you drink slowly and intensely.

INGREDIENTS

juniper berries ....
ginger ....
coriander ....
exotic plant extracts ....

COMBINE WITH

Fentimans Tonic Water and a sprig of thyme, fresh coriander or coriander seeds

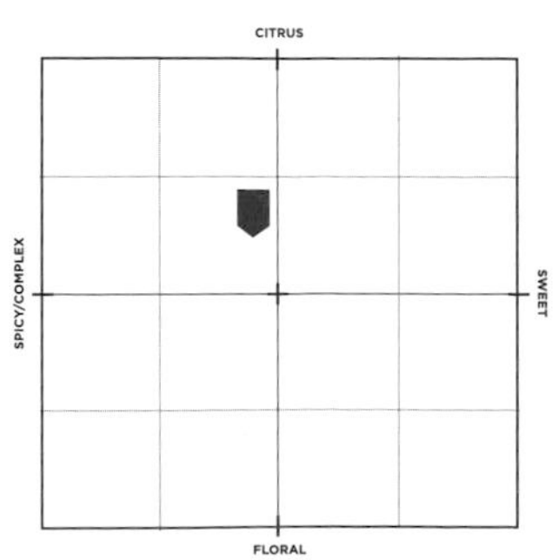

UNITED KINGDOM

40 %

SACRED GIN

THE VACUUM ONE

ORIGIN

Sacred Gin is one of the standard bearers of microdistilleries, a sub-trend of the gin revival. Creators Ian and Hillary Hart produce the gin in their own terraced house in North London, where they have an artisan distillery. Sacred Gin is Ian's brainchild, brought to life in 2008 after he lost his job as a head-hunter. He dusted off his degree in natural sciences and started to concentrate on vacuum distillation. He tried out his gin on friends at the local pub and, on the 23rd attempt, it was unanimously declared a success. Sacred Gin is produced under a very low pressure, but this does not compromise the quality; quite the contrary. Each of the twelve organic botanicals are macerated in the finest quality English grain alcohol, and then separately distilled in glassware under high pressure. This process ensures the fresh and luxuriant character, and is above all highly unusual in the world of gin. The name 'Sacred' comes from one of the botanicals: Olibanum or 'Boswelia Sacra' in Latin (a type of incense).

TASTE AND AROMA

Spicy in the nose with citrus notes. Soft tastes of nutmeg and juniper berry, leading to an elegant finish.

INGREDIENTS

juniper berry ....
freshly cut lemon ....
cardamom ....
nutmeg ....
incense Boswelia Sacra ....
and others

COMBINE WITH

Fever-Tree Indian Tonic Water, grated nutmeg and/or cinnamon stick

OTHER GINCREATIONS

- Sacred Cardamom Gin / 40% / spicy
- Sacred Orris Gin / 40% / floral

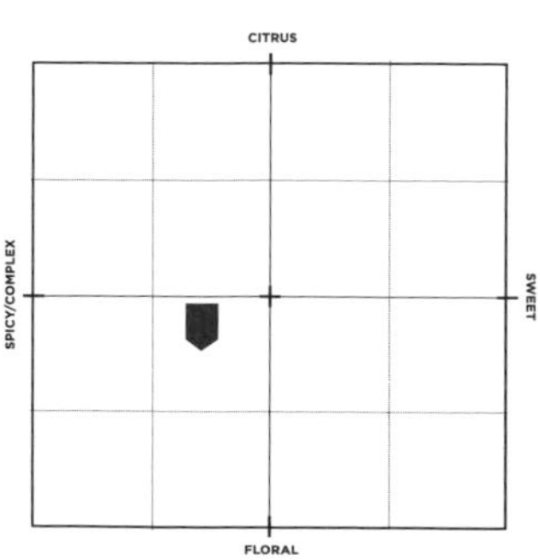

SACRED

Tanqueray
MALACCA GIN
LIMITED EDITION
BOTTLE №: GR 0638

UNITED KINGDOM

40 %

TANQUERAY MALACCA

THE PHOENIX ONE

ORIGIN

Tanqueray Malacca was for years seen as the little brother of the widely known Tanqueray London Dry Gin. Founded in 1997 – based on a recipe from 1839 – the gin was taken off the market in 2001, despite its growing popularity amongst gin lovers. Following this, record amounts were paid on the black market by people wanting to get their hands on a bottle of this iconic gin. In 2013, the label was relaunched to the general public. The reintroduction issue of this spicy gin consists of a mere 100,000 bottles worldwide. An homage to the recipe from 1839, taken from the notes of Charles Tanqueray, the gin was developed during his trade missions to the Far East, with herbs and spices from all four corners of the world. Nowadays, trying to locate a bottle is like looking for a needle in a haystack. But definitely worth the effort!

TASTE AND AROMA

Tanqueray Malacca is a lighter and fruitier gin, with less juniper but more grapefruit aroma than its big brother. The gin is soft and round with a prominent cinnamon, almost candy-like taste. The finish is simple and clean.

INGREDIENTS

No information available

COMBINE WITH

Gents Swiss Roots Premium Tonic and grapefruit zest

CHARLES TANQUERAY

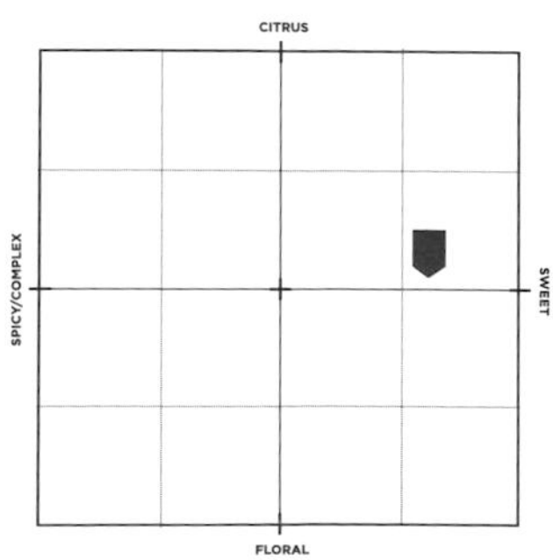

41.7 %

VL92 GIN

THE RETRO ONE

ORIGIN

VL92 Gin was borne out of a quest of two entrepreneurs, Leo Fontijne and Sietze Kalkwijk, who went in search of the ultimate gin. This Dutch artisan gin uses malt wine (25%) in its production, the original ingredient of jenever, and is therefore strongly reminiscent of the origins of jenever and gin. The gin is named after an historic Dutch sailing ship which was used for transporting exotic spices, too daring for the local jenever recipes of the time, but perfect for VL92 Gin. On 15th May 2012, the first batch of VL92 Gin was delivered to London, arriving in style on the original ship.

TASTE AND AROMA

The malt wine is responsible for the boldness, the complexity is delivered by the play of the botanicals, and the surprise is brought about by the coriander leaf. The inspired addition of malt wine cannot be found in any other gin.

INGREDIENTS

malt wine ....
juniper berry ....
coriander leaf ....
and various other botanicals

COMBINE WITH

Fentimans Tonic Water and a sliver of ginger

OTHER GINCREATION

- VL92 YY Gin / 45% / matured

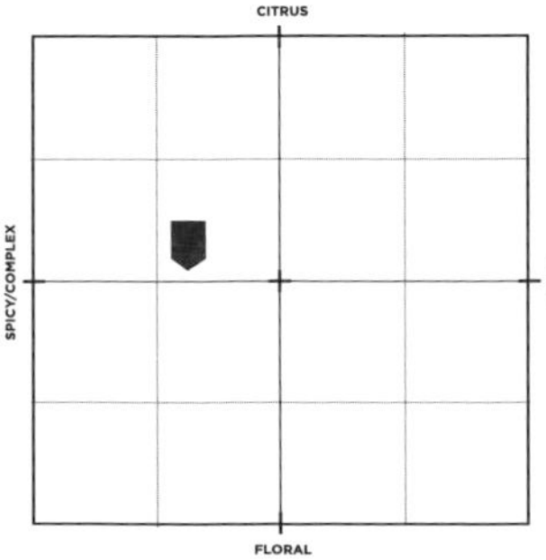

VL92 GIN
ginstooksel:
XX
XY
YY
moutwijn
korianderblad
28 JUL 2013
41,7% alcohol per volume
1000ml.

Zuidam
INTERNATIONAL SPIRITS CHALLENGE 2012 GOLD
Small Batch
DUTCH COURAGE
Dry Gin
Zuidam Dutch Courage Dry Gin is handcrafted in the distillery of the Van Zuidam Family where two generations of master distillers combine the most exquisite ingredients to create an exceptional gin. No effort was spared in the search for perfection from the use of the very best botanicals to the careful distillation in very small batches, everything was done to create the ultimate dry gin.
Product of Holland
Distilled from Grain
1 Liter
44,5% Alc. by Vol.

44.5 %

ZUIDAM DUTCH COURAGE

THE HISTORICAL ONE

ORIGIN

Zuidam Distillers is one of the last remaining independent distilleries in the Netherlands, and the family-run business makes its own distillate and extracts using traditional methods of working and production. The name of the gin is a historical reference to the shot of jenever given to the soldiers in the thirty years' war, before they were sent into battle. Zuidam Dutch Courage Dry Gin has been awarded many times at big international competitions.

TASTE AND AROMA

On the nose, strong and spicy aromas with a core of earthy juniper, filled out with exotic herbs. The taste is earthy with a hint of citrus and dried herbs. A bittersweet and intense finish.

INGREDIENTS

juniper berry ....
coriander ....
angelica ....
oranges and lemons
from Spain ....
Madagascan vanilla ....
Indian liquorice ....
cardamom pods
from Ceylon ....

COMBINE WITH

Thomas Henry Tonic Water and a liquorice stick

OTHER GINCREATIONS

- Zuidam Dutch Courage Aged Gin 88 / 44% / matured
- Zuidam Dutch Courage Old Tom's Gin / 40% / sweet retro gin

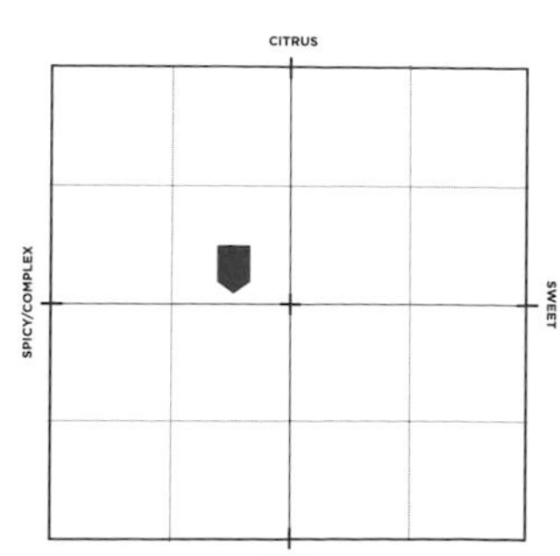

THE PRACTICAL: IN THE MIX

Gin, and of course tonic, have now become so incorporated in the world that it is high time that we put the theory into practice, and show you how it should be done: the right proportions, tools and garnishes.

Put on some laid back music, grab a gin & tonic and move to the beats of this ideal partnership. The pure love which has manifested for decades; passion since the first meeting, a moment of rest and then a rekindled 'love at second sight'. And believe us, this renewed passion is one that makes the sparks fly, one that invites delirious dancing or can, just as in the game of love, sometimes maintain a kind of 'coolness'. A love where both partners challenge each other, enhance and lift each other up and encourage creativity. But stay open-minded as there is a third player in this relationship — Mr or is it Mrs Botanical? (We will leave this choice to your own imagination) — may often accompany the couple and can even improve them; a couple with just that little bit extra, which you will notice in your glass...

HOW IT SHOULDN'T BE...

Let us give you a couple of silly examples: a bowl of cornflakes with champagne or a bag of chips with caviar. To say the least, these are strange combinations, but also combinations that have virtually no common ground with very few similarities as far as taste interest or creativity go. Although it must be said, each product individually has its own qualities, but they just don't work when put together. Some things are just not meant to be. Just like chips and caviar do not provide the basis for a long-term relationship, some gins do not blend well with certain tonics.

HOW TO FIND THE PERFECT MIX AND USE THE G&T FLAVOUR CROSS

First of all, you need to find out who you are in terms of which gin you enjoy the most. Happiness lies in your own hands, as they say, and happily the search for your personal favourite gin is a lot of fun. To begin with, taste as many as you can, which of course can be done at the same time as enjoying the summer on a terrace, going dancing and investigating the range on offer at the disco, or relaxing by the open fire at home. Of course take this book with you and discover, read and record. However, don't forget that every journey of discovery has its ups and downs, sometimes a gin will sound lovely when you read about it, but disappoint when you taste it, or the other way round. Look at it as a quest that may last throughout your whole life, and may well change direction, but one thing we can promise you: your own Holy Grail exists! After that, it becomes even more fun and maybe even easier, because this book will steer you in the right direction, give you lots of inspiration to find the right tonic and show you how to make and serve the ultimate gin & tonic.

As you now know, the secret behind the perfect mix is actually quite simple. It is all about analysing the ingredients in both the gin and the tonic. On the following pages, we will introduce an original way of examining flavours: the G&T flavour cross.

G&T FLAVOUR CROSS

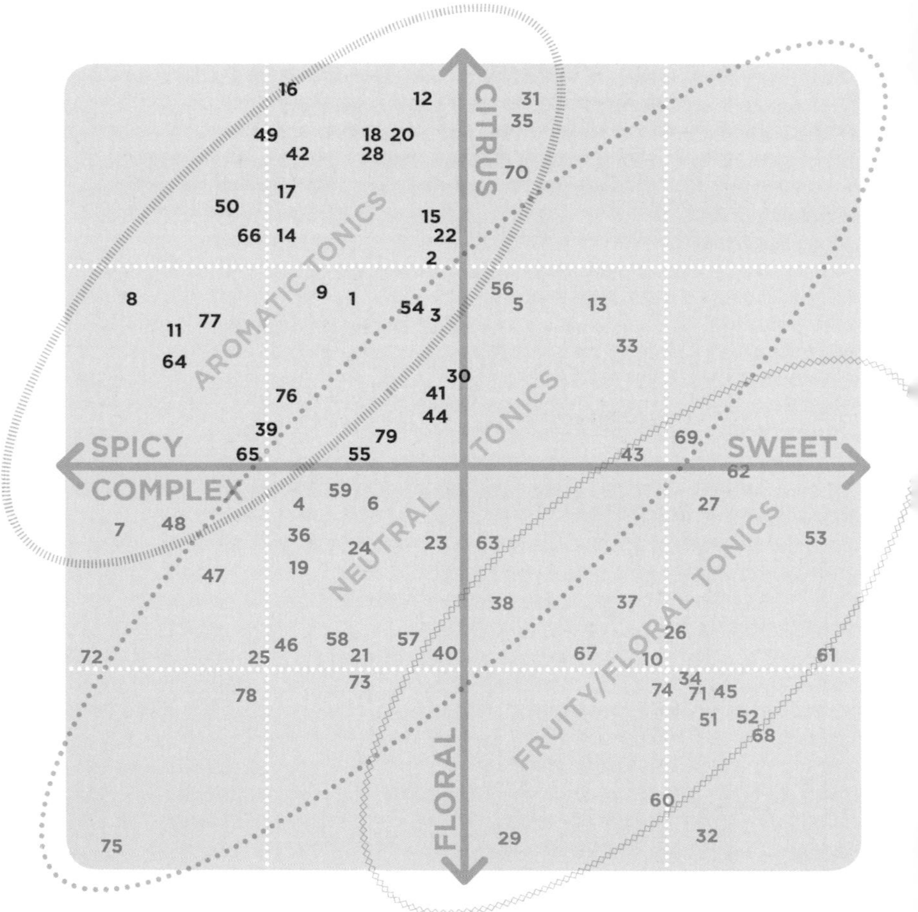

Have you already taken a good look at the G&T flavour cross? This innovative new version shows the combination of the flavours of gin and of tonic, it is an absolute first and very easy to read and interpret.

LET'S PRACTICE!

First, take your favourite gin of the moment or go and get the bottle you were given as a present, but if you are not sure which tonic to combine it with, it's OK, we will wait for you....

Have you got it? Right, now get the G&T flavour cross with the gin universe and the tonic tastes. Open the bottle, smell the aroma, taste the pure gin. But hang on, we haven't explained how to correctly taste gin yet...

TASTING THE GIN

Although humans can distinguish between many different tastes, there are actually only four different kinds of taste papillae, each specialised in detecting a specific taste: sweet, salty, sour and bitter. All the flavours we can distinguish are combinations of these four basic tastes. Now, there is also a fifth taste, 'umami' or savoury that can be added to the list. Although this was scientifically recognised in 1980 as one of the basic tastes, it is only since 2010 that people have started to refer to umami as the fifth taste.

The five basic tastes however, are only a part of how we perceive tastes. For humans, the sense of smell plays an important role in taste. A smell can give a certain expectation of what you are about to taste. So it is going to be interesting to see if the gin lives up to those expectations or not.

And so, to work...

THE GLASS

The glass can help with the tasting. It is preferable to use a tulip-shaped glass with a wide base but narrower at the rim as this will better help the aromas channel towards the nose. This type of glass is called a snifter, but a similarly shaped wine or sherry glass will do just as well. A tumbler (a broad glass with a thick bottom and straight sides) is not so good for tasting as the aromas dissipate quickly.

THE GIN

Pour about 30 ml of gin into the glass. You can also add a little water as this dampens down the alcohol and enhances the taste of the botanicals used.

ROLL

Roll the gin around the glass. This adds oxygen and allows the aromas to gather on the edge of the glass. By doing this it will allow you to perceive the bouquet of the gin more effectively.

THE NOSE

Put your nose into the glass – literally – and sniff in the fragrance. A few common terms used to identify the aromas in gin are: citrus, fruity, floral, earthy, spicy, sweet and woody.

Note:
A strong chemical odour is an indication that you are dealing with a poor-quality gin.

THE TASTE

Take a little sip and swirl the gin around in your mouth to evaluate the elementary tastes. Then let the gin rest on the tongue before rolling it around in your mouth again, allowing you to analyse all the flavours.

The first sip should feel warm and pleasant with the subtle flavour of juniper berries. Take the time to give all the flavours a chance to come through, because as you already know, there is a whole range of botanicals used in the development of a gin.

Following this, try to find the dry taste of the gin. A dry feeling on the back of your tongue often means that there have been a lot of herbal botanicals used, such as angelica or orris root.

Many commonly-used terms to describe the tastes of gin are first and foremost the four 'arms' in our flavour cross: citrus, sweet, floral, and spicy/complex. But tastes are also often described as earthy, peppery, exotic and so on.

THE FINISH

Finally, a feature of a good gin is that it should always leave a fresh and clean finish. The juniper berry flavour shouldn't hang around for too long. When you are ready to take your next sip, the previous one should only be a memory, gins with this quality are often said to be soft.

GIVING THE GIN A PLACE ON THE FLAVOUR CROSS, AND FINDING THE RIGHT TONIC

We have already placed a lot of gins on the flavour cross, but if you have discovered a good gin of your own, after tasting you will want to give your discovery its own place on the flavour cross. Focus mainly on the citrus, sweet, floral and herby/complex tastes. The closer your gin is to the centre of the cross, the closer it is to the classic London Dry taste. If you find it impossible to place your gin anywhere on the flavour cross, it is more than likely an exotic gin. These types of gin need to be individually assessed when it comes to the choice of tonic.

A QUICK RECAP:

CLASSIC LONDON DRY

London Dry gins find themselves in the central part of the flavour cross and so should not be coupled with a strongly pronounced tonic. They are better partnered with a more neutral tonic such as Fever-Tree Indian Tonic Water, Thomas Henry Tonic Water or a Schweppes Premium Mixer Original Tonic. A neutral tonic will perfectly enhance the classic flavours of a London Dry without overpowering it.

CITRUS GIN

These gins are inordinately suited to aromatic tonics, and an aromatic tonic with a citrus note is absolutely ideal. For example, combine with Fentimans Tonic Water infused with lime leaves, amongst other things. These ingredients perfectly highlight the citrus notes in your gin.

SWEET GIN

The average sweetness of these types of gin are best combined with the flavours of a fruity tonic, such as 1724 Tonic Water and Indi Botanical Water.

FLORAL GIN

The typical characteristics and botanicals used in these types of gin, with the light fruitiness and beautiful floral bouquets, are very much at home with the soft and fruity composition of tonics such as 1724 Tonic Water and Indi Tonic Botanical Water.

SPICY GIN

Spicy gins clearly display a pronounced palette of aromas and flavours, and because of this complex diversity, they blend perfectly with an aromatic tonic such as Fentimans Tonic Water. But one could also argue that because these types of gin are so complex and multi-layered, they only need the slightest lift. This is certainly understandable: the spiciest of gins like Monkey 47 of Gansloser Black Gin – are so great already, a neutral tonic *is all they need.*

DON'T FORGET TO EXPERIMENT!

We are focusing on 100% natural tonics, but you should absolutely explore for yourself the vast range of gins and the countless brands of tonic that are available. For example, think about the gins which use elderflower as an ingredient, such as Darnley's Gin, Knockeen Gin, Zephyr Gin, etc. These gins go very well with Thomas Henry Elderflower Tonic.

The sky is the limit, and your own creativity and experience will certainly bring about knowledge. Experimentation is free, and don't forget that there are new brands of gin and tonic emerging almost every week, providing enough material for endless mixing and matching, and discovering surprising new combinations.

Once you have found your perfect pair (or sublime mix), we can proceed with the ideal way of serving this melodious couple. We begin with the classic way of serving and the correct proportions. Don't worry, we will discuss 'the perfect' serve shortly, including of course the garnish.

THE CLASSIC GIN & TONIC

Let's begin with the basics: a gin & tonic, nothing more and nothing less. The recipe is simple, but still deserves the appropriate attention. Something simple can so easily be diminished by not taking the time or paying too little attention. So pay attention and you will never forget it. Sloppiness is no excuse in the world of cocktails, where even the basics are an art form. The classic measurements used are: 1 measure of gin to 4 measures of tonic. The tonic must complement the essence and purity of the gin and not dominate.

— 1 measure gin: 50 ml
— 4 measures tonic: 200 ml tonic
— A lot of ice

The bigger the ice cubes, the better, as water is actually the enemy of gin & tonic so you need to do everything possible to make sure the ice melts as little as possible.

And lemon or lime, we hear you say... Well really that depends on the natural flavours of the gin. This distinguishes it from, for example vodka. Without a doubt the juniper berry is the protagonist, but very often this taste is supported by lemon or lime. In other words, the citrus taste is already present. If however, you wish to enhance this flavour or add a little more citrus to a gin where this flavour is not strong enough, then by all means you should do so. *De gustibus et coloribus non disputandum est*—in matters of taste, there can be no disputes. Our advice? When you do decide to add lemon or lime to a gin & tonic, just add the peel or zest of the fruit, otherwise the juice and the acid will overpower the 'real' taste of the gin.

Note:
The purists and connoisseurs amongst us will doubtless prefer a slightly stronger gin & tonic. In that case the ratio can easily be adjusted to 1 measure of gin to 2 or 3 measures of tonic, or even 1 measure of tonic. But to get the optimal enjoyment out of the phenomenon that is gin & tonic, the 1 to 1 proportion is the minimum requirement.

PERFECT SERVE

Just as a meal should look appealing to stimulate the appetite, a gin & tonic should be just as tempting and invite you to quench your thirst. Spain is the birthplace of contemporary gastronomy (it is no coincidence that they have dominated the international restaurant guide lists), and so the Spanish have also elevated the gin & tonic to an art form. Moreover, 'gintonic' is a way of life in Spain, it is omnipresent, a 'ginsanity' that is impossible to ignore. About five years ago, it was the interest of Spanish chefs, and above all the bartenders, who gave the drink a serious boost, and it became incorporated into Spanish culture. Now, locals and tourists alike can enjoy the ritual that is all part of the perfect serve...

WHAT DO YOU NEED?

THE GLASS

Gin & tonic is served in a large *copa de balon* or a balloon glass. This is basically a large wine glass in the shape of a balloon. *Copa de balon* comes from Spain, as the name suggests. In this land of gastronomic pioneers, serving gin & tonic in any other type of glass is simply not done. In the Lowlands, gin & tonic is also served in a tumbler – a low, wide, cylinder-shaped glass. However, a balloon glass is preferable because our favourite long drink warms up much faster in a tumbler. We hold the balloon glass by its foot or stem (just like a wineglass) to avoid warming up the glass by direct hand contact. If you don't happen to have a balloon glass, then use a red wine glass. The conical shape does justice to the gin & tonic. But if you don't mind some good advice from us – purchase a few balloon glasses. Nowadays, they are easy to obtain and they will elevate your favourite gin & tonic to a higher level

Forget about the long drink glass, because it traps your gin in the bottom of the glass. A *copa de balon*, red wine glass or even a tumbler ensures that the intermingling of the gin with the tonic will only benefit the fusion of the drink. Moreover, a wide glass opens the aroma and helps to capture it in the glass due to the slightly narrowing form toward the top of the glass. Every detail counts.

THE ICE

Large ice cubes made from 'clean water' that hasn't come into contact with other products. Ice will quickly take on the smells and flavours of other products kept in the same freezer. The larger the ice cube, the less chance it will melt, and as mentioned earlier, you don't want your gin & tonic diluted down by water. Here it is a case of the more, the better. By all means fill your glass to the brim with ice cubes, a gin & tonic should be cold!

Note:

You can of course cool the glass by first rolling ice cubes around in the glass. Make sure you replace the ice cubes with fresh ones after cooling.
A creative spirit? Try freezing a botanical in the ice cube itself. Not only does it look pretty, but it also won't have much effect on the taste of your gin & tonic.

THE GIN

There is no such thing as the best gin in the world. Everyone has their own personal taste. 5 cl (50 ml) gin is the standard measure and is easy to judge with a jigger as they mostly hold 5 cl (50 ml). If your personal choice has a higher alcohol percentage (+45%), we recommend that you use a little less gin.

THE TONIC

The starting point is 1 measure of gin to 4 measures of tonic. This means 50 ml of gin with 200 ml tonic is the ideal partnership. Not all bottles of tonic contain 200 ml, however. Fentimans for example, only has 125 ml, while Q Tonic comes in a bottle of 237 ml. You should always ask that your gin and tonic is served separately so that you can pour your own drink, and your friends can then enjoy any leftover tonic. Too little tonic? Well, then you can drink your gin & tonic with a bit more zing. Do you drink gin & tonic mostly at home? In which case there is no problem, as you are the bartender and after reading this book you will know exactly how to serve your perfect gin & tonic. Pour the tonic against the side of the glass: this will keep the bubbles at their best, or make use of a bar spoon, allowing the tonic to gently flow over the spoon handle and into the glass.

GARNISHING A GIN & TONIC, SENSE OR NONSENSE

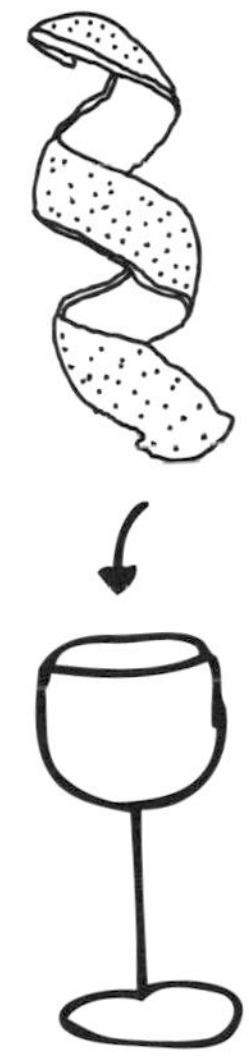

As we have already discussed, making a salad of your favourite gin & tonic is not the idea. We will leave the discussion about whether to use a garnish or not, for now. You and you alone can decide what finally goes into your gin & tonic. First and foremost, the garnish is for the attractive presentation of the glass, but can also highlight a particular taste or provide an additional taste that is missing.

Lime, lemon, rhubarb or olives go well with a dry gin. In principle, you can add any type of garnish to a dry gin or a gin with an extra portion of juniper berries, because the gin doesn't have a distinct taste. You use botanicals in this case to add that particular taste. Grapefruit, lemon zest, cucumber or rose petals go perfectly well with a floral gin. For a herbal gin use for example rosemary, thyme, mint, basil or coriander. Fruits, such as raspberry, are used mainly to liven up the glass. Make sure that you never crush the fruit, but add it whole to your gin & tonic.

If you decide to garnish your gin & tonic, don't forget a simple but essential rule: Wash the fruits, herbs and other garnishes. Another important rule when garnishing with citrus fruits (lemon, lime or orange) is to always use the peel or the zest since it contains the oil of the fruit and doesn't have the bitterness of the pith.

A traditional zester is used to cut very fine slivers from a citrus fruit. Using a classic peeler, it is very easy to cut off larger slivers. Of course a good knife is just as indispensable. How you will cut and what you will create is entirely up to you.

We do, however, want to take a closer look at one of the most common ways to cut a citrus fruit, namely the twist. Cut the peel of a citrus fruit with a peeler, hold the ends with both hands and twist the zest in opposite directions over the glass to press out the oils. Afterwards drop the twist into the glass.

If you decide to add herbs to your gin & tonic, don't exaggerate. One twist of the pepper mill, one star anise, three juniper berries, one or two rasps of nutmeg are more than adequate. In general, one to three different garnishes will suffice. One is just enough, two is a dynamic duo and three is a jolly trio. More than three is simply too much company!

To assist you in finding your way, we have listed the most common herbs and we will show you which ones combine best with which gins. Nowadays, it is easy to acquire pots of herbs in the supermarket or in a liquor store – they are filled with a selection of common herbs for your perfect gin & tonic.

JUNIPER BERRIES

You will find juniper berries in every gin, so you can use them in any gin & tonic combination.

COMBINE WITH all gins.

USE three to four (crushed) juniper berries.

HIBISCUS

The hibiscus shrub is native to the Mediterranean area and to sub-tropical regions around the world. Its trumpet-shaped flowers are large and eye-catching. They give your gin & tonic an elegant, attractive and floral touch.

COMBINE WITH floral gin.

USE three to four petals.

ROSE PEPPER

The decorative rose pepper is the sun-dried pip of the fruit that grows on the 'shinus molle', a small South American tree, and it gives your gin & tonic a light, refreshing and spicy flavour. Watch out: Rose pepper may cause an allergic reaction in people with tree nut allergy.

COMBINE WITH floral or sweet gin.

USE two to three crushed berries.

CARDAMOM

Cardamom is related to the ginger family, has a sweet and tangy smell and tastes like bergamot, lemon and camphor. When the seeds are crushed, they fully enhance your gin & tonic with a warm and herbal taste.

COMBINE WITH herbal gin.

USE a few crushed pips.

CINNAMON

Cinnamon has a herbal and warm taste and it is frequently used in cooking. In gin & tonic cinnamon provides a sweet-citrus contrast.
COMBINE WITH floral or sweet gin.
USE one cinnamon stick.

CITRUS RIND

In the past, an orange rind was used mainly for decorating a gin & tonic. Nowadays, there is a trend to expand on the citrus character in gin. Therefore, the rinds of various citrus fruits are added, such as sweet and sour orange, lemon, lime, grapefruit, mandarin, kumquat and more.
COMBINE WITH all gins.
USE four rinds.

CORIANDER SEEDS

Coriander seeds originate in the Middle East and are frequently used there in cooking. They are often added as flavouring to dark beers, but they also play a major role in quite a number of gin recipes. During distillation, coriander seeds release a herbal flavour of sage and lime.
COMBINE WITH all gins.
USE a few seeds.

STAR ANISE

Star anise is used as a spice – whole or milled. The spicy and intense taste is in the rind of the fruit. Star anise has a strong smell of anise and adds this same strong and spicy flavour to your gin & tonic.
COMBINE WITH herbal and citrus gins.
USE one star anise.

LIQUORICE

Liquorice is often called the 'sugar stick candy' of the master distiller and it contains sugars, bitters and a substance that produces the typical woody taste. Its practical and binding role makes it suitable for all types of gins. Moreover, Liquorice softens the mouth feel.

COMBINE WITH all gins.

USE one piece of Liquorice (maximum two, depending on the size).

THE FINISH

If you drink your gin & tonic as an aperitif, it is important to enjoy it as fizzy as possible. That is why the tonic must be added gently to the glass (poured down the side) and it is recommended not to stir the gin & tonic.

If you opt to enjoy your gin & tonic after a meal, do stir your creation a bit with a bar spoon or a stirrer in order to reduce the carbon effect. Two or three times is sufficient to avoid burping. And our most important tip for a perfect finish is to drink it in good company.

FIVE STEPS TO A PERFECT GIN & TONIC

1

Take a *copa de balon*, a red wine glass or tumbler. Put the glass in the refrigerator for a couple of hours. An alternative is to fill the glass with ice, stir it with a bar spoon until it is sufficiently cooled and then pour out the ice and melted water. Never use the ice that you used to cool your glass for serving your gin & tonic. Additional tip: you can tell that a glass is well cooled if it looks foggy.

2

Fill the glass to the rim with ice. The bigger the ice cubes the better. Rub a citrus zest lightly around the rim. Make sure though that the zest is a piece of the peel without the flesh of the fruit. The zest contains the oil of the fruit.

3

Choose a garnish (or garnishes) and add to the glass.

4

Take a jigger or bar measure and pour 50 ml of your favourite gin on top of the ice and herbs. If the alcohol content is higher than 45, you can pour slightly less: 40 ml.

5

Finally pour 200 ml of tonic, but do this gently to preserve the bubbly effect. You can do that by pouring the tonic down the inner side of the glass. Another trick is to take a bar spoon or swizzle stick, cover the tonic bottle and gently spill the tonic down the length of the stick into the glass.

ULTIMATE SERVE

You now know how to serve a perfect gin & tonic, but there's always room for improvement. That's why we give a moment's thought to the ultimate perfect serve! A perfect serve lifted to a higher level or a serving method that will really astound your guests. It's not about garnishes that you didn't even know existed or about garnishing your gin & tonic with 1001 different types of herbs. Nope, the ultimate trick is to find the ingredient that simply makes your gin & tonic better. With the right method of cutting and handling, you guarantee that the perfect serve is an outright WOW.

Please allow us to explain with a few examples, starting with Hendrick's Gin, which is where is all began. As you know by now, Hendrick's is served with a cucumber. No ice cubes, no citrus slices, but with a long cucumber ribbon! Cut the cucumber along its length. Use a cheese slicer to get perfect ribbons that swirl around in your glass. The ribbon is not only for decoration, it also gives your drink the taste of cucumber, which is what you are looking for when serving Hendrick's Gin.

Another example is the way BCN *Barcelona* Gin is served. As you have learned earlier, BCN Gin comes from the winery that produces the world famous Spanish Priorat wine. The local *Carinyena* and *Garnatxa* grapes are distilled to acquire a basic alcohol of BCN Gin. To make BCN Gin truly excel, add a dash of red wine when serving it, preferably from the Priorat region. Fill a red wine glass with three ice cubes, pour in a dash of red wine and swirl the glass. Then pour out some of the wine through a cocktail strainer, but make sure to leave some in the glass. Keep the ice cubes because they have absorbed the taste of the wine. Now cut a lime wedge and twist it over the glass, rub it along the rim and then drop it into the glass. Add a sliced dark grape and fill the glass to the top with ice

cubes. Complete with 30 ml of BCN Gin and 200 ml of neutral tonic. The result is a gin & tonic with a light pink colour that beautifully expresses the wine character of BCN Gin.

In other words, always find a spectacular way to mirror the DNA of your gin. Furthermore, as an experienced gin lover, you could venture into using contrasting garnishes. Take your cue from the cleverness you find among chefs. For example, serve a sweet gin, such as Fifty Pounds or Old English Gin with a salty or salt-alloy garnish, such as glasswort or sea lavender. These natural contrasts create a mini ecstasy!

Want to take this a step further? Examine the chemical makeup of your gin, comparable to food pairing. That's how the chemist Stuart Bale discovered that the most appropriate garnishes for Gin Mare are mango and black pepper. The presence of thyme, rosemary and basil is also a great hit in this gin, but he discovered that the high levels of pinene in mango and black pepper are also found in juniper berries and Mediterranean herbs. Mango and black pepper are therefore the ultimate garnish match for Gin Mare.

You achieve the *Ultimate Serve* by using the right tools and the right garnishing. By combining these elements, you get a gin & tonic that meets all expectations. Aim high and amaze both friend and foe.

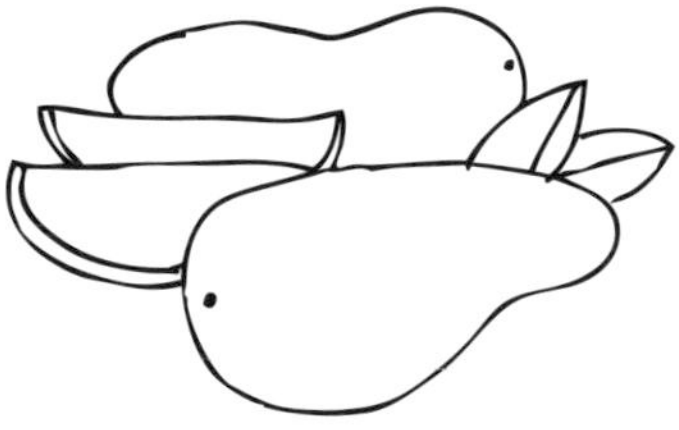

If you want to bestow your favourite gin the attention it deserves, then surf the Internet for the perfect serve of your brand. You will find countless videos that give the perfect serve that extra touch. In all fairness, we have to admit that the Internet also shows many misinterpretations of the perfect serve. You will have to select the ones that are reliable, but after reading this book, that shouldn't be a problem.

GINLICIOUS: FOOD & GIN & TONIC

People who are of the opinion that gin & tonic is destined to stand all alone have got it wrong. Many dishes, from tapas to desserts, find an ideal companion in gin & tonic. Gin & tonic not only sharpens the palate, but also offers a totally new taste sensation. Gin is definitely a bottle full of possibilities: a gin & tonic can either perfectly complement the flavours in your meal, or can act as an ingredient in the recipe, or both. Gin has inspired many a gastronome to create surprising combinations, and it is no longer possible to imagine the culinary world without it.

Pull up a chair and get ready for this 'ginlicious' experience. The chefs serving up this feast are Hermes Vanliefde and his side-kick Peter Laloo, managers of the unique Rock-Fort in Bruges. They really know how to get the most out of the bottle, and create magic both on the plate and in the glass standing next to it...

To form the perfect link between the dish and the gin & tonic, we serve them 'clean', without garnish.

Each recipe is for four people.

GIN-TONIC:
HENDRICK'S GIN + FENTIMANS TONIC WATER

RECIPE:
TUNA TARTARE, GRANITA OF APPLE AND ROSE WATER, WITH CUCUMBER

The cucumber taste that is so redolent in Hendrick's Gin is mirrored in this dish. The freshness of the granita offers a delightful contrast, and simultaneously forms the perfect link to the gin & tonic.

PREPARATION

Combine all the ingredients for the sauce, mix and pass through a sieve. Finely chop the tuna and mix with 2 to 3 tablespoons of the sauce. Season to taste with pepper and salt. Next, add the chopped shallot, chives and sesame seeds. Combine thoroughly.

Mix all the ingredients for the granita together in a shallow freezer-proof container. Place in the freezer but check after an hour or so and loosen with a fork as the ice crystals form.

Soak the dried seaweed in lukewarm water. Allow to drain thoroughly and combine with a little of the sauce. Garnish the tuna with the seaweed, cucumber and apple slices. Finish with the Hendrick's granita.

INGREDIENTS

200 g tuna (from the Mediterranean)
salt and pepper
1 large French shallot, chopped
2 tsp. chopped fresh chives
20 g dried seaweed
½ cucumber, finely diced
1 Granny Smith apple, in slices
1 tbsp. sesame seeds

Sauce

30 g grated fresh ginger
60 ml sushi-vinegar
100 ml Arbequina olive oil
30 ml soy sauce
a little sesame oil

Granita

200 ml apple juice
40 ml Hendrick's Gin
100 ml white wine
1 tsp. rose water
3 tbsp. cane sugar syrup

GIN-TONIC: **GERANIUM GIN + 1724 TONIC WATER**

RECIPE: **FRESH GOAT'S CHEESE WITH JUNIPER BERRY, PRESERVED LEMON AND HONEY**

Goat's cheese and juniper is a wonderful combination, and the connection to the gin goes without saying. The preserved lemons perfectly complement the floral and slightly herby notes in the Geranium Gin, which contains, amongst other ingredients, the oil of the geranium plant. The dish is finished off with a garnish of geranium petals.

PREPARATION

Pre-heat the oven to 180 °C.

Cut eight lengthways slices of the courgette on a mandolin, and then cut the slices into thin ribbons. Season with salt and pepper.

Season the goat's cheese with the juniper berries, pepper and salt, spoon the honey over the cheese and grill until soft, or brown with a blow torch.

Arrange the courgette-spaghetti on the plates, place the goat's cheese on top and finish with a slice of preserved lemon and the geranium petals.

INGREDIENTS

1 courgette

4 goat's cheese

4 dried juniper berries

pepper and salt

4 slices preserved lemons (available from speciality suppliers or Moroccan stores)

4 tbsp. honey

20 (approx.) geranium petals

GIN-TONIC: **FIFTY POUNDS GIN + 1724 TONIC WATER**

RECIPE: **GLASS NOODLES WITH SEAFOOD AND SEAWEED**

Fifty Pounds Gin is a sweet gin which combines perfectly, or perhaps contrasts with, the saltiness of the sea flavours of the seafood. The seaweed and samphire also play their part perfectly.

PREPARATION

Combine all the ingredients for the vinaigrette and keep in a squeezable dressing bottle.

Steep the dried seaweed in lukewarm water and allow to drain well. Then mix with the vinaigrette.

Cook the cockles and mussels for a short time, in a pan or on a plancha covered by a lid.

Briefly cook the glass noodles and allow them to cool under cold-running water. Then mix with the seaweed and vinaigrette. Remove the oysters and mussels from their shells, but leave the cockles whole, and arrange all the ingredients on a plate.

INGREDIENTS

100 g dried seaweed
20 cockles
20 Bouchot-mussels
150 g glass noodles
4 Oysters (Gillardeau)
12 fresh coriander sprigs
gomasio (mix of white and black sesam mixed with salt)
pepper
a knob of butter

Vinaigrette

2 tbsp. grated fresh ginger
2 tbsp. sushi-vinegar
2 tbsp. soy sauce
9 tbsp. Arbequina olive oil
a little sesame oil

GIN-TONIC:
G'VINE FLORAISON + FEVER-TREE INDIAN TONIC WATER

RECIPE:
VERJUICE MARINATED FOIE GRAS, MUSCAT GRAPES, RAISINS, JAMÓN IBÉRICO, BREAD CRUNCH AND FENNEL

The basis of G'Vine Floraison Gin is the Ugni Blanc grape. The verjuice (the juice of unripened grapes) used in this dish perfectly complements the gin. The fattiness of the foie gras is counterbalanced by the acidity of the verjuice. The flavours of grapes (and raisins) are also echoed in the dish.

PREPARATION

For the bread crunch: in the peanut oil, fry the bread cubes with the garlic and rosemary. Allow to drain for two days, then blitz into fine crumbs.

Cut the raw foie gras into slices. Marinate for 15 minutes in the verjuice, season with salt and pepper, the raisins and grapes.

Arrange the foie gras on a plate, garnish with the Jamón Ibérico, a tablespoon of the bread crunch, a few sprigs of fennel leaf and dress with a little of the juice from the grapes and raisins.

INGREDIENTS

100 g foie gras
200 ml verjuice (juice of unripened grapes)
pepper and salt
24 dark raisins
12 Muscat grapes, quartered
4 slices Jamón Ibérico
a few fresh fennel leaf sprigs

Bread crunch

1 small stale white loaf, roughly cut into cubes
1 clove garlic
1 sprig fresh rosemary
1 litre peanut oil

GIN-TONIC:
GIN MARE + 1724 TONIC WATER

RECIPE:
HAND-PEELED ZEEBRUGGE PRAWNS, CHERRY TOMATOES, ARBEQUINA OLIVES AND BASIL

The bouquet of Gin Mare is reminiscent of a bunch of ripe tomatoes. The cherry tomatoes in this recipe are therefore the perfect partner, forming a bridge between the prawns and the gin. The botanicals in Gin Mare include, amongst others, rosemary, thyme, Arbequina olives and basil. The rosemary and thyme flavours are present in the vinaigrette, and the dish is finished with basil and olives, which matches the gin and tonic seamlessly.

PREPARATION

First make the vinaigrette. Warm the white wine vinegar slightly to about 50 °C, along with the tomato, shallot and fresh herbs. Allow to infuse for 15 minutes off the heat and then pass through a sieve. Add the olive oil.

Blanch the cherry tomatoes in boiling water, then plunge into a bowl of iced water. Peel before adding to the vinaigrette.

Arrange the tomatoes on the plate and garnish with the olives, prawns and basil leaves.

INGREDIENTS

20 cherry tomatoes
16 Arbequina olives
100 g cooked hand-peeled Zeebrugge prawns
12 sprigs fresh small leaf basil

Vinaigrette

50 ml white wine vinegar
1 tomato, peeled and chopped
1 shallot, finely chopped
fresh thyme (according to taste)
fresh rosemary (according to taste)
fresh oregano (according to taste)
60 ml Arbequina olive oil

GIN-TONIC:
BLUE GIN + FENTIMANS TONIC WATER

RECIPE:
WILD DUCK WITH BEETROOT, POMEGRANATE, CLOVES AND BLACK PEPPER

The spicy finish of Blue Gin, with its surprisingly earthy tone, combines beautifully with the wild duck, cloves and black pepper. The gin is also used in this recipe's preparation.

PREPARATION

Pre-heat the oven to 180 °C. Cook the duck filet with plenty of black pepper and the cloves, then finish by baking in the oven for about 12 minutes. Add the pomegranate vinegar and the Blue Gin to the pan. Remove the duck filets and keep warm.

Finish the sauce off in the pan with the brown stock and a knob of butter.

Cook the beetroots in water with salt and vinegar. Once cooked through, remove the skins and then reheat in a pan with some butter, sugar and pomegranate vinegar.

Arrange the sliced duck and beetroot on the plates, finish with the sauce, a few pomegranate seeds and sprigs of fresh mint. Season with a final grind of fresh black pepper.

INGREDIENTS

2 wild duck filets
black pepper (freshly ground)
2 cloves
2 x 1 tbsp. pomegranate vinegar
60 ml Blue Gin
500 ml beef stock
a knob of butter
8 small beetroots
a pinch of salt
2 tbsp. distilled white vinegar
3 tbsp. brown sugar
a knob of butter
500 ml water
1 fresh pomegranate
4 sprigs of fresh mint

GIN-TONIC:
FILLIERS TANGERINE SEASONAL EDITION + FENTIMANS TONIC WATER

RECIPE:
CEVICHE OF SEA BASS, CITRUS, TOASTED CORN AND CORIANDER

Tangerines are used in the making of this seasonal edition of Filliers Gin. Filliers Tangerine Seasonal Edition has a soft, fruity taste, with clear accents of fresh orange and tangerine. The citrus flavours in the gin are reflected by the mix of citrus fruits in the dish, which at the same time combine flawlessly with the ceviche of sea bass.

PREPARATION

First prepare the ceviche by dissolving the palm sugar in a little water. Next add the lime zest, lime juice and mandarin or orange juice.

Make the coriander oil by combining the roughly chopped coriander with the grape seed oil and warm to 80 °C before passing through a sieve.

Remove the dark parts of the sea bass and cut into thin slices.

Divide the ceviche into the serving bowls and arrange the slices of sea bass on top. Finish with the coriander oil, red onion, chili peppers and the toasted corn.

INGREDIENTS

+/- 280 g sea bass filet............
1 red onion, chopped...............
1 red chili pepper, chopped....
a handful of toasted corn or crunchy corn chips (health food store)........................
4 kumquats (small elongated orange-like fruit)..........................

Coriander oil
1 bunch fresh coriander..........
100 ml grape seed oil...............

Ceviche
1 tbsp. palm sugar.....................
juice and zest of 1 lime............
juice of 2 mandarins or 1 orange................................
3 tbsp. Arbequina olive oil .....

GIN-TONIC:
MOMBASA CLUB GIN + FENTIMANS TONIC WATER

RECIPE:
CRÈME OF WHITE CHOCOLATE, GRAPEFRUIT, GRANITA OF MOMBASA CLUB GIN, STAR ANISE, CANADA DRY AND VERBENA

Gin is also excellent when included in the preparation of a dessert, and here is a good example. Based on Mombasa Club Gin, this spicy granita counterbalances the rich crème of white chocolate. The citrus hints in the gin are enhanced by the grapefruit and the spicy notes are highlighted by the use of star anise and the ginger of the Canada Dry.

PREPARATION

Mix the egg yolks with the sugar. Warm the milk and cream together, then add to the egg yolk mixture. Continue to heat to 85 °C and then add the soaked gelatine leaves. Sieve the mixture and strain over the white chocolate pastilles. Gently stir until a smooth consistency is reached and the temperature has reduced to about 40 °C. Then fold in the softly whipped cream.

Mix all the ingredients for the granita together in a shallow freezer-proof container. Place in the freezer but check after an hour or so and loosen with a fork as the ice crystals form.

Divide the crème of white chocolate into four cocktail glasses. Segment the pink grapefruit and arrange on top of the crème. Finish off with the granita and a few sprigs of verbena.

INGREDIENTS

Crème of white chocolate

- 30 g egg yolks
- 12 g white sugar
- 70 ml semi skimmed milk
- 70 ml whipping cream (35%)
- 300 g white chocolate (pastilles)
- 3.5 g gelatine leaves
- 500 ml softly whipped, whipping cream (35%)

Granita

- 250 ml Canada Dry
- 50 ml Mombasa Club Gin
- 1 star anise
- 30 ml ginger syrup
- 50 ml sweet white wine
- 2 pink grapefruits
- a few sprigs fresh lemon verbena

STOLLEN 1930

AUSTRIA - KUFSTEIN

WWW.AURACHER-LOECHL.AT/DE/BAR-KUFSTEIN

Kufstein (Tirol) might be one of smallest cities in Austria, but it has one of the biggest gin collections, namely in Stollen 1930. The bar, with its collection of 528 different types of gins has even made it into the *Guinness Book of Records*. The manager of the well-known Auracher Löchl restaurant and hotel remodelled the dark tunnels under the hotel into a hip bar for night owls and gin lovers. When entering Stollen 1930, you actually feel like you're in a 1920/1930 scene, accompanied by music that instantly makes you want a classic cocktail or gin-tonic. Also after skiing, this bar is the place to be.

BAR VOLTA GENT

BELGIUM - GHENT

WWW.VOLTA-GENT.BE

Bar Volta is located above the restaurant with the same name in the former electric power conversion station and named after Alessandro Volta, the inventor of the electric battery. The energy is exceedingly buoyant, the gastronomy reaches high peaks, the hip choices for the interior are refreshing, and the jazzy lounge music completes the picture. Moreover, since it opened, this bar is considered one of the gin pioneers of Belgium, thanks to mixologists Eric Veldhuis & co-star Ben Wouters who used to work in Bar Volta. Shaking cocktails was once their unshakable skill, but gin & tonic became their new calling. This wonderful philosophy and the great gin menu are still there today and there is plenty to discover.

CAFÉ AKOTEE

BELGIUM - DE HAAN

WWW.CAFEEAKOTEE.BE

A visit to Café Akotee in De Haan is worthwhile – if only for their more than 120 gins and 20 tonics. Café manager Gunther Jonckheere, better known as 'Bolle', serves every gin professionally, accompanied by the necessary explanations. Café Akotee has existed for more than 20 years and is the regional G&T hotspot, with regular gin tastings. From the start, Bolle has been a fan of gin, but it was Sam Galsworthy (Sipsmith), Henrik Hammer (Geranium Gin) and Alexander Stein (Monkey 47) who really fanned the 'gin fire' during a seminar in 2011. This was followed by several renovations of Cafée Akotee in order to do justice to the fast-growing collection of gin bottles. Bolle continues to explore the world of gin, both locally and abroad, so as to offer his customers the latest gins in an appropriate manner. Whether you're a layman or a seasoned gin lover, Bolle can always surprise you with a gin & tonic made to your taste, accompanied with the story behind each gin.

GILT

DENMARK - COPENHAGEN

WWW.GILT.DK

Gilt is one of the most popular bars in Copenhagen and it knows how to create a perfect mix of the classic and modern cocktail culture. The menu offers season-based drinks that include berries, roots, nuts and fruits. A small bar, proving that Scandinavian gin is also on the rise. Typical Danish ingredients are mixed in a gin & tonic. Gilt also infuses its gins with all sorts of botanicals, including lavender. All the cocktail syrups are also produced in-house.

GIN & TONIC BAR

GERMANY - BERLIN

WWW.AMANOGROUP.DE/EN/EAT-DRINK/GIN-TONIC-BAR

What's in a name? Yes indeed, this bar in the Amano Hotel in Berlin serves fantastic gin & tonics. According to the Gin & Tonic Bar, the king of cocktails is perfect after work, during dinner, or as a night cap. You can expect more surprising innovations with gin as the protagonist. Gin & tonic infused with tea? Yes, in the Gin & Tonic Bar in Berlin you can try this exceptional mix. Head barman Stjepan Sedlar makes sure you won't forget this surprising combination quickly.

GOLDENE BAR

GERMANY – MUNICH

WWW.GOLDENEBAR.DE

High end and rock & roll go hand in hand at this award-winning (including, amongst others, Bar des Jahres 2013, Mixology Bar Award 2012 and 2013) bar. The bar opened under the management of head barman Klaus Stephan Rainer in 2010, in the 'Haus der Kunst' (House of Art). Classic and modern cocktails complement an innovative food concept under the direction of Chef Michael Heid. A top cocktail bar with an extensive menu, somewhat hidden behind an historic façade, and DJ sets, surfers and celebrities ensure a sizzling atmosphere. Klaus Stephan introduced the idea of adding aromatic homemade tea blends to gin & tonic, creating a type of gin & tonic tea. Many bartenders follow a workshop to develop their own blend. One certainly worth a try is the '24h Ginmillo Tea'. This is an infused gin (Tanqueray N°10) with chamomile, topped up with warm Fever-Tree Indian Tonic Water and finished off with sugar candy.

THE GIN JOINT

GREECE - ATHENS

WWW.THEGINJOINT.GR

The Gin Joint is located near the lively entertainment quarter of Karytsi Square in the centre of Athens. In 2011, the popular gin bar was chosen as the best bar in the Bar Academy Show during the Xenia Fair. The atmosphere and interior design of the bar reminds you immediately of the 1930s. The music from the same period makes you want to get a gin & tonic right away. In addition to the many classic cocktails made with top-quality spirits, the Gin Joint also has more than 60 gins on its menu from around the world. In 2012, barman Vasilis Kyritsis won first place in the World Class, an international initiative of Diageo Reserve Brands in which the world's best known cocktail mixers and bartenders compete against each other. At The Gin Joint you drink an undeniable gin & tonic, just as the drink should be.

LISBONITA GIN BAR

PORTUGAL - LISBON

WWW.TABERNAMODERNA.COM

Lisbonita Gin Bar is a part of the tapas restaurant, La Taberna Moderna. Its interior consists mainly of wood and reminds you of a traditional Portuguese tavern, but the atmosphere is extremely open and friendly. The food is superb: traditional but with a modern twist. Also their gin-tonic is fantastically served. With more than 70 types, you're sure to find your favourite. And if you have no idea which gin to choose, the waiters will recommend one. Go for the classic gin & tonic or a cocktail that doesn't appear on the menu. Depending on the inspiration of the barman, he will concoct the most delicious creation for you. And don't forget to order your drink at the bar, because just watching how your favourite gin & tonic is made is worthwhile. Once you taste it, we are convinced it won't be your last.

BOBBY GIN

SPAIN - BARCELONA

WWW.BOBBYGIN.COM

"The perfect gin & tonic does not exist" is written on one of the walls of Bobby Gin. Nevertheless, the gin & tonic creations in this bar come pretty close. This place-to-be is managed by Alberto Pizaro, award-winning mixologist and bartender par excellence. From the most delicious gin & tonics, to smoked cocktails and various infusions of botanical deliciousness, Bobby Gin is one of the must-visit bars in Barcelona for every gin lover. The retro interior is warm and welcoming. Certainly try out 'Bobby's Spring': a gin & tonic with Bobby's Spring Gin (an in-house creation of a variety of gins with an infusion of hibiscus flower and olive tree leaf), Schweppes Heritage Indian Tonic Water, finished off with strawberry and grapefruit zest.

BRISTOL BAR

SPAIN - MADRID
WWW.BRISTOLBAR.ES

Owners Ellie (United Kingdom) and Fran (Spain) embody Spanish gin culture in their Bristol Bar. The variety of gins on offer is overwhelming and the atmosphere is buzzing. The décor of the interior of the Bristol bar is 'old school', with a black and white marble topped bar, Bordeaux red leather sofas and a life-size portrait of Queen Victoria on the wall. But isn't old school the new cool?! Gin is the order of the day here. All the 'usual suspects' can be found on the menu, but there are also a few gems to discover. Above all, Bristol Bar has its very own gin, and also its own cocktail lounge, 'Gintonize'. Modern Spanish dishes sit comfortably alongside your favourite gin & tonic and if the choice is just too difficult to make, the (Ellie) Baker's Top 10 Gin & Tonic will offer you solace. You should definitely try the 'Royal Pink-Ish' specially designed for the wedding of Prince William and Kate Middleton. This gin & tonic combines Ish Gin, Schweppes Original Premium Tonic Water and cranberry juice, finished off with lime and half a strawberry.

PURE C

THE NETHERLANDS - CADZAND

WWW.STRANDHOTEL.EU

It was Sergio Herman (Chef of Oud Sluis***) who put gin & tonic on the map in Flanders and in the Netherlands. Back in 2005, Sergio, or his maître sommelier at that time, went twice a week to London to check out Hendrick's Gin. While bars and discos served only classic drinks in those days, Sergio also discovered the different varieties of gin that were available in Spain. Barman and mixologist Vainius Balcaitis gets his inspiration from Sergio's approach to cocktails, namely combining them with fresh herbs and spices. In his gin & tonics, Vainius tests the limits with unbridled energy and serves his creations in a non-conforming way. Take for example the Brecon Botanicals Gin with Fever-Tree Tonic, served with a mini burlap sack into which you can place the added botanicals and personalise your gin & tonic.

TUNES BAR

THE NETHERLANDS - AMSTERDAM

WWW.CONSERVATORIUMHOTEL.COM/
RESTAURANTS-AND-BARS/TUNES-BAR

With its chic décor and sparkling ambiance, Tunes Bar is an elegant, yet informal refuge in the lively museum area of Amsterdam, where you'll be served unique champagnes, exclusive cocktails and delicious sushi with the appropriate sake. But gin & tonic is the real signature drink of the Tunes Bar. Here you can choose from a selection of 30 different types of gins. Every Wednesday, a new gin & tonic is in the spotlight. In the evenings, the comfortable furniture with its rich upholstery combined with the subtle lighting provides a modern, stylish and intimate atmosphere. Tunes Bar, located in the Conservatorium Hotel, has recently been named not only the best hotel bar in Amsterdam, but also the winner of the Best Style Bar Award and Best Interior Design Award by the VENUEZ Hospitality & Style Awards.

GRAPHIC BAR

UNITED KINGDOM - LONDON

WWW.GRAPHICBAR.COM

This gin bar in Soho offers more than 100 gin varieties. The entire length of the bar is filled almost exclusively with gins, and the menu or rather 'gin bible' provides information on every gin they have available. Graphic Bar houses, in their own words, the biggest gin collection in the world, and strives to serve the perfect Gin & Tonic and Martini: these two cocktails don't mask the taste of the gin. Moreover, you will always find the right tonic and the right garnish with every gin. Art meets bar in Graphic as the décor changes regularly, each time assembled by a different, trendy artist. Graphic Bar is one of the first 'gin-craze' bars in London and they are very happy to work with staff from the Iberian Peninsula, so as to take gin & tonic to a new level.

PORTOBELLO STAR

UNITED KINGDOM - LONDON

WWW.PORTOBELLOSTARBAR.CO.UK

The first bar with its own gin, namely Portobello Road N°171, is located in the Notting Hill area. From the outside it looks just like a regular English pub, and it is not immediately apparent that there is a real cocktail bar inside. And to be fair, the inside décor of the Portobello Star is very pub-like. But the cocktails and the gin & tonics are of an extremely high quality. Mixologist Jake Burger definitely knows his trade. Gin lovers can also book a 'Ginstitute' session, which includes a tour of the mini gin museum, followed by a comprehensive history lesson and an introduction to the development of gin. Last but not least, you get the chance to try out your own gin formula.

THE STAR AT NIGHT

UNITED KINGDOM - LONDON

WWW.THESTARATNIGHT.COM

The Start at Night in the heart of Soho is the base of the London Gin Club, founded in March 2012. The bar itself was opened in 1933 and has kept much of its original charm. Discover more than seventy gin varieties, including their own 7 Dials London Dry Gin. Constantly in search of premium gins and super-premium gins you can taste the exclusivity. The focus of this bar is, without a doubt, on the quality, and the 'gin menu' is constantly kept up-to-date. Every gin & tonic is served in a 'coppa' glass and matched with the right tonic and garnish. The signature gin is undeniably the 7 Dials Gin with Fever-Tree Indian Tonic Water and frozen raspberries which are 'cracked' by hand.

BATHTUB GIN & CO

UNITED STATES - SEATTLE

WWW.BATHTUBGINSEATTLE.COM

Bathtub Gin & Co in Seattle is nestled in the cellar of the Humphrey Apartments in Belltown. This small bar, fully designed in a speakeasy style, was established in 2009 in the former boiler room of the building. The intimate bar is multilevel: upstairs is a small bar with gins from every corner of the globe, downstairs are comfortable couches and a library. Bathtub Gin & Co is an affectionate bar (it even has a bathtub!) and somewhat mysterious, but with perfectly served cocktails and gin & tonics. The name of the bar refers to the bathtub used for making gin during the Prohibition Era. The real reason why owners Marcus Johnson and Jessica Gifford opened the bar was to be able to pour their friends a perfect gin & tonic. Apparently they have lots of friends, because Bathtub Gin & Co is always full.

MADAME GENEVA

UNITED STATES - NEW YORK

WWW.MADAMGENEVA-NYC.COM

This bar was named after the nickname that gin acquired during the Gin Craze in London. This spot gives a slight impression of British colonialism in the middle of Manhattan, more specifically in the Bowery. The bar feels like a hidden room for governors in 19th century Singapore. The dark lounge with side panelling, lamps, the gramophone in the corner and the sultry atmosphere do justice to this hip bar. There are many cosy corners where you can sit by candlelight and have profound discussions over your gin & tonic. That's because gin & tonic is indeed a central feature. Nowhere in New York will you find a bigger and tastier selection of gin cocktails. Fans of classic gin & tonic will certainly find something suitable here, but Madame Geneva goes even further. Try a gin & tonic with celery bitters and homemade tonic water based on cucumber. For those who truly want to taste a memorable drink, we recommend one of their gin & jam brews. This is not a music jam, but the edible jam. Indeed, Madame Geneva mixes Beefeater Gin with seasonal jams. Also try a Madam's Treats (light bites) that go well with...

THE FLINTRIDGE PROPER

UNITED STATES –
LA CAÑADA FLINTRIDGE

WWW.THEPROPER.COM

This bar is located in California, more precisely in La Cañada Flintridge. This small town is not particularly known for its lively nightlife, so it might surprise you to know that this suburb is the home base of one of the world's biggest gin collections, at least according to the owners. The Flintridge Proper feels almost like a private club. After entering the restaurant, you come to a bar that looks like it was taken straight from the film The Great Gatsby. What immediately strikes you is the more than 200 gins propped up at the back of the bar. In addition, The Flintridge Proper makes its own gin. Flintridge Native Botanicals Gin is distilled from local botanicals, which are found mainly within a radius of 15 km of the bar. And if gin is not your thing, we are certain that the barmen will convince you otherwise, as they do their best to turn you into a gin lover. And believe us ... they are good at their job.

GINCYCLOPEDIA

This list provides a summary of gins currently available worldwide. However, as new gins are popping up almost every week it is by no means exhaustive, rather more of a snapshot of how it is at the moment. It will hopefully prove to be a useful tool for your initial investigations.

Note: producers are often (deliberately) vague about production information and so this list also has its limitations. Only gins of 40% ABV make it onto the list, as this is our own idiosyncratic bench mark of quality and passion.

NAME	Derivatives	Place of origin	Alc%	Year	Brand owner/ distillery	Number of botanicals	(Known) botanicals
1 & 9 GIN		France	40		Distillerie Des Terres Rouges	10	juniper berry, coriander, orris root, orange, cinnamon
1836 RADERMACHER GIN		België	43		Radermacher	11	jeneverbes, bergamot, citroenschil, koriander, engelwortel, sinaasappelschil, kardemom, lavendel, vlierbes, kaneel en den
25 ELCKERLIJC SILVER EDITION GIN		Belgium	40		Heynsquared VOF	5	juniper berry, sloe, porcini, heather, ground elder
5TH DISTILLED GIN	Fire - Red Fruits	Spain	42		Destilleries del Maresme	4	blueberries, raspberries, strawberries, blackberries
	Wind - Floral		42		Destilleries del Maresme	4	flowers, spices and botanical elements
	Earth - Citrus		42		Destilleries del Maresme	4	grapefruit, orange, mandarin, lemon
6 MOMENTS PREMIUM GIN		Belgium	40		De Moor Distillery	16	juniper berry, angelica root, coriander, cinnamon, cardamom , pepper, lime, sweet orange, bitter orange, orris, liquorice, nutmeg, clove, ginger, lemon balm, rose
	6 Moments Gin Sense Unlimited		40			17	juniper berry, angelica root, coriander, cinnamon, cardamom, black pepper, lemon, orange, orris root, liquorice, nutmeg, clove, ginger, balm, roses and lemon grass
7D ESSENTIAL LONDON DRY GIN 0.7L		Spain	41		Comercial S.A. Tello	12	juniper berry, bitter orange, thyme, peppermint, cinnamon, lemon, chamomile, spearmint, sweet orange, lavender, mandarin orange, coriander
7 DIALS GIN		UK	46			7	juniper berry, coriander, angelica root, marsh-mellow root clementine, cardamom and almond
12 BRIDGES GIN		USA	45		Integrity Spirits/ Distillery Row	12	

NAME	Derivatives	Place of origin	Alc%	Year	Brand owner/ distillery	Number of botanicals	(Known) botanicals
12/11 GIN		Spain	42.5	2011	Benevento Global/ Destilerías Liber	11	juniper berry, mandarin, rose, sage, lemon, angelica root, cardamom, coriander, thyme, rosemary
	12/11 Aurum Gin						Extra: gold flakes
ADLER BERLIN DRY GIN 0,7L		Germany	42		Preußische Spirituosen Manufaktur	unknown	juniper berry, lavender, coriander, ginger and lemon peel
	Adler's Reserve / KPM Edition		47				
ADNAMS DISTILLED GIN		UK	40	2010	Adnams Brewery	6	juniper berry, orris root, coriander seed, cardamom pod, sweet orange peel and hibiscus flower - See more at: http://adnams.co.uk/spirits/our-spirits/distilled-gin/#sthash.ARyNwTPb.dpuf
	Adnams First Rate Gin 0.7L		48				
	Adnams Sloe Gin		26				
ALAMBICS GIN (13YO)		Scotland	65.6		Alambics Classique	unknown	
ALVERNA HOLY GIN		Italy	47		Sanuario della verna monastery	4	juniper berry, citrus, savory, orange peel
AMATO WIESBADEN GIN		Germany	43,7	2014	Manoamano Bar	unknown	juniper berry, coriander, citrus
AMSTERDAM DRY GIN GOLD		The Netherlands	43		The Goldeen Arch D+G378istillery	unknown	
ARCTIC VELVET PREMIUM GIN		Greenland/ Switzerland	40		ThoCon AG	25	juniper berry, coriander, caraway seed, nutmeg
ATOMIC GIN		Belgium	40		Atomic Distillers / RC2	23	juniper berry, Dolomite herbs, Sicilian lemon, tangerine
AVIATION GIN		USA	42		The House Of Spirits distillery	unknown	lavender, indian sarsaparilla
A.V. VAN WEES THREE CORNER GIN		The Netherlands	42		Van Wees	2	juniper berry and lemon
BAHIA GIN		Spain	40	2011	Kiskaarly S.L.	12	lemom, sweet & bitter orange
BANKES GIN		UK	40		Langley Distillery	10	orris, cinnamon, coriander, juniper berry, nutmeg, lemon peel , engelen-wortel, liquorice, cassia, orangeschil
BARBERS GIN		UK	40		Timbermill Distillery	4	juniper berry, coriander, thyme, angelica wortel
BARR HILL GIN		USA	45		Caledonia Spirits	unknown	juniper berry, honey
	Barr Hill Honey gin						
BAVARKA BAVARIAN GIN		Germany	46		Lantenhammer Distillery	unknown	
BAYSWATER GIN		Spain	43		Casalbor	unknown	juniper berry, coriander seed, angelica root, orris powder, lemon peel, orange peel, lquorice, cassia and nutmeg
BCN GIN		Spain	40		Aquavida Llops	7	grapes, rosemary, citrus, fennel, figs, juniper berry, pine shoots

NAME	Derivatives	Place of origin	Alc%	Year	Brand owner/ distillery	Number of botanicals	(Known) botanicals
BECKETTS LONDON DRY GIN		UK	40			6	juniper berry, lime, orange, coriander, mint, orris root
BEDROCK GIN		UK	40		Spirit Of The Lakes	unknown	juniper berry, coriander seed, lemon and orange peel, angelica root, liquorice root powder and cinnamon
BEEFEATER		UK	40		Pernod Ricard/ Beefeater Distillery	9	juniper berry, angelica root, angelica seeds, coriander seeds, liquorice, almonds, orris root, seville oranges, and lemon peel
	Beefeater24		45			12	
	Beefeater's Burrough's Reserve		43	2013			
	WET by Beefeater						
	Beefeater London Market (Limited Edition)		40				
BELGIN FRESH HOP		Belgium	40		VDS	4	fresh hop, juniper berry, coriander, lemon peel
	Belgin Ultra 13		41.4		VDS	13	juniper berry, cloves, angelica, orange, bergamot, vanilla, cinnamon, gentian root, lemon pee , lime peel, cardamom, fresh hop, coriander
BELLRINGER GIN		USA	47		Frank-Lin Distillers Products Ltd	unknown	
BERKELEY SQUARE GIN	Berkeley Square Still No. 8 Release Small Batch Gin	UK	40		G&J Greenall	8	juniper berry, coriander, basil, angelica root, lavender, cubebs, kaffir lime leaves and sage
	Berkeley Square Slow 48 Hour Distilled Gin		40		G&J Greenall	unknown	juniper berry, basil, lavender, kaffir lime
BIERCÉE GIN		Belgium	44		Biercée	18	poppies, cocoa, fresh fruit, juniper berry, cloves, hops, hyfope, ambrette, angelica root, cumin, caraway, fennel, coriander, malt wine, vanilla, lavender, amis vert
BIG GIN		USA	47		Captive Spirits	9	juniper berry, coriander, bitter orange peel, grains of paradise, angelica, cassia, cardamom, orris, Tasmanian pepper berry
	BIG Gin Bourbon Barreled		47				
BIG BEN DELUXE LONDON DRY GIN		India	42.8		Mohan Meakin Ltd / Solan brewery	unknown	
BILBERRY BLACK HEART'S GIN		USA	45		Journeyman Distillery	9	juniper berry, bilberries
BLACK GIN		Germany	45		Gansloser Distillerie	74	
	Black Gin Distiller's Cut		60				
	Black Gin Edition 1905		45				
	Red Gin Edition		40	2015			

NAME	Derivatives	Place of origin	Alc%	Year	Brand owner/ distillery	Number of botanicals	(Known) botanicals
BLACK DEATH GIN		UK	40		G&J Greenall	unknown	
BLACKWOOD'S VINTAGE DRY GIN		Shetland Islands, UK	40		Blavod Drinks Ltd	13	wild water mint, angelica root, sea pinks, juniper berry, meadow sweet, coriander, cinnamon, liquorice, citrus peel, nutmeg, oris root, violet flowers, turmeric
	Blackwood's Vintage Dry Gin		60				
BLADE GIN		USA	47		Old World Spirits	5	cardamom, juniper berry, lemon peel, orange peel and pepper
BLANC OCEAN/TIDES GIN		Spain	40		Blanc Gastronomy	11	juniper berry, gentian, coriander, angelica root, lemon vervain, cinnamon, orange, lemon, citrus aurantium, bergamot and grasswort
BLEU D'ARGENT GIN		France	40		GCF	9	juniper berry, citrus
BLIND TIGER GIN		Belgium	47		Deluxe Distillery	12	juniper berry, coriander seed, liquorice root, lemon peel , orange blossoms, green cardamom, ginger, horseradish, orris root, angelica root, cubeb pepper
BLOOM PREMIUM LONDON DRY GIN		UK	40		GJ Greenall's	4	juniper berry, honeysuckle, chamomile and pomelo
BLOOMSBURY	Lemon	UK	45		Bloomsbury Wine & Spirit	unknown	
	Orange		45				
BLUE GIN		Austria	43		Reisetbauer	27	lemon rind, angelica root, cilantro seeds, turmeric, liquorice
BLUECOAT GIN		USA	47	2007	Philadelphia Distilling	secret	juniper berry, orange peel, lemon peel, 3rd citrus peel - "more than 6 and less than 20"
	Bluecoat Barrel Reserve		47				
BOBBY'S GIN		The Netherlands	42		Herman Jansen	8	juniper berry, clove, coriander, lemon grass, cinnamon, cubeb pepper, fennel, rose hip
BOË SUPERIOR GIN		Scotland	47		VC2 brands	14	juniper berry, coriander, angelica, ginger, orris root, cassia bark, chinese cinnamon, grains of paradise, orange and lemon peel, cardamom seeds, liquorice, almonds, cubeb berry
BOMBAY SAPPHIRE		UK	40	1987	Bacardi-Martini/ G&J Greenall	10	almond, lemon peel, liquorice, juniper berry, orris root, angelica, coriander, cassia, cubeb and grains of paradise
	Bombay Dry		40	2010			
	Bombay Sapphire East		42	2012		12	Extra: lemon grass, Vietnamese pepper
	Star of Bombay		47	2015		10	New: bergamot, ambrette seeds
BONNIE&CLYDE GIN		Belgium	44/47.7	2014		unknown	malt, wheat, citrus/malt juniper berry
BOODLES GIN		UK	40		Proximo Spirits/ G&J Greenall	9	juniper berry, coriander seed, angelica root, angelica seed, cassia bark, caraway seed, nutmeg, rosemary, sage

NAME	Derivatives	Place of origin	Alc%	Year	Brand owner/ distillery	Number of botanicals	(Known) botanicals
BOOTLEGGER 21 NEW YORK GIN		USA	47		Prohibition Distillery	5	juniper berry, coriander, lemon verbana, orris root, bitter orange
BORDIGA DRY GIN		Italy	42		Cav. Pietro Bordiga	8	juniper berry, coriander, cardamom , thyme, citrus
	Bordiga Smoke Gin		42				
	Bordiga Rose Gin		42				
BOTANIC PREMIUM LONDON DRY GIN			40		Williams & Hurbert/Langley Distillery	14	Boeddha's hand, juniper berry, tangerine, thyme, coriander, lemon, cinnamon, peppermint, camomile, anise, sweet orange apple, almond, cardamom , mango.
	Botanic Ultra Premium London Dry Gin 0,7L		45				
BOTANICAL AND HOPPY GIN		Denmark	44		Mikkeller Spirits/ Braunstein Distillery	unknown	juniper berry, lemon grass, angelica root, cardamom, oranges, hops
BOTH'S OLD TOM GIN		Germany	47		Haromex / The Both Distillery	unknown	
BOUDIER GIN		France	40		Gabriel Boudier	unknown	
	Boudier Sloe Gin		25				
BOXER GIN		UK	40		Green Box Drinks	11	juniper berry, sweet lemon, sweet orange, angelica root, orris root, liquorice root, cinammon, cassia bark, nutmeg, coriander, bergamot
BRECON SPECIAL RESERVE GIN		UK	40		Penderyn Distillery	11	Welsh Spirit, juniper berry, orange peel, cassia bark, liquorice, cinnamaon bark, angelica root, nutmeg, corianders seeds, lemon peel, orris root
BREILPUR LONDON DRY GIN		Switzerland	45		Breil Pur SA	unknown	juniper berry, Alpenroos, chocolade munt
	Breilpur Sloe Gin						
BRIDGE GIN		Spain	38		Montana Perucchi	6	juniper berry, coriander, ginger, cardamom, komijn,orange peell
BROCKMANS GIN		UK	40		Brockmans Distillery	10	juniper berry, coriander, blueberries, blackberries, orange peel
BROKEN HEART GIN		New Zealand	40		Broken heart spirits	11	citrus, rosemary, juniper berry
BROKER'S PREMIUM LONDON DRY GIN		UK	40	1998	Broker's Gin Ltd/ Langley Distillery	10	juniper berry, coriander, angelica root, orris root, cassia bark, cinnamon, liquorice, nutmeg, orange peel, lemon peel
BROOKLYN GIN		USA	40		Brooklyn Craft Works	2	juniper berry, citrus
BRUUT! GIN		Belgium		2014	Spirits By Design	unknown	

NAME	Derivatives	Place of origin	Alc%	Year	Brand owner/ distillery	Number of botanicals	(Known) botanicals
BULLDOG GIN		UK	40	2006	Bulldog Gin Company/ G&J Greenall	12	juniper berry, dragon fruit, poppy, lavender, lotus leaves, coriander, angelica root, orris root, cassia bark, almond, liquorice, lemon peel
	Bulldog Gin Extra Bold		47				
BURLEIGH'S LONDON DRY GIN		UK	40		45 West Distillers	11	silver birch, dandelion, burdock, elderberry, orris, juniper berry
	Burleigh's Navy Strength Gin						
	Burleigh's Distillers Cut Gin						
BUTLER'S GIN		UK	40		Ross William Butler	10	juniper berry, fresh lemongrass, cardamom, coriander, cloves, cinnamon, star anise, fennel, lemon and lime
CADENHEAD'S CLASSIC GIN			50				
CADENHEAD'S OLD RAJ		Scotland	46		WM Cadenhead's	unknown	juniper berry, saffron
	Cadenhead's Sloe Gin		46				
	Cadenhead's Old Raj		55				
CAORUNN SMALL BATCH GIN		Scotland	41.8		Balmenach Distillery	6	juniper berry, rowan red berry, heather, bog myrtle, dandelion, apple
CAP ROCK ORGANIC GIN		USA	41		Peak Spirits	12	juniper berry, apple, lavender, roses
CARDINAL GIN		USA	42	2010	Southern Artisan Spirits	11	angelica, apricot kernals, cardamom, cloves, coriander, frankinsence, juniper berry, mint, orange, orris root, spearmint
	Cardinal Barrel Rested		42	2013			
CASTLE GIN	The First	Switzerland	43		MQ Wines	unknown	
	The Roses		43				
CHASE ELEGANT CRISP GIN			48		Chase Distillery	10	juniper berry, coriander, angelica, liquorice, orris, orange, lemon, hops, elderflower and bramley apple
	Extra Dry Gin		40			10	juniper berry, cinnamon, nutmeg, ginger, almond, coriander, cardamom, cloves, liquorice and lemon
	Seville Orange Gin						
	Summer Fruit Cup						elderflowers, raspberries and blackcurrants
CHIEF GOWANU NEW-NETHERLAND GIN		USA	44	2013	New York Distilling Company	unknown	juniper berry, cluster hops
CINDERELLA GIN		Belgium	40	2014	Jan Broer/Heyn-squared VOF	9	Herb-Robert, fleece flower, kaffir lime, juniper berry, swine cress
CITADELLE GIN		France	44	1998	Cognac Ferrand	19	juniper berry, coriander, almond, cassia bark, cardamom, grains of paradise, violets, fennel, cinnamon
	Citadelle Réserve Gin (6-9MO)		44.7	2008			

NAME	Derivatives	Place of origin	Alc%	Year	Brand owner/ distillery	Number of botanicals	(Known) botanicals
CITY OF LONDON DRY GIN		UK	40	2012	City of London Distillery	7	juniper berry, coriander seed, angelica root, liquorice root and fresh oranges, lemons and pink grapefruit
	City of London 'Square Mile Gin'		40+				
COCKNEY'S GIN		Belgium	44.2	2013	VDS	15	juniper berry, coriander, angelica root, cumin, paradise seed, liquorice, yuzu, pomelo, bitter orange
COLD RIVER TRADITIONAL GIN		USA	47	2010	Maine Distilleries	7	juniper berry, coriander, lemon peel, orange peel, orris root, angelica root and cardamom
COOL GIN		Spain	42.5	2011	Benevento Global/ Destilerías Liber	12	
COPPERHEAD GIN		Belgium	40	2014	Filliers Grain Distillery	5	angelica, juniper berry, cardamom , orange peel, coriander
CORSAIR ARTISAN GIN		USA	46		Corsair Artisan Distillery	unknown	angelica, coriander, juniper berry, lemon, orange, orris root
	Corsair Barrel Aged Gin (3M)						
COTSWOLDS DRY GIN		UK	46		The Cotswolds Distillery	9	juniper berry, coriander, angelica root, lavender, grapefruit, lime, black pepper, cardamom , bay leaf
COVENT GARDEN PREMIUM LONDON DRY GIN		UK	42			16	
CRATER LAKE GIN		USA	47.5		Bendistillery	unknown	
CREAM GIN		UK	43.8		Whistling Shop/ Master of Malt	unknown	
CREMORNE 1859 COLONEL FOX DRY GIN		UK	40		Cask Liquid Marketing/ Thames Distillery	6	juniper berry, coriander, angelica, cassia, liquorice and bitter orange peel
D1 DARINGLY GIN		UK	40		D.J. Limbrey Distilling Company	unknown	juniper berry, coriander, citrus peel, nettles
DACTARI ORIGINAL GERMAN GIN		Germany	40		Dactari Fine Nature Products	unknown	
DAMRAK GIN		The Netherlands	41.3		Bols	17	juniper berry, citrus, honeysuckle
DANCING PINE GIN		USA	40		Dancing Pine Distillery	6	
DARNLEY'S VIEW GIN		Scotland	40	2010	Wemyss Whisky Company	6	juniper berry, lemon peel, coriander seed, angelica root, elderflower and orris root
	Darnley's View Spiced Gin		42.7	2012			
DE BORGEN HOLLAND GIN		The Netherlands	48		Hooghoudt Distillery	unknown	
DEATH'S DOOR GIN		USA	47		Death's Door Spirits	3	juniper berry, coriander and fennel
DESERT JUNIPER GIN		USA	41	1998	Desert Juniper Company/ Bendistillery	unknown	

NAME	Derivatives	Place of origin	Alc%	Year	Brand owner/ distillery	Number of botanicals	(Known) botanicals
DH KRAHN GIN		USA	40		American Gin Company	6	coriander seed, galangal (ginger), grapefruit, juniper berry, lemon peel and orange peel.
(DICTADOR) COLOMBIAN AGED GIN	White	Colombia	43	2013	Destileria Columbiana	unknown	
	Dark / Gold		43	2013			
DINGLE GIN		Ireland	42.5	2013	Dingle Distillery	unknown	juniper berry, rowan berry, angelica, coriander, rowan, fuschia, bog myrtle, heather, chervil and hawthorn
DIPLOME DRY GIN		France	44		BeBoDrinks	unknown	juniper berry, coriander, whole lemons, orange peel, angelica, safron,orris root, fennel
DODD'S LONDON DRY GIN		UK	49.9	2014	The London Distillery Company	8	juniper berry, angelica, fresh lime, bay laurel, green and black cardamom , red raspberry, honey
DOL GIN		Italy	45	2014	Plunhof		
DOORNKAAT GERMAN DRY GIN		Germany	44		Berentzen Gruppe	unknown	juniper berry, lemon, coriander, lavender
DOROTHY PARKER GIN		USA	40	2013	New York Distilling Company	unknown	elderberries, dried hibiscus petals, cinnamon and citrus
DOUBLE YOU GIN		Belgium	43.7	2013	Brouwerij Wilderen	21	juniper berry, hop, rose, blossoms, coriander
D.R.K.N.S.S. GIN		Belgium		2015		8	juniper berry, malt, hop, cacao, orange, mandarin, fennel, poppy
DRY FLY GIN		USA	40	2007	Dry Fly Distilling	unknown	appel, munt, juniper berry, hop
DUIN GIN		Belgium	43	2015	Mr Swing / Spirits By Design	6	juniper berry, lavender, kardmom, angelica root, iriswortel, duin-doornbes
EDGERTON ORIGINAL PINK DRY GIN		UK	47		Edgerton Distillers Ltd	14	pomegranate, coriander, angelica, juniper berry, orris root, sweet orange peel, cassia bark, nutmeg, damiana herb, grains of paradise
EDINBURGH GIN		Scotland	43		Spencerfield	9	juniper berry, coriander, angelica root, orris root, lemon peel, pine cone, heather, thistle
	Raspberry Gin						
	Elderflower						
ELEPHANT GIN		Germany	45		Robin Gerlach, Tessa Wienker, Henry Palmer	14	juniper berry, cassia, orange, ginger, lavender, elderberry, piment bes-sen, apples, pine needles,Baobab fruit, Buchu fruit, Leeuwenstaart, Duivelsklauw
ENTROPIA GIN		Spain	40		Entropia Liquors	unknown	juniper berry, coriander, ginseng, guarana, hibiscus, orange peel, lemon peel, liquorice root, nutmeg
ETHEREAL GIN		USA	43		Berkshire Moun-tain Distillers	unknown	changes every batch
ET ALORS PREMIUM GIN		Belgium		2014		23	

NAME	Derivatives	Place of origin	Alc%	Year	Brand owner/ distillery	Number of botanicals	(Known) botanicals
EVER GIN		Spain	43			9	juniper berry,rosemary, peppermunt, orange en lemon peel , angelica root, cardamom, coriander
FAHRENHEIT GIN		France	40		Gabriel Boudier	unknown	juniper berry, coriander, orange & lemon peel, angelica seed, orris, fennel
FARMER'S ORGANIC GIN		USA	46.7		Crop Harvest Earth Co	secret	juniper berry, elderflower, lemon grass, coriander, angelica root
FEEL! MUNICH DRY		Germany	46		Korbinian Achternbusch	17	
FERDINAND SAAR DRY GIN		Germany	44		Avadis Distillery/ Capulet & Montague LTD		juniper berry, lavender, thyme, sloe, rosehip, angelica, hop blossom, rose, almond shell, coriander, ginger
	Ferdinand Goldcap Gin		49				
	Ferdinand Quincy Gin		30				
FEW AMERICAN GIN		USA	40	2011	FEW Spirits	11	juniper berry, citrus (lemon & orange peel), Tahitian vanilla, cassia, grains-of-paradise and homegrown hops
	Barrel Aged Gin (4MO)		46.5				
FG 20-3		Belgium	46	2012	Stokerij De Moor	23	
	The oriGIN		49.3		De Moor Distillery	23	
FIFTY POUNDS GIN		UK	43.5		Fifty Pounds Co	unknown	juniper berry, coriander, savory, grains of paradise, orange & lemon peel, liquorice, angelica root
FILLIERS DRY GIN 28		Belgium	46		Filliers Graanstokerij	28	
	Filliers Dry Gin 28 Tangerine Seasonal Edition		43.7				
FINSBURY PLATINUM DRY GIN		UK	47		Borco International/ Langley Distillery	unknown	
FORDS LONDON DRY GIN		UK	45		The 86 Co/Thames Distillers	9	juniper berry, lemon peel, pomelo, jasmine
FOREST DRY GIN	Autumn	Belgium	42			unknown	peer, lavender, tangerine
	Winter		45			unknown	
	Spring		42			24	peer, mandarijn, rozeblaadjes, juniper berry, citrus, coriander
	Summer		45			unknown	blood orange, bergamotessence, ginger
FOXDENTON DRY GIN		UK	48	2009	Foxdenton Estate Company	unknown	juniper berry, angelica root, orris root, coriander seeds, lemon peel, lime flower
	Foxdenton Blackjack Gin						
	Foxdenton Raspberry Gin						
	Foxdenton Damson Gin						
	Foxdenton Sloe Gin						

NAME	Derivatives	Place of origin	Alc%	Year	Brand owner/ distillery	Number of botanicals	(Known) botanicals
G&CIN		Spain	40		Destilerías Acha	unknown	
G/10		France	40		Hervé Erard Spirits	10	
G-VINE	Floraison	France	40		EuroWineGate	10	vine flower, juniper berry, ginger, liquorice, cassia bark, green cardamom, coriander, cubeb berries, nutmeg and lime
	Nouaison		43.9			10	vine blossom, juniper berry, ginger, liquorice, cassia bark, green cardamom, coriander, cubeb berries, nutmeg and lime
GALE FORCE GIN		USA	44.4		Triple Eight Distillery	unknown	anise, cassia, juniper berry, lemon, lemongrass, mint, orange
GENIUS GIN		USA	45		Genius Liquid	unknown	juniper berry, cardamom, coriander, lime zest, lavender, lemon leaf
	Navy Strength		57			unknown	
GERANIUM GIN		UK	44		Hammer & Son	unknown	juniper berry, geranium oil, coriander, lemon peel, angelica root, orris root, anise, cinnamon
	Geranium55 Gin						
GET BACK GIN	Blue Gin	Spain	40		Destilerías Acha	unknown	
	Pink Gin		40				
GILPIN'S EXTRA DRY GIN		UK	47		Westmorland Spirits Ltd	6	juniper berry, sage, borage, 3 citrus peels
GILT GIN		Scotland	40		Gilt Gin Co	unknown	
GILT SINGLE MALT SCOTTISH GIN		Scotland	40		Gilt Gin Co/Strathleven Distillers	unknown	
GIN BELET		Belgium		2014			
GIN DEL PROFESSORE		Italy		2014	Jerry Thomas Project		
GIN MARE		Spain	42.7		Global Premium Brands	5	juniper berry, thyme, basil, rosemary, olives
GIN SEA		Spain	40		Manuel Barrientos	10	juniper berry, cardamom, coriander, thyme, chamomile, liquorice, peppermint, lemon, sweet orange, bitter orange
GIN SUL		Germany	43		Altonaer Spirituosen	unknown	juniper berry, coriander,rosemary, lemonen, lavender, cinnamon, piment, Zonneroosje
GINA GIN		Spain	40		Worldskyandarts	4	juniper berry, coriander
GINIE GIN LIQUEUR		Germany	35		Edelbrennerei Scheibel		
GINIU		Italy		2013		7	juniper berry, curryplant, bes mastik, myrthe, thyme, rosemary, bay leaf
GINSELF		Spain	40		Gin Al Punto	9	sweet orange, bitter orange, lemon peel, angelica root, angelica seed, orange blossom, tiger nut, juniper berry & mandarin

NAME	Derivatives	Place of origin	Alc%	Year	Brand owner/ distillery	Number of botanicals	(Known) botanicals
GLORIOUS GIN		USA	45	2010	Breuckelen Distilling	5	juniper berry, lemon, rosemary, ginger, grapefruit
GOA GIN		UK	47		World Wide Distillers	8	juniper berry, coriander, carraway seed, angelica root, nutmeg
GOLD 999.9		Spain	40		The Water Company	10	tangerine, almonds, ginger, violet, coriander, angelica root, cinnamon, gentian, poppy, juniper berry
GOLDEN MOON GIN		USA	45		Golden Moon Distillery	unknown	
GOODMANS GIN		The Netherlands	44	2014	Paul & Gerda de Goede	unknown	
GRANIT BAVARIAN GIN		Germany	42	2015	Brennerei Pen-ninger	28	juniper berry, lemon zest, coriander, cardamom, melissa, spignel, gentian
GREENALL'S LONDON DRY GIN		UK	40	1760	G&J Greenall Distillers	8	juniper berry, coriander, lemon peel, angelica, orris, liquorice, cassia bark and bitter almonds
GREENBRIER GIN		USA	40		Smooth Ambler Spirits	unknown	citrus peel, juniper berry and pepper
GREEN HAT GIN		USA	41.1		New Columbia Distillers	unknown	juniper berry, citrus, coriander, grains of paradise, celery seed
GREYLOCK GIN		USA	40		Berkshire Mountain Distillers	7	
GROUND CONTROL GIN		Belgium	45	2015	Open Up Distillery	30	
GUGLHOF ALPIN GIN		Austria	42	2010	Brennerei Guglhof	unknown	blackberries, flour berries, alpine rose bleed
HANA GIN		USA	40		Branded Spirits	unknown	
HANAMI DRY GIN		The Netherlands	43	2014	The Melchers Group	9	juniper berry, japanese cherry blossoms
HASWELL LONDON DRY GIN		UK	47		Rainbow Chaser Ltd	9	juniper berry, angelica, coriander, savory, lemon peel, grains of pardise, bitter orange peel, sweet orange peel, liquorice
HAYMAN'S LONDON DRY GIN		UK	40		Hayman Distillers	10	unknown
	Hayman's 1820 Gin Liqueur		40				
	Hayman's 1850 Reserve Gin (5WO)		40				
	Hayman's Old Tom Gin		40				
	Hayman's City of London		40				
	Hayman's Royal Dock Gin		57				
	Hayman's Sloe Gin		26				
HEAVEN&HELL GIN		Belgium	41.6	2014	Serge Hannecaert	unknown	
HENDRICK'S GIN		Scotland	41.5		William Grant & Sons Ltd	11	extra infusion of rose petals & cucumber

NAME	Derivatives	Place of origin	Alc%	Year	Brand owner/ distillery	Number of botanicals	(Known) botanicals
HENTHO GIN		Belgium	44	2014	Hendrik & Thomas Coenen	12	
HERNÖ GIN		Sweden	40.5	2012	Hernö Brenneri	8	juniper berry, coriander, meadow-sweet, cassia, black pepper, vanilla, lemon peel, lingonberries
	Hernö Navy Strength		57	2013			
	Hernö Juniper Cask Gin			2013			
	Hernö Old Tom Gin						
HOXTON GIN		UK	43		Gerry Calabrese	unknown	coconut, grapefruit, juniper berry, orris, tarragon and Ginger
SPIRIT OF HVEN ORGANIC GIN		Sweden	40		Spirit of Hven Distillery	unknown	juniper berry, grains of paradise, citrus, Sichuan pepper, aniseed, guinea pepper
IBZ PREMIUM GIN		Spain	38		Familia Mari Mayans	unknown	juniper berry, rosemary, thyme, citrus
IMAGIN		Sweden	40	2011	Facile & Co	12	
INDIAN SUMMER GIN		Scotland	46		Duncan Taylor Ltd	unknown	juniper berry, saffron
INVERROCHE GIN CLASSIC		South Africa	43		Inverroche Distillary	unknown	
	Inverroche Gin Verdant		43			unknown	
	Inverroche Gin Amber		43			unknown	
ISFJORD ARCTIC GIN		Greenland	44	2007	Isjford Distillery	12	juniper berry, angelica, lemon grass, cardamom, orange
ISH LONDON DRY GIN		Spain	41		The Poshmakers	11	juniper berry, coriander seed, angelica root, almond, orris root, nutmeg, cinnamon, cassia, liquorice, lemon and orange peel
	Ish Limed London Dry Gin		41				
JENSEN'S BERMONDSEY GIN		UK	43		Bermondsey Gin Ltd	unknown	coriander, orris root, angelica, liquorice, juniper berry
	Jensen's Old Tom Gin		43				
JINZU GIN		UK	41.3	2013	Dee Davies/ Cameron Bridge Gin Distillery		juniper berry, coriander, Japanese herbs
JODHPUR		UK	43		Beveland Distillers	13	angelica, bitter almonds, coriander, cassia bark, juniper berry, lemon peel, liquorice root, orris root, orange peel, ginger, pomelo peel
	Jodhpur Reserve (2YO)		43				
JOSEPHINE GIN		France	40		Camus Cognac	unknown	
JUDGES LONDON DRY GIN		UK	40		Cale distillers	unknown	
JUNIPER GREEN ORGANIC		UK	43		Organics Spirits Co/ Thames Distillers	4	juniper berry, coriander, savory and angelica root

NAME	Derivatives	Place of origin	Alc%	Year	Brand owner/ distillery	Number of botanicals	(Known) botanicals
JUNIPERO GIN		USA	49.3	1996	Anchor Distilling Company	secret	
K-25		Spain	45		Destilerías Acha	unknown	
KIMERUD GIN		Norway	47		Family Johnsen	20	juniper berry, coriander, lemon peel , walnut, mint, rose root
KING OF SOHO GIN		UK	42		West And Drinks Ltd Thames Distillers	12	
KINROSS GIN SPECIAL SELECTION		Spain	37,5		Teichenné Liqueurs	unknown	
	Citric & Dry		40			8	juniper berry, coriander, cardamom, orange, cinnamon, angelica root, lemon zest, iris
	Wild Berry Fruits		40			7	juniper berry, coriander, cardamom, orange, lemon, raspberry, angelica root
	Tropical Exotic Fruits		40			11	juniper berry, coriander, cardamom, orange, mango, angelica root, lemon zest, pomelo, yuzu, pineapple, passion fruit
KNOCKEEN HEATHER GIN		UK	47.3		Knockeen Hills	unknown	heather, juniper berry, coriander, angelica root, savoury
	Knockeen Hills Elderflower Gin		43				
KOVAL GIN		Germany	47		Koval Distillery	unknown	
KRAAIKE GIN		Belgium	40	2014	Craywinckelhof	unknown	
LACLIE FRERES GIN		France	48		Maison René Laclie	unknown	
LANGLEY'S NO. 8 DISTILLED LONDON GIN		UK	44		Langley Distillery	8	juniper berry, nutmeg, coriander, orange, lemon, cassia
LANGTONS NO.1 GIN		UK	40	2012	Tim Moor & Nick Dymoke-Marr/G&J Distillers	11	
LARIOS (12) PREMIUM GIN		Spain	40		Beam Global	12	juniper berry, nutmeg, angelica root, coriander, Mediterranean lemon, orange, tangerine, mandarin, clementine, grapefruit, lime and orange blossom
LARKS GODFATHER GIN		Australia	40		Lark Distillery	unknown	juniper berry, pepper berry
LEBENSSTERN DRY GIN		Germany	43		Lebensstern Bar/ Freihof Distillery	unknown	
	Lebensstern Pink Gin		43				
LEOPOLD'S AMERICAN SMALL BATCH GIN		USA	40	2002	Leopold Brothers	5	juniper berry, coriander, orris root, California pomelos, Valencia oranges
LEVEL PREMIUM GIN		Spain	44		Teichenné	8	
LIBERATOR SMALL BATCH GIN		USA	42		Valentine Distilling	9	

NAME	Derivatives	Place of origin	Alc%	Year	Brand owner/ distillery	Number of botanicals	(Known) botanicals
LIGHTHOUSE BATCH DISTILLED GIN		New Zealand	42		Greytown Fine Distillates	9	secret
	Hawthorn Edition		57				
LOBSTAR MARIN GIN		Belgium	40	2014	Kristof Marrannes/ Spirits By Design	unknown	crayfish, juniper berry
LONDON HILL DRY GIN		UK	43	1785	Ian Macleod Distillers/ Langley Distillery	unknown	juniper berry, citrus peels and coriander seeds
LONDON N° 1 ORIGINAL BLUE GIN		Spain	47		Gonzalez Byass	13	juniper berry, anglica, cinnamon, almonds, coriander
LOOPUYT 1772 DRY GIN		The Netherlands	45.1	2014	P. Loopuyt & Co Distillers	12	juniper berries, lavender, cardamom, nutmeg, cinchona, coriander, raspberries, orange, pomelo, Inca berries, mulberries, goji berries
LUBUSKI GIN	Classic Gin	Poland	40	1987	Henkell & Co. Vinpol/ Lubuski Distillery	14	juniper berry, coriander, angelica root, citrus peel, liquorice, cassia bark, bitter almonds, cardamom, cinnamon, star anise, cumin, calamus (myrtle), marigold flowers, bay leaf
	Lime Gin		40				
M5 GIN		Spain	48		Bodegas Vinícola Real	26	
MG 1835 ORIGINAL DRY GIN		Spain	43		Destilerías MG	unknown	
MACARONESIAN (WHITE) GIN		Spain	40		Destileria Santa Cruz	unknown	juniper berry, cardamom, angelica root, liquorice, lemon peel, orange peel
MADAME GENEVA GIN BLANC		Germany	44.4		Kreuzritter GmbH	3	
	Madame Geneva Rouge Gin		41.9			46	
MAGELLAN BLUE GIN		France	44		Angeac Distillery	11	cloves, cinnamon, coriander, cardamom, orris root & flower, cassia, liquorice, juniper berry, orange peel, grains of paradise, nutmeg
MARTIN MILLER'S DRY GIN		UK	40	1999	The Reformed Spirits Co	10	Florentine iris, juniper berry, cassia bark, liquorice, coriander, angelica root, bitter orange peel, lemon peel, lime peel, cucumber
	Martin Millers, 'Westbourne Strength,' Dry Gin		45.2	2003			
MASCARO GIN 9		Spain	40	2010	Antonio Mascaro	1	juniper berry
MASONS YORKSHIRE DRY GIN		UK	42		Karl Mason	unknown	
MASTER'S SELECTION		Spain	40		Destilerías MG	unknown	
MAYFAIR LONDON DRY GIN		UK	40		Mayfair Brands/ Thames Distillery	5	juniper berry, coriander, angelica, orris, savoury
MEYER'S GIN M1		Belgium	38	2014	Spirits By Design	unknown	juniper berry, kiwi berry
	Mayer's Gin M2		43	2015		unknown	juniper berry, asparagus

NAME	Derivatives	Place of origin	Alc%	Year	Brand owner/ distillery	Number of botanicals	(Known) botanicals
MIKKELLER BOTANICAL GIN		Denmark	44		Mikkeller Spirits/ Braunstein	unknown	juniper berry, lemon grass, angelica root, cardamom, orange, hop
MOMBASA CLUB LONDON DRY GIN		UK	41.5		Imperial British East Africa Company	unknown	juniper berry, angelica root, coriander seeds, cassia bark
	Mombasa Colonel's Reserve						
MONKEY 47 DRY GIN		Germany	47		Black Forest Distillers	47	
	Monkey 47 Sloe Gin		47				
	Monkey 47 Distillers Cut		47				
MONOPOLOWA VIENNA DRY GIN		Austria	44		Altvater Gessler - J.A. Baczewski	unknown	caraway seed, coriander seed, fennel seed, ginger, lemon peel and orange peel
MRDC RIVER ROSE GIN		USA	40		Mississippi River Distillery	unknown	juniper berry, citrus, lavender, rose petals, cucumber
MYER FARM GIN		USA	42.7		Myer Farm Distillers	10	juniper berry, coriander, cinnamon and citrus
MYRTLE GIN (10YO)		Scotland	47		Spirit of the Coquet	unknown	Northumberland myrtle
N GIN VLC		Spain	39		DHV Destilados	10	juniper berry, orange, lemon, mandarijn, rose petals, liquorice, coriander seed, angelica root, cardamom, salvia
	N gin two		39				
NB GIN		Scotland	42	2013	NB Distillery Ltd	8	juniper berry, coriander, angelica root, paradise seed, lemon peel, cassia bark, cardamom, violet root
NEW AMSTERDAM GIN		USA	40		New Amsterdam Spirits Co	20	
NGINIOUS SWISS BLEND GIN		Switzerland	45	2014	Oliver Ullrich & Ralph Villiger	18	
	Nginious Vermouth Cask Finish Gin		43				
N°0 LONDON DRY		Spain	41		Number Zero Drinks	11	juniper berry, coriander, angelica, lavender, orris, cinnamon, cinchona (containing the quinine) from Peru
N°209 GIN		USA	46		Distillery N°209	between 8 & 11	juniper berry, bergamot, orange, lemon peel, cardamom pods, cassia bark, angelica root, coriander seeds
N°3 LONDON DRY GIN		The Netherlands	46		De Kuyper Royal Distillers	unknown	
NOG gin		Belgium	46	2014	Ben Bruyneel	unknown	juniper berry, hop, poppy, coriander, orange, lemon, cacao
NOLET'S DRY GIN SILVER		The Netherlands	47.6		Nolet Distillery	unknown	Turkish rose, peach, raspberry
	Nolet's Dry Gin - The Reserve	The Netherlands	52.3				

NAME	Derivatives	Place of origin	Alc%	Year	Brand owner/ distillery	Number of botanicals	(Known) botanicals
NORDÉS GIN		Spain	40		Atlantic Galician Spirits	unknown	verbena, lemon peel, eucalyptus leaves, sage, juniper berry, cardamom, quinine, ginger, hibiscus, liquorice, tea
NORTH SHORE DISTILLER'S GIN	N°6 & N°11	USA	45	2007	North Shore Distillery	unknown	
NOTEWORTHY GIN		Canada	43		The Dubh Glas Distillery	unknown	
NUT GIN		Spain			Emporda	13	juniper berry, coriander, cardamom, angelica root, lemon peel, orange peel, green walnuts, fragrant nutmeg, rosemary, thyme, olive tree leaves, cinnamon and liquorice
NUTMEG GIN		Austria	44		Oliver Matter/ Erlebnis Brennerei	unknown	
O WANNBORGA GIN		Sweden	40.1		Destileria Wannborga	9	juniper berry, angelica root, coriander, cardamom, nutmeg, cinnamon, white pepper, lemon peel, bitter orange peel
OLD BUCK GIN		South Africa	43		Henry Tayler & Ries Ltd.	unknown	
OLD ENGLISH GIN		UK	44		Hammer & Son	unknown	
OLD LADY'S GIN		France	40		Marie Brizard	unknown	
OLIVER CROMWELL 1599 PREMIUM GIN		The Netherlands	40		Aldi Stores Ltd.	unknown	
OMG GIN		Czech Republic	45		ZUSY Ltd	16	juniper berry, linde, melisse, lavender, paradise grain, coriander, angelica root, sweet flag
ONE KEY GIN		Singapore	40		Abnormal Group Singapore	unknown	juniper berry, ginger, coriander, exotic plant extracts
ONLY GIN		Spain	43		Campeny Destilleries	11	juniper berry, jasmine, veronica, violet, rose petals, lavender, orange blossom, mallow, pansies, lemon balm, hibiscus
OPIHR ORIENTAL SPICED LONDON DRY GIN		UK	40		Quintessential Brands/G&J Greenall Distillers	4	juniper berry, cubebe pepper, black pepper, coriander
ORIGIN SINGLE ESTATE LONDON DRY GIN	UK	UK	40		Master of Malt	1	juniper berry
	Croatia						
	Macedonia						
	Albania						
	Kosovo						
	Bulgaria						
	Italy						
OXLEY DRY GIN		UK	47		Oxley Spirits Co	unknown	
PALLADIAN DRY GIN		UK	40		Mayfair Distillery	unknown	

NAME	Derivatives	Place of origin	Alc%	Year	Brand owner/ distillery	Number of botanicals	(Known) botanicals
PALMERS LONDON DRY GIN		UK	40		Alcohols Ltd/ Langley Distillery	10	unknown
PÈRE ALBERT GIN		Belgium	41.8	2014		5	juniper berry, coriander, cumin, lime, rose leafs
PERRY'S TOT NAVY GIN		USA	57		New York Distilling Company	8	juniper berry, cinnamon, cardamom, star anise, lemon, orange & grapefruit peel, wild flower honey
PH. COLLET GIN		Belgium	46		Phillip Collet/de Moor Distillery	11	juniper berry, rosemary, orange apple, green tea, coriander
PINCKNEY BEND GIN		USA	46.5		Pinckney Bend Distillery	9	juniper berry, coriander seeds, orris root, angelica, liquorice, and three different kinds of dried citrus
PINK 47 GIN		UK	47		Old St Andrews Ltd	10	juniper berry, coriander, angelica root (2), lemon peel, orange peel, orris root, liquorice, almond, cassia bark, nutmeg
PINK CLOUD GIN		Belgium	45	2014	Bosteels Brewery		
PJ DRY GIN		Belgium	40	2014	PJ Frooninckx / Belgian Spirits Company	unknown	juniper berry, grain, orange
	PJ Elderflower Gin		40			unknown	juniper berry, grain, orange, elder-berry, lemon
PLATU LONDON DRY GIN		UK	39		Platu Premium Spirits	10	juniper berry, coriander seed, orris root, liquorice, angelica root, cinna-mon, nutmeg, orange, cassia, lemon
PLYMOUTH GIN		UK	41.2		Plymouth Distillery	unknown	
	Plymouth Gin Navy Strength		57				
	Plymouth Sloe Gin						
POPPIES GIN		Belgium	40		Stokerij Rubbens	unknown	poppies
PORTOBELLO ROAD N° 171 LONDON DRY GIN		UK	42		Jake Burger/ Thames Distillers Ltd	unknown	
PORT OF DRAGONS		Spain	44		Premium Distillery	unknown	almond, angelica, anise, cardamom, coriander, ginger, hazelnut, hibiscus, juniper, lemon, lime, liquorice, nutmeg, orange, poppy, rose, vanilla, fennel
PROFESSOR CORNELIUS AMPLEFORTH'S BATHTUB GIN		UK	43.3		Master of Malt	unknown	juniper berry, orange peel, coriander, cinnamon, cloves and cardamom
RAFFLES LONDON DRY GIN		Scotland	40		William Maxwell Distillery	13	juniper berry, coriander seeds, angelica root, orange & lemon peel, cassia bark, ginger, nutmeg, liquorice root, almonds, cinnamon bark, fennel and cardamom seeds
RANSOM OLD TOM GIN (6-9MO)		USA	44		Ransom Spirits	6	juniper berry, orange peel, lemon peel, coriander seed, cardamom pods and angelica root

NAME	Derivatives	Place of origin	Alc%	Year	Brand owner/ distillery	Number of botanicals	(Known) botanicals
REVAL DRY GIN		Spain	40		Remedia Distillery	unknown	
REVENGE NAVY GIN		Italy	57				juniper berry, coriander, cardamom , orris root, lemon, red currant
RIGHT GIN 0.7L		Sweden	40		Altamar Brands/ Right Distillery	unknown	bergamot
ROARING FORTIES GIN		New Zealand	40		South Pacific Distillery	unknown	
ROBY MARTON'S GIN		Italy	47	2014	Roby Marton / Bassano del Grappa	10	juniper berry, citrus, cinnamon, liquorice, anise seed, rose pepper, horseradish, ginger, red fruits, clove
ROB'S MTN GIN		USA	44		Spring44 Distilling Inc	unknown	juniper berry, coriander, orris root, orange peel, kaffir lime leaf, basil, peppermint, Unicorn Tears
ROUNDHOUSE GIN		USA	47		Roundhouse Spirits	unknown	juniper berry, coriander, citrus peel, star anise, angelica, orris root, sencha green tea, lavender, hibiscus and chamomile
	Roundhouse Imperial Barrel Aged Gin (10M)						
SACRED GIN		UK	40		Sacred Spirits Company	12	juniper berry, citrus, cardamom, nutmeg, frankincense
	Sacred Cardamom Gin						
	Sacred Orris Gin						
SAFFRON GIN		France	40		Gabriel Boudier	unknown	juniper berry, saffron, coriander, lemon, orange peel, angelica seeds, orris, fennel
SALICORNIA OCEAN/ TIDES GIN		Spain	40		Blanc Gastronomy	11	juniper berry, gentian, coriander, angelica root, verbena (lemon verbena), cinnamon, orange, lemon, citrus aurantium (bitter orange), bergamot and samphire
SANTAMANIA GIN		Spain	41		Santa Mania Distillery	10	juniper berry, plums, grapes, coriander, cinnamon, cardamom, lime, lemon, angelica root, raspberry
SEAGRAM'S EXTRA DRY GIN		USA	40		Seagram & Sons	unknown	
	Distiller's Reserve (6MO)		51	2006			
SEARS CUTTING EDGE GIN		Germany	44		MBC International Premium Brands	unknown	
SECRET TREASURES GIN 'OLD TOM STYLE'		Germany	40		Haromex	unknown	
SHARISH GIN		Portugal	40		Antonio Cuco	7	juniper berry, apple, coriander, citrus, vanilla, cinnamon, lemon verbena
SHORTCROSS GIN		Ireland	46		Rademon Estate Distillery	unknown	juniper berry, elderberry, apple, coriander seed, orange, cassia

NAME	Derivatives	Place of origin	Alc%	Year	Brand owner/ distillery	Number of botanicals	(Known) botanicals
SIKKIM INDIAN BRITISH TEA	Private	Spain	40			unknown	juniper berry, red tea, floral aromas, coriander
	Bilberry		40				juniper berry, red tea, flower essences, blackberries, blueberries, coriander, orris, calamus, bitter orange peel
SIPSMITH LONDON DRY GIN		UK	41.6	2009	Sipsmith Distillery	10	Macedonian juniper, Bulgarian coriander seeds, French angelica root, Spanish liquorice root, Italian orris root, Spanish ground almond, Chinese cassia bark, Madagascan cinnamon, Seville orange, Spanish lemon peel
	Sipsmith Sloe Gin		29				
	Sipsmith Summer Cup		29				
	Sipsmith VJOP (Very Juniper Over Proof)		52				
	Sipsmith Blue Label		44.1				
SIX RAVEN GIN		Germany	46		Alandia & Co	unknown	
SKIN GIN		Germany	42		Martin Jens & Mathias Rüsch	7	juniper berry, coriander, lime, lemon, pomelo, orange, Moroccan mint
SLOANE'S DRY GIN		The Netherlands	40		Toorank Distilleries	9	orange, angelica root, orris root, coriander seeds, juniper berry, vanilla, cardamom, liquorice, lemon
SMOOTH AMBLER BARREL AGED		USA	49.5		Smooth Ambler Spirits	unknown	
SOUTH GIN		New Zealand	48.2	2005	42Below	9	juniper berry, lemon, orange, coriander seed, angelica leaves, orris root, gentian root, manuka berries, and kawakawa leaves
(THE) SPECTATOR GIN		UK	42.4		The Spectator Magazine	unknown	juniper berry, Earl Grey tea, melisse
SPIRIT HOUND GIN		USA	42		Spirit Hound Distillers	9	juniper berry, fennel seeds, Sichuan peppercorns, cloves, cinnamon, star anise
SPRING GIN		Belgium	40		Manuel Wouters/ Filliers Graanstokerij	13	coriander, lemon and orange peel, star anise, black pepper, cardamom, ginger, rhubarb, pine buds, delicate orange blossom, cinnamon, angelica
	Spring Gin Gentleman's Cut		48.8				
	Spring Gin Ladies' Edition		38.3				
	Spring Black Pepper			2014			
	Spring Mediterannée			2015			
SPRING 44 GIN		USA	44		Spring44 Distill-ing Inc	4	juniper berry, coriander, nutmeg, agave nectar
	Old Tom gin		44				juniper berry, coriander, lemon grass, orris root, pomelo, rosemary, galangel root
	Mountain gin		44				

NAME	Derivatives	Place of origin	Alc%	Year	Brand owner/ distillery	Number of botanicals	(Known) botanicals
SQUARE MILE LONDON DRY GIN		UK	47		City of London Distillery	8	
STEED GIN		UK	44		Cial. Fuente Anguila Ltd	unknown	juniper berry, coriander, angelica root, lemon peel, orange peel, cinnamon, cardamom, Florence lily
ST GEORGES GIN	Terroir Gin	USA	45		St George Spirits	unknown	Douglas fir, California bay laurel, coastal sage
	Botanivore Gin		45			19	angelica root, bay laurel, bergamot peel, black peppercorn, caraway, cardamom, cilantro, cinnamon, citra hops, coriander, dill seed, fennel seed, ginger, juniper berry, lemon peel, lime peel, orris root, Seville orange peel, star anise
	Dry Rye Gin		45			unknown	rye
STUDER SWISS ORIGINAL GIN		Switzerland	40			unknown	juniper berry, lemon grass, angelica root, cubebe pepper, lavender, coriander, ginger
	Studer Swiss Golden Snow Gin		40			unknown	Extra: gold flakes
SUAU GIN		Spain	43		Bodega Suau/ Bodegas y Destillerias de Mallorca		oranges, lemons, almonds, juniper berry, coriander, angelica, orris, liquorice root
SYLVAN GIN		USA	47		Koval Distillery	13	juniper berry, citrus, white pepper
SW4 GIN		UK	40	2009	Park Place Drinks Ltd/ Thames Distillery	12	juniper berry, lemon, orange, coriander, savory, orris powder, cinnamon, cassia, nutmeg, almonds, liquorice root and angelica
TANN'S GIN		Spain	40	1977	Campeny Destilleries	10	juniper berry, coriander, cucumber, rose petals, cardamom, mandarin peel, orange blossom, lemon peel, liquorice, raspberry
TANQUERAY DRY GIN		UK	40		Diageo	4	secret
	Tanqueray N° Ten Dry Gin		47.3	2000			
	Tanqueray Dry Gin Rangpur		41.3	2006			
	Tanqueray Malacca			1997			
	Tanqueray Old Tom		47	2014			
TARQUIN'S DRY GIN		UK	42		South Western Distillery	12	juniper berry, orange zeste, Devon violets
TASMANIAN GODFATHER GIN		Australia	40		Lark Distillery	unknown	pepper berry
TELSER LIECHTENSTEIN DRY GIN		Lichtenstein	47		Telser Brennerei	11	juniper berry, coriander, angelica root, cinnamon, ginger, lemon peel , orange (bitter/Curaçao), camille, lavender, elderberry
THE BITTER TRUTH PINK GIN		Germany	40		The Bitter Truth	unknown	
	The Bitter Truth Sloeberry Blue Gin		28				

NAME	Derivatives	Place of origin	Alc%	Year	Brand owner/ distillery	Number of botanicals	(Known) botanicals
THE BOTANICAL'S LONDON DRY GIN		UK	42.5		Langley Distillery	14	juniper berry, coriander, cassia, orange, lemon, cinnamon, orris, angelica, liquorice, nutmeg, grapefruit, lemon blossom, orange blossom
THE BOTANIST DRY GIN		Scotland	46		Bruichladdich	22	orris root, cassia bark, coriander seed
THE DUKE MUNICH DRY GIN		Germany	45		The Duke Destillerie	13	juniper berry, coriander, lemon peel, angelica root, lavender, ginger, orange blossom, pepper
THE EXILES IRISH GIN		UK	41.3		Protege International	unknown	shamrock, red clover flowers, honeysuckle flowers, rowan berries, bog myrtle, juniper berries
THE ORIGINAL		Germany	43		Michael Scheibel	unknown	
THE STING SMALL BATCH LONDON DRY GIN		UK	40			10	
THE TRADEWINDS 'CUTLASS' GIN		Australia	50		Tailor Made Spirits Company	unknown	lemon myrtle
THREE CORNERS VAN WEES DRY GIN		The Netherlands	42		Van Wees	unknown	
TORK GIN		Italy	42.8		F&G	unknown	juniper berry, coriander, orris root, citrus
TWO BIRDS COUNTRYSIDE LONDON DRY GIN		UK	40	2012	Union Distillers Ltd	unknown	
UNCLE VAL'S BOTANICAL GIN		USA	43		35 Maple Street	5	juniper berry, cucumber, lavender, lemon, sage
UNGAVA PREMIUM CANADIAN GIN		Canada	43.1		Ungava Gin Co	6	crowberry, wild rose hips, Labrador tea, Arctic blend, cloudberry
UNTITLED RESERVE GIN		Germany	41.5		Gebr. Both	unknown	
	Untitled Old Tom Gin		41.5				
	Untitled Sloe Gin		28				
UPPERCUT GIN		Belgium	49.6		Manuel Wouters/ Zuidam Distillers	unknown	juniper berry, liquorice, vervain, strawberry leaf, Damiana leaf, nettle
V2C DUTCH DRY GIN		The Netherlands	42			10	juniper berry, orange, liquorice, bay leaf, ginger, coriander, angelica root, cardamom, lemon, St. John's wort
	V2C Oaked Dutch Dry Gin		42			unknown	
	V2C Orange Dutch Dry Gin		42			unknown	
	V2C Sloe Dutch Dry Gin		42			unknown	
VAN GOGH GIN		The Netherlands	47	1999	Royal Dirkzwager Distilleries	10	coriander, liquorice, angelica, juniper berry, grains of paradise, almonds, lemons, cassia bark, orris, cubeb berries
VALLENDAR PURE GIN		Germany	40		Brennerei Hubertus Vallendar	unknown	
VIBE GIN		Belgium	43	2014	Vibe Distillers	unknown	juniper berry, anise, ginger, jasmine, orange, lemon

NAME	Derivatives	Place of origin	Alc%	Year	Brand owner/ distillery	Number of botanicals	(Known) botanicals
VL-92 GIN		The Netherlands	41.7	2011	Van Toor Distileerderij	unknown	fresh coriander leaves
VONES GIN		Spain	40		LAJ Spirits	11	juniper berry, coriander, angelica, lemon peel, orange peel, liquorice root, cassia, cinnamon, nutmeg, Florencia root, chestnuts
VOORTREKKER DUTCH GIN		The Netherlands	40		Unique Brands	8	juniper berry, liquorice, vanilla, angelica root, ginger, orange, lemon peel, coriander seed
VOR PREMIUM GIN		Iceland	47		Eimverk Distillery	unknown	juniper berry, Iceland moss, empetrum
VORDING GIN CEDAR WOOD INFUSED		The Netherlands	44		Thomas Vording	4	juniper berry, orange, cinnamon, cedar
VOYAGER SMALL-BATCH DRY GIN		USA	42		Pacific Distillery	unknown	juniper berry, orris root, citrus, angelica, cardamom and cassia
WANNBORGA O-GIN		Sweden	40.1		Wannborga Bränneri	9	juniper berry, coriander, white pepper
WARNER EDWARDS HARRINGTON GIN		UK	44		Falls Farm	11	juniper berry, elderberry
WENNEKER ELDERFLOWER GIN		The Netherlands	40		Wenneker Distilleries	6	juniper berry, elderberry, coriander, orange peel, lemon peel, lime blossoms
WESTWINDS GIN	The Sabre	Australia	40		Gidgegannup Distilleries	12	juniper berry, lime peel, lemon myrtle, Lelzaad
	The Cutlass		50			unknown	juniper berry, cinnamon myrtle, Australian tomato
WHITE LAYDIE GIN		USA	40		Montgomery Distillery	unknown	juniper berry, citrus, orris root, angelica root, cardamom
WHITLEY NEILL DRY GIN		UK	42	2005	Whitley Neill Ltd/ The Sovereign Distillery	7	baobab fruit and cape gooseberries
WINDSPIEL PREMIUM DRY GIN		Germany	47		Eifelion	unknown	
WINT & LILA GIN		Spain	40		Casalbor Wines & Spirits	10	juniper berry, coriander, angelica root, cinnamon, orange, lemon, orange blossoms, mint
WOOD'S TREELINE GIN		USA	40	2012	Wood's High Mountain Distillery	unknown	
	Treeline Barrel Rested Gin		45	2014			
	Mountain Hopped Gin		45.75	2015			
XELLENT GIN		Switzerland	40		Diwisa Distillery	27	juniper berry, Edelweiss, lemon melisse, lavender, Swiss rye
XORIGUER GIN		Spain	38		Destillerias Xoriguer	secret	
ZEPHYR GIN	Blu Gin	UK	40		Zephyr Imports	unknown	elderberries, gardenia
	Black Gin		44			unknown	exotic botanicals

NAME	Derivatives	Place of origin	Alc%	Year	Brand owner/ distillery	Number of botanicals	(Known) botanicals
ZUIDAM DRY GIN		The Netherlands	43.5		Zuidam Distillers	9	angelica root, cardamom, coriander seed, orris root, juniper berry, lemon peel & orange peel
	Zuidam Dutch Courage		44.5				
	Dutch Courage Aged 88 Gin (9M)		44				
	Dutch Courage Old Tom's Gin		40				

NAME	Derivatives	Place of origin	Alc%	Year	Brand owner/ distillery	Number of botanicals	(Known) botanicals

NAME	Derivatives	Place of origin	Alc%	Year	Brand owner/ distillery	Number of botanicals	(Known) botanicals

NAME	Derivatives	Place of origin	Alc%	Year	Brand owner/ distillery	Number of botanicals	(Known) botanicals

NAME	Derivatives	Place of origin	Alc%	Year	Brand owner/ distillery	Number of botanicals	(Known) botanicals

NAME	Derivatives	Place of origin	Alc%	Year	Brand owner/ distillery	Number of botanicals	(Known) botanicals

NAME	Derivatives	Place of origin	Alc%	Year	Brand owner/ distillery	Number of botanicals	(Known) botanicals

ALPHABETICAL INDEX

ALPHABETICAL INDEX PER TYPE

COLOPHON

WWW.LANNOO.COM

Register on our web site and we will regularly send you a newsletter with information about new books and interesting, exclusive offers.

Text:
Frédéric Du Bois, Isabel Boons

Photography:
Kris Vlegels & Wim Kempenaers

Illustrations:
Emma Thyssen

English translation:
Fran Oosterbaan-Clarke & Bracha De Man

Design:
KIET

Layout:
Keppie & Keppie

If you have questions about gin & tonic
send an e-mail to: info@miraflor.be
If you have observations, please contact our
editorial office: redactielifestyle@lannoo.com

2nd print run
D/2015/45/91 – NUR 447
ISBN: 978 94 014 2560 5